USING
PLANTS
FOR
HEALING

An American Herbal

USING PLANTS FOR HEALING

by Nelson Coon
Author of **Using Wayside Plants**

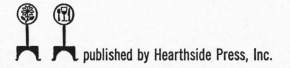

published by Hearthside Press, Inc.

CONTENTS

USING
PLANTS
FOR
HEALING

CHAPTER I

A POINT OF VIEW

LTHOUGH the last decade or two has seen a great revival of interest in plant remedies, little useful information is available for Americans. Most herbal treatises are almost world-wide in their scope, or are limited to Great Britain, Germany, Switzerland, or Mexico. Either way, they are quite unrelated to plant life of the United States. To fill the gap, this book is written specifically for Americans, for those who feel that their fathers "knew a thing or two" about practical home remedies, and who would like to investigate this ancient knowledge. It presents to the nature lover of the United States an assessment of the medicinal properties of the flora to be found in our woods, roadsides, gardens, and yards. As background for this investigation, the book discusses also the medical lore of the American Indians and its use by early settlers.

To say that this is a book about *American* medicinal plants, however, one must realize the semantic problems of "American" and understand one definition of the word. Too commonly do people from the States claim the sole right to this title, whereas in fact it is a continental term. "North American" is equally troublesome in that Mexico and Canada are alike entitled to this geographic designation. Therefore, to prevent confusion, "United States," or "the States" is used most frequently throughout this book. "American," when used, is to be understood as "United States."

Actually, however, the plants discussed are further reduced to those commonly found in the territory stretching from the Atlantic to the

9

Rockies, with only a sampling of notable plants which are at home in subtropical areas, desert country, or the peculiar climatic conditions of California. Of course, since the southern strip of Canada is climatically similar to our northern tier of states, many of the plants mentioned may be found there; just as plants along our southern borders are found in Mexico, and many species of plants from our North grow in Mexico's mountain regions.

From the readers of the author's previous book, *Using Wayside Plants,* many queries have come as to why certain plants were not there discussed. Without doubt, some readers will question the selections made here also. But the fact is that any book in this field must be highly selective or inordinately long. A list has been made of some 1500 plants with reputed medicinal value growing in one state alone; a recent letter from a researcher in the field of possible plant cures for cancer tells of reported values in nearly 3000 plants, distributed throughout the world; while a list of all plants used medicinally by the various tribes of American Indians would be equally long. Hence, it has been necessary to select the plants which seem to be most commonly known, most widely used, and about which there has grown up at least a body of empirical knowledge. Also, many of them have scientific and pharmacological acceptance.

Names of the plants differ locally even more than knowledge of them does, for common names are by no means standardized. Thus it has been necessary to make arbitrary selections of the common names which seemed to the author to be most often heard. Also (and this may be strange to the amateur) it has been necessary to choose among the scientific names for each plant, for botanists are by no means agreed about the most authoritative name for many species. This problem of selection was solved by using a single authority for scientific names, Gray's *Manual of Botany,* eighth edition, largely rewritten and expanded by M. L. Fernald, and published in 1950.

If the question of plants, their locale, and their names has posed a problem in the preparation of this book, so has the discussion of their medicinal properties. Some plants which once enjoyed the widest repute, today would be questioned even by the most ardent herbalist. Certain other plant drugs, respectable current entries in the *United States Pharmacopoeia,* have had claims made for them in the past which go far beyond presently known values. Our aim has been to include only the plants which have a generally wide acceptance today.

A decision made easily was to eliminate plants of a highly poison-ous nature, and to provide suitable cautionary remarks for margin-ally poisonous ones. Plants of slight documentation, hallucinatory plants, and many plants of Indian medicine were also omitted, al-though pharmacological uses of plants by these first Americans is an interesting story, touched upon lightly in Chapter II.

Use of the book

Because the range of plants mentioned is so highly selective, the book does not constitute a medical encyclopedia, nor does it spell out prescriptions for any diseases.

Instead, it should be read as a brief history and general introduc-tion to herbal medicine, a practical guide to the use and preparation of simple herbal remedies, and a three-way reference for the recogni-tion of herbs and a knowledge of their medicinal properties. This reference includes Chapter IV, a glossary which defines and com-ments on a number of physical conditions that have been the subject of herbal treatment; Chapter V, which lists specific plants used in treatment of these conditions; and Chapter VI, "Plant Portraits," which discusses and gives an illustration for each of the plants separately.

The reader's own use of plant drugs will be dictated by his needs, beliefs, location, and circumstances. The plant portraits pre-sented in Chapter VI are intended as only a guide to much that is known or believed about the selected plants. The illustrations which supplement the verbal portraits have been drawn by the author to act not as a guide to identification but as a "memory jogger." The gross characteristics of each plant have been shown as accurately as possible within the limits of pen-and-ink, but the herb-gatherer should arm himself also with regional plant guides when they are available.

Taking into account the element of faith in healing

Suggestions for the use of dried plant material have been made on the simplest basis, with the feeling that the extraction of active prin-ciples is done best in a pharmacological manner, and that use and prescription of these extractions should be under the guidance of physicians. Simple infusions of certain plants, where so indicated, have been found to be of considerable value in malfunctions of the human body, but, in the familiar phrase on the label of many items from the drug store, "A physician should be consulted if prompt relief is not obtained."

This last statement does not contradict the author's belief in the curative value of even marginally acceptable plant drugs; for more than chemistry is involved in healing. The best doctor in the world, with the most chemically potent drugs, can often do little for the patient who is without hope or faith. And natural processes, given time, will often work wonders in the restoration of health with or without medicines. To these factors one can impute the claims for cures which are otherwise without scientific basis.

Of course, the importance of faith in healing is no new idea. Philosophers have written about it for centuries. The Stoic Roman philosopher Seneca wrote, "It is part of the cure to wish to be cured," and the founder of Christianity said, "Thy faith hath made thee whole."

Many Christian rituals reflect belief in this principle. The Roman Catholic church provides formal application of the healing power of faith in its rite of extreme unction. The Episcopal church has a pre-scribed service in its *Book of Common Prayer* called "The Laying on of Hands." The Emmanuel movement in the Episcopal church at the turn of the century was an effort to put healing back into the place into which Christ elevated it. In discussing his attitude toward this place of the Christian religion and faith in healing, the founder of the movement, Rev. Elwood Worcester, has said:

> "We are not skilled physicians—we are teachers of religion; and we believe that religion is a reality, that it has ideas and emotions which can release psychic forces strong enough to create a unified state of mind in which inhibitions, weaknesses, disharmonies incline to disappear, with consequent beneficial reaction on the physical organism. . . . If cure there is to be, it must come from within."

And the Christian Science church goes beyond these and other move-ments in making the process of healing a central belief; its successes have undoubtedly had an unacknowledged influence on all healing practices of our century. Certainly the power of religious faith today as a part of the whole of healing should not be dismissed.

On a nonreligious basis, the understanding of the relationship of mind and body, although rooted in ancient Greek practice, led to an important twentieth century movement—psychosomatic medicine. It reinforced the belief that healing can come from oneself rather than from drugs, either botanical or chemical. It must be said that many perceptive doctors (the country doctors of popular image, for instance) have long recognized the importance of faith as therapy, but today, quite differently from a century ago, psychiatry and religion give them active support.

In conclusion, it is interesting to read about the rites practiced in a few remote parts of Mexico, in which, using the forms and trappings of the Mass, a priestess, or *curandero*, eats hallucinatory mushrooms for the purposes of giving herself extrasensory powers and, with them, the ability to prophesy and heal. In his book, *Mushrooms, Russia and History*, W. Gordon Wasson contends that such rites have been conducted around the world for untold centuries, and that in them are the true beginnings of all religious observances. We might also see in them the original merger of medicine, religion, and herbal remedies, to help us put these three in proper relationship today.

The place of home remedies in medicine

The patient who finds that some of the "miracle" drugs have alleviated one condition only to produce a worse one, may well be interested in trying some of the remedies which "Grandma used to take." Or—taking advantage of modern medical knowledge—it would seem sensible to use inorganic chemicals reinforced by organic plants— science and nature thereby working as allies.

The value of plant drugs is assessed in *Cancer Chemotherapy Report No. 7*, issued by the Public Health Service. Discussing plant remedies for cancer, the assistant chief of research in that field, Jonathan L. Hartwell, a friend of the author, writes:

> "To sum up, the empirical application of plants to the ailing human body over thousands of years has resulted in certain observed effects interpreted as beneficial, and has culminated in the development of many useful drugs for a number of diseases. If there is any hope in a chemical treatment for cancer, it is reasonable to believe that such an agent is as likely to originate from a plant as from pure synthesis."

In broader terms, E. Vincent Askey, M.D., a former president of the American Medical Association, puts plant remedies in perspective with medical science. In an article in *This Week*, December 19, 1960, he acknowledges the mass of evidence on simple remedies which Grandma has handed down:

> "Home remedies probably always will have a place in the treatment of mankind's aches and pains. Physicians do not expect and do not desire that patients shall dash to the doctor with every minor discomfort, every trifling injury, every small ache or pain. It is sensible to care for such things by simple, safe home means.
>
> "Folk medicine has to its credit many important contributions to scientific medicine. It will continue to have a strong appeal as long as gaps in our scientific knowledge exist. . . .
>
> "Another reason for strong faith in folk medicine is that some of it was definitely effective in a percentage of cases—digitalis for 'dropsy' due to heart weakness, quinine for malarial fever, citrus juices to prevent scurvy, . . . relief of asthma with ma-huang (ephedrine).
>
> "Psychological factors are important, too. Perhaps no force is so persuasive in favor of folk medicine as the overwhelming desire of the normal person to get well. . . ."

Dr. D. C. Jarvis, whose book, *Folk Medicine*, has been read by millions, suggests that popular reliance on herbal medicine stems partly from our observation that wild and domestic animals use them instinctively. He writes:

> "I have come to marvel at the instinct of animals to make use of natural laws for healing themselves. They know unerringly which herbs will cure what ills. Wild creatures first seek solitude and absolute relaxation, then they rely on the complete remedies of Nature—the medicine in plants and pure air. A bear grubbing for fern roots; a wild turkey compelling her babies in a rainy spell to eat leaves of the spice bush; an animal, bitten by a poisonous snake, confidently chewing snakeroot—all these are typical examples. An animal with fever quickly hunts up an airy, shady place near water, there remaining quiet, eating nothing but drinking often until its health is recovered. On the other

hand, an animal bedeviled by rheumatism finds a spot of hot sunlight and lies in it until the misery bakes out."

Scientific investigation has confirmed the medicinal value of most of the plants which sick animals select instinctively. This suggests the virtue of another animal instinct—their use of food as medicine. In his journals, Thoreau wrote, "A man may esteem himself happy when that which is his food is also his medicine." And now scientific research seems to agree with both Thoreau and the animal world! We know for instance, that plants, and plants only, can transmute inorganic elements into the organic substances which become the food of animals (hence our meat) and of man (in the form of grains, fruits, and vegetables). Thus, when we use plants medicinally, we are employing active organic substances which are in harmony with our own physical composition. Chemical drugs are inert materials which are often incompatible with the chemistry of our bodies—this is an added reason for the continuing use of herbal medicines.

Another factor adds validity to reliance on plant medicines: herbal doctors generally believe that small doses continued for a long time are more effective than large quantities administered at once. This theory agrees with some of the normal modern chemotherapy.

One of the most prolific current writers on herbal medicine, Mrs. C. F. Leyel, states that the fundamental objective of herbal doctors, after making a diagnosis, is to purify the bloodstream and create a normal functioning of the ductless glands. Then, using herbs which have specific spheres of influence on the human body, to endeavor to make the body function properly. Professional herbal doctors contend that their treatment is especially suited to deal with chronic complaints. The plant medicines, being administered in small doses usually of low potency, are slow in effect, but, Mrs. Leyel says, "the slow process of herbal treatment effect more radical and complete cures than other more rapid methods."

In the past few decades, herbal doctors and pharmaceutical researchers, by scientific analysis, have eliminated the magic associated with many medicinal plants. Herbal practitioners in England, particularly, have been active not only in this direction, but also in endeavoring to exclude from their materia medica, poisonous plants. Many have been educated botanically as were the eighteenth century doctors who studied at the great University of Edinburgh.

In summary

Modern herbal doctors, aware of the general limitations of their field, are eager to cooperate with the more orthodox physicians. Although many medical doctors—and laymen as well—ally herbalism with superstition, nevertheless plant medicines are having a tremendous revival today and far greater acceptance than would have been thought possible a generation ago. George Sarton, Harvard professor and author of *An Introduction to the History of Science*, sums up:

> "The remembrance of these astounding folk discoveries . . . should sober our thoughts when we criticise too freely the old pharmacopoeias. It is easy to make fun of medieval recipes: it is more difficult and may be wiser to investigate them. Instead of assuming that the medieval pharmacist was a benighted fool, we might wonder whether there was not sometimes a justification for his strange procedure."

For those who believe in the cyclic nature of all things, as does the author, this brings us full circle.

With this statement, I conclude the preface and direct the reader to the pages which follow, in the hope that he will read them with the balanced viewpoint which I have proposed. In *Using Wayside Plants*, I pointed out that true conservation of our national heritage of trees and plants is fostered by knowledge, appreciation, and careful usage. I hope my readers, while they study the medicinal plants of our country, will strengthen their love of America and its many resources.

A word of appreciation

Finally, a word of appreciation to those who have helped me with the preparation of this book. These include many correspondents who have made suggestions or contributed personal experiences; my researcher, Mrs. Annie W. Couperus; my several "Nancy" typists; the librarians at Houghton Library of Harvard University, at the Massachusetts Horticultural Society, at the Massachusetts College of Pharmacy; several doctors, scientists and herbal enthusiasts who have read and helped criticize the manuscript; publishers who have granted reprint permissions; many writers and illustrators of the immediate and ancient past without whose books this one would have been impossible; finally, and not least, Nedda Casson Anders of Hearthside Press for her encouragement and wise counsel.

Nelson Coon

October, 1962
Vineyard Haven
Island of Martha's Vineyard
Commonwealth of Massachusetts

CHAPTER II

A DIP INTO THE PAST

*He preferred to know the power of herbs and their value
for curing purposes, and, heedless of glory, to exercise that
quiet art.*

Vergil, *Aeneid*, Book XII-I-396

BY TAKING a detour into history we will make our present-
day search for therapeutic plants more interesting and
meaningful. This chapter provides that backward look,
with special reference to plant medicine in America since
1492. To tell that story, one has to go back to the very beginnings of
civilized existence, back to a time about which only educated guessers can write.

Prehistoric to Roman times

On this particular subject, one of the best guessers is E. A. Wallis
Budge. We quote several paragraphs from his fascinating book, *The
Divine Origin of the Craft of the Herbalist.*

"It has already been said that many ancient nations thought
that the gods themselves were the first herbalists, and that it
was they who had taught their vicars upon earth how to heal
the sicknesses of man-kind by means of certain herbs and plants.
More than this, they thought that the herbs and plants which the
gods employed in their work of healing were composed of or

contained parts of the bodies of the gods. And as the operation or effect of a medicine became more assured, or more potent, if a formula was recited at the time when it was administered to the patient, the god or goddess supplied, according to the general belief, the words which constituted the formula which was recited by the herbalist. Thus the medicine itself, and the knowledge of how to administer it, and its healing effect, came directly from the gods. It is then clear that the gods were the earliest herbalists and physicians.

"It is impossible to say exactly which nation possessed the oldest gods of medicine. Of the Chinese gods of medicine little seems to be known. Some authorities claim that an Emperor of China called Huang-ti, who reigned about B.C. 2637, composed a treatise on medicine, and that another emperor, Chin-nong (B.C. 2699), composed a catalogue of Chinese herbs, or a sort of pharmacopeia."

Going beyond the clouded past of prehistory, one finds that our medical heritage from Europe actually has its beginning in Egypt. We are indeed fortunate to have a record of herbal medicine in the land of the Pharaohs. Apparently ancient Egyptian doctors practiced a combination of faith healing and herbalism, supplemented with magic. Proof of this survives in a papyrus translated by George Ebers, a German of the late nineteenth century.

Contemporaneously, the medical knowledge of the Greeks was advancing. Five hundred years before Christ, the father of medicine was born in Greece. To Hippocrates goes the credit for putting medicine on a scientific basis, separating fact from superstition and fancy, basing his theories on bedside observation. Also from the Greeks has come down to us the substantial work *An Enquiry Into Plants,* written about 370 B.C. by Theophrastus, a pupil of Plato, and fellow pupil of Aristotle. A section in his book on "The Juices of Plants, and of the Medicinal Properties of Herbs," is especially relevant to the present discussion. For such an early period, his was, indeed, a respectable bit of botanical observation.

Three hundred years later, the Roman poet, Vergil, in his *Georgics,* contributed a great deal to plant knowledge. His comments on the properties and growth of plants are worthy of attention today.

This combined Egyptian, Greek, and Roman knowledge was recorded in the first century of the Christian era by Dioscorides, a

De Lattuca.

Woodcut illustration from early printed herbal—Peter Crescentius (Venice 1471), suggesting lettuce as possible cure for snake bite.

Greek surgeon in the Roman army. His writings were extensive and showed a knowledge not only of plant remedies used in Rome but of those from many corners of the great empire.

Europe

It is, in a way, a sad commentary on the advance of civilization that the work of Dioscorides remained the basis of all European medical practice for nearly fifteen hundred years. Right into the twentieth century, many of Dioscorides' recommendations were still known and used by doctors and herbalists. In part, his writings were also used as a source by the Greek physician Galen (about 130 A.D.) for the system of medicine which we inherited.

However, not even the ancient herbal knowledge was spread widely throughout Europe until the advent of the printing press in the middle of the fifteenth century. The whole field of medicinal and herbal knowledge was given a new impetus by the invention of printing, and by the ability thus provided to disseminate the old knowledge of Dioscorides as well as the more up-to-date knowledge of the Moorish world.

In connection with the invention of printing, it is interesting to note that the twelfth complete work printed after the Bible was a book by one Peter Crescentius, with the title *De Agricultura*. This book, published in Venice in 1471, contained, despite its name, complete, woodcut-illustrated references to the useful and medicinal plants of southern Europe. This "catch-all" was quickly followed by more careful writings, of a number of meticulous Germans, especially the medical treatise *Ortus Sanitatus* published in 1491. Europe in the sixteenth century saw a great expansion and copying of such works and the publication in 1597 of *Gerard's Herbal* in English, was especially noteworthy for us. All things considered, seventeenth century explorers in the new world of America must have been, for their time, well informed about useful medicinal plants.

Mexico

Among the first of the explorers, who were the earliest colonists, the Spanish learned a great deal about the native medicine in their conquered lands. We are now fortunate in having facsimile copies of the well-illustrated manuscript of Aztec medicine written in Latin in 1552 by one Juan Badianus, a native doctor who had been educated by priests. His work, reflecting solely Indian practices, is dedicated to a doctor Francisco Hernandez, who, a few years later with a royal appointment, was able to explore and write about the whole of Mexican medical practice with a completeness still appreciated and studied. The exhaustive and interesting story of early Mexican medical knowledge is beyond the province of these pages even though much of this knowledge must surely have spread north from Mexico; but it does merit careful investigation elsewhere.

On a visit to Mexico in 1961, the author found many stalls selling medicinal herbs in the great public markets that are so important to the people of that country. The available varieties of dried plant material differed greatly from the plants mentioned in this present book, but the dependence on herbal material by more primitive members of the Indian population was obvious. In the two largest cities of Mexico, one finds herbal practitioners with extensive offices and consulting rooms. Evidence is great that, despite 400 years of European medical practice, the knowledge of local plant medicines is still treasured by the descendants of this and other ancient cultures.

Hawaii

Similarly, in our newest state, there exists a native flora which we cannot here investigate, but which must be mentioned. Hawaii typifies many formerly isolated countries in which the materia medica of necessity was almost exclusively indigenous, and varied greatly from that used elsewhere. In precolonial days in Hawaii, the medicine man, in addition to being an herbalist, had to be well-schooled in the importance of the spiritual or magical numbers. With a fifteen year apprenticeship and the study of three hundred plants known to have been used, he was able to cure or kill by psychological as well as by herbal means. But in Hawaii, naturally, the plants were all tropical. Members of the nightshade and pepper families were important, as were morning glory species, taro roots, forms of hibiscus, roots of some trees and the juice of others. Considering the known virility of the Hawaiian peoples in the days before European diseases took their toll, who can say that our modern medical armamentarium is any more efficient for our time than was theirs for its more primitive civilization? And yet how their remedies differed from those of Europe.

America

Thus, one sees that cultures all over the fifteenth century world had developed herbal practices of their own, yet exchange of this knowledge outside the Roman Empire was at a minimum. Although both China and India had a well-developed herbal lore long before Europe came out of the Dark Ages, the spice trade brought little exchange of this knowledge between East and West. It did bring to the West spices with medicinal flavors and possible stomachic values, many of which became important ingredients in medieval specifics.

When the search for spices led the early explorers to America, they found a land rich in medicinal herbs. In 1602, an Englishman, Gosnold, explored and named the island of Martha's Vineyard off Cape Cod and discovered sassafras growing there. Economic historians contend that the cargo of sassafras which he transported to Europe was probably the first American export.

The importance of medicinal plants in early America, and particularly of sassafras, is recorded by another Englishman, Whitaker, who wrote in his *Good News From Virginia* (1612) that he found many plants such as "pine, pitchtrees, soape ashes, cedar, ash, maple and cypress" and "sassafras which is called by the inhabitants *Winauk*, a kinde of wood of most pleasant and sweet smell, and of rare virtues in phisick for the cure of many diseases."

A much more extensive discussion of Colonial medicine as seen by a contemporary in the years from 1638 to 1660, is found in a pamphlet appearing in London in 1672 by John Josselyn, *New England Rarities Discovered . . . and Chyrurgical remedies wherewith the natives constantly used to cure their distempers, wounds and sores.*

Indian medicine

From works such as that just noted we see that the herbal knowledge of the English soon merged with the purely empiric and less mythological lore of the Indians. The untutored Redmen living in the country were entirely dependent upon nature, and had learned to live with and by it. In 1621, a writer in England commented:

"The French relations of their voyages to Canada, tell us that the Indians and themselves falling into a contagious disease; of which Phisitians could give no reason or remedy, they were all in a short space restored to their health merely by drinking water; in which Saxifrage [Sassafras? Ed.] was infused and boyled; which was discovered to them by the natives; and wee justly entertain beliefe that many excellent medicines either for

DR. JAMES M. SOLOMON, JR.,

INDIAN PHYSICIAN.

Seventh Son of old Dr. James M. Solomon, of Attleboro, Mass.

TREATS ALL DISEASES WITH ROOTS, HERBS AND BARKS.

Locates Diseases without asking questions.

YOU CAN BE CURED NOW.

DR. SOLOMON has had years of experience in every class or form of disease. He has treated more cases annually than any other physician in the world, curing thousands of persons who were considered incurable; and has raised from the deathbed thousands who had lost all hope. Those who once said "I WILL TRY NO MORE," are to-day his converts

No CALOMEL, QUININE, or other SLOW POISONS, but Nature's own remedies have power over disease.

DR. SOLOMON IS PERMANENTLY LOCATED AT

75 COURT STREET, BOSTON, MASS.

Where he can be consulted daily from 9 a. m. to 6 p. m. **Consultation Free.**

Typical of the late nineteenth century, this advertisement by an herbal doctor invokes, as evidence of his special

conservation of Nature in her vigour or restauration in her decadence may be communicated unto us. . . ."

Whatever the early English settlers may have known of *Gerard's Herbal* and of hand-me-down folk medicine, they soon became aware of the empiric knowledge of their Indian neighbors. It is in part this knowledge that makes American folk medicine quite different from European.

To be sure, the knowledge of all of the plant medicines of the Indians is a matter not too well known. The official medicine men of the Indians were not given to advertising the nature of their cures as were their imitators of the nineteenth and twentieth centuries. For the little we know of seventeenth and eighteenth century usages, we must turn to travelers, priests, and merchants and to a few of the physicians of a more inquiring turn of mind. One reporter on life in the New Netherlands, although not a doctor, found easily some thirty plants which he said were valuable to the Indians, including polypody, sweet flag, sassafras, mallow, violet, wild indigo, Solomon's seal, milfoil, ferns, agrimony, wild leek, snake root, and prickly pear.

A careful researcher of early American medical history is William B. Fenton, who, in the 1942 Annual of the Smithsonian Institution, summarizes what is known about the herbalism of the Iroquois Indians.

He offered "a partial list of the more important plants used among the Iroquois" (Scientific names omitted—Ed.):

maidenhair fern	crane's bill	wild indigo
white pine	ground pine	sumac
Indian turnip	hemlock	Jersey tea
blue flag	sweet flag	basswood
white oak bark	bellwort	leatherwood bark
Indian poke	sweet gale	willow-herb
wild ginger	slippery elm	ginseng
golden seal	gold thread	sarsaparilla
black cohosh	Canada anemone	tobacco
papoose root	mayapple	water-hemlock
bloodroot	sassafras	angelica
cherry bark	avens	

The above list of plants comes from only one of the great tribes, but the records indicate that, given the differences in flora and climate, Indian practices had certain similarities throughout America.

A few further examples of the variety of Indian remedies will make the point clear. As cardiac stimulants, the North Carolina Indians used an infusion of yaupon holly *(Ilex vomitoria)* while the Dakota and Winnebago Indians depended upon bee balm *(Monardo punctata)*. The Delawares for the same purpose used pokeweed *(Phytolacca decandra)*, and the Pawnee Indians used a morning glory *(Ipomoea leptophylla)*. Another example, for a simple thing like a diuretic Ottawas used wintergreen *(Chimaphila)*, while the Chippewas used decoctions of yellowwood *(Zanthorhiza)*; the Tewa Indians depended upon cedar *(Juniperous monosperma)*, and the Plains Indians, sarsaparilla *(Aralia nudicaulis)*. The authority for these facts, M. B. Gordon, says his research has shown that the Indians definitely added 59 drugs to our modern pharmacopoeia; including cascara sagrada, lobelia, puccoon, cohosh, pipsissewa, and dockmackie.

It is regrettable that a much fuller appreciation of the contributions of America's Indians was so long delayed in our country and that observation of the positive aspects of their knowledge was so casual. Regrettable, too, that the tribal system and tribal antagonisms prevented the development of more uniform practices among these peoples. Linguistic differences must also have hampered the exchange of the medicinal knowledge which they possessed.

One of the earliest efforts to explore the herbal knowledge of the Indians was made at the end of the seventeenth century. In an enlightened area of Philadelphia, the suburban community of Germantown, lived a Bavarian, one Johann Kelpius (1673-1708), who became interested in the flora of his adopted country and established what is deemed to be the first arboretum in the United States. His main objective was to test the plant drugs of America which he had discovered through contact with the Indians.

Early colonial-pioneer America

As one would expect, the effect of seemingly magical cures on the native Indians by their own doctors was not lost on the early settlers, who, even in the best circumstances, were quite isolated from European trained doctors. Actually, the belief in the *Doctrine of Signatures* in which the shape or color of a plant determined its probable use was not too far in the background of seventeenth century European practice nor—as we know all too well from what happened at Salem—neither was a belief in witchcraft. Except for the veneer of what one might designate as Roman cultural civilization, the colonist and his Indian neighbors were actually not too far apart in medical beliefs.

Hence we find that the colonists' knowledge of European herbal medicine, bolstered by an underlying belief in magic and witchcraft, provided, when placed alongside the similar knowledge of the Indians, a situation where cross-borrowings could take place quickly and extensively. This is easily confirmed by exploring the folklore of peoples such as those in the southern mountains who, long isolated from the main track of progress, are still using herbal medicines; or by noting the home remedies which have been handed down in household compendiums or cookbooks, in old diaries, and by word of mouth.

For a quick look at the history of folk medicine in the south, we can turn to a recent article by Supreme Court Justice William O. Douglas. In the *National Geographic Magazine*, June, 1962 ("The People of Cades Cove") he writes that the early settlers of the Tennessee mountains (the Great Smokies) were "heavily dependent on homemade remedies." Among other plant medicines he mentions are:

Buds of the Balm of Gilead tree made a salve for soreness and aches.
Onion poultices for pneumonia, chest colds and croup.
Tea made from rue leaves for stomach worms.
Crushed jewelweed . . . for poison ivy.
Honey and alum for sore throat.
Tea made of ground ivy for the croup.
Catnip tea or mustard poultice for colds.
Wads of cobweb on wounds to staunch blood.
Tea from spikenard roots for backache.
Tea from the bark of the wild cherry for measles and colds.

Justice Douglas concludes: "While there was an herb school in the Smokies, there was also the alcohol school. The latter said herbs 'hain't a bit of use without just a grain of whiskey.' " This alcohol theory is quite widespread although somewhat dependent on one's religious convictions or cultural heritage.

Or one can look at what happened to a community of Americans whose isolation made them more than normally dependent on folk and Indian medicine. The author's island off the New England coast, a community of fisherfolk and farmers in the eighteenth century, was for periods of time without a resident physician. Joseph Chase Allen, a knowledgeable folklorist of Martha's Vineyard, has offered a sample list of some of the remedies mentioned to him in his younger days by the "oldtimers," and we can imagine that these are only representative of a much larger knowledge.

Cranberries—Crushed to use as a poultice
Celandine—Bathing inflammations with crushed plants
Catnip tea—For soothing babies
Tansy tea—General remedy for adults
Balm of Gilead buds—Soaked in rum as a healing liniment
Blackberry juice—For diarrhea
Pennyroyal—To cause abortion

The "worts"

Thorough-wort ⎫ Used internally for various
Kidney-wort ⎬ —purposes and externally for
Blood-wort   ⎭ piles

Mullein root—Used as a soothing syrup for coughs
Onions, boiled—Wrapped around affected part as a frostbite cure
Sassafras root tea—A general specific

The patent medicine era

These and many others were folk remedies. Official approval did not come until a notable physician, Benjamin Rush of Philadelphia, investigated and wrote about the materia medica of the Indians. With his work, and the experiences of many individuals, popular confidence in Indian medicine grew and remained strong during the early nineteenth century. "Yarb" doctors, red or white, were prominent in many communities, and soon compilers began to publish guides to Indian medicines. A few of the titles are: *Indian Doctor's Dispensatory*, 1813, Cincinnati; Selman's *Indian Guide to Health*, 1836; Foster's *North American Indian Doctor*, 1838.

In fact a positive attitude toward the Indian medicine man persisted up to the second decade of this century. One notes the success for thirty or more years of the famous Kickapoo Indian Medicine Company. It's a success which could not have been attained without public confidence that "the Indians knew the answers." Today on television we are sold various nostrums which quite likely are no better than some "Indian Medicine," with the difference that endorsement by the medical profession rather than by the Indians, is implied.

Some Americans who appreciated the combination of Indian and colonial herb practice wrote about it. One such, Dr. Samuel Thomson (1769-1843) of New Hampshire, in 1822 produced an 800-page manual at the then almost prohibitive price of $20.00.

Dr. Thomson is worth more than passing mention. He was not a quack; although self-taught, his prescriptions were so useful that they were widely copied. In 1813, having found certain compounds of plant medicines valuable in easily diagnosed circumstances, he had them patented, and thus started the vogue for patent medicines. This patenting, he claimed was not for personal profit nor credit, but to protect the public from the misrepresentations of his imitators.

It can easily be understood that a doctor without credentials in the early nineteenth century (or in any century for that matter) would be a thorn in the side of the graduates of medical schools, and Dr. Thomson's life was filled with litigations. But, curiously, the years seemed to have justified his convictions. For example, one claim made by the doctor was for the peculiar efficacy of *Lobelia inflata*, a plant which soon appeared in the *Pharmacopoeia* and has remained a reputable drug until the present time. In fact, of 65 major plants from which his medicines were compounded, at least fifty species are still valued.

Returning from Washington with his patent, Dr. Thomson stopped in Philadelphia to discuss his ideas with Dr. Rush, and especially with Dr. Benjamin Smith Barton (1766-1815), a physician and scientist, who had written *Materia Medica of the United States*. It is from a work such as his that we know a great deal of the Indian medical lore.

The successes of Thomson and the writings of Barton and others focussed public interest on medicinally useful American plants. Soon there appeared other works on the subject, some scientifically founded, others purely popular. Of the former, notable was *Good's Family Flora*, which was issued in parts (as was the custom of the time), by Peter P. Good of Elizabethtown, New Jersey. Another was

The Complete Herbalist, or *The People Their Own Physicians By The Use Of Nature's Remedies,* by Dr. O. Phelps Brown of Jersey City, New Jersey.

The circulation of such writings stimulated the use of plant drugs, but there were few sources for their purchase in quantity, except as people went into the woods themselves or grew the plants in their gardens. For a good description of the gathering of medicinal herbs by settlers in isolated areas in the eighteenth and nineteenth centuries, we turn again to an article by Joseph Chase Allen, September 1, 1961, in the Martha's "Vineyard Gazette."

> "Not quite all the herbs they collected were to be found in the swamps. . . . The thoroughwort, still heavy with its greenish-white blooms, kidney wort, with its pink clusters, and bloodwort, also pink, these were to be found rooted in the soft, black mud. . . . Celandine, with its tiny orange trumpets, grew almost in the water . . . and withe-wood, the bark of which was saved and dried for the annual spring tonic. Long before sulphur was available, the rude forefathers of the hamlet had mixed up pulverized withe-wood bark and either steeped it or blended it with molasses to be taken as a conditioner. . . . On their way to and from the very wet places, the herb-gatherers collected other things. Catnip, in its second bloom, apt to be heavier, and certainly with more and larger leaves. . . . There were tansy, leaves and blooms, yarrow, both the pink and white, and baskets of wild cherry twigs. These last, steeped while yet green, produced a bitter tea . . . for the appetite, they said.
>
> "On the higher, drier land, they gathered pennyroyal, which was always regarded as a 'woman's medicine.'
>
> "Somehow the preparation and even the application of herb remedies never appeared to attract any particular attention. It was accepted as a part of life. . . ."

The Shakers

However diligently the country folk might gather their herbs in the late eighteenth and early nineteenth century, city people had no access to the bounties of forests and fields. Into this gap, in a most responsible way, stepped the Church of the United Society of Believers (known commonly as the Shakers). Its five thousand members working together in the East and Midwest, were prime friends of the Indians and were the first to pioneer in the mass production of herbs. They specialized successfully in the growing and honest merchandising of a wide variety of drug plants.

To meet the demand for drugs recommended by Thomson and others, two Shakers, in 1820, laid out a "physic garden" in New Lebanon, New York. By 1857, a visitor to the Shaker settlement was able to report that in one season seventy-five tons of medical plants were grown, dried, pressed, packed, and shipped to every state, as well as to London and Australia. In fact, a list issued just prior to the Civil War offers 354 kinds of medicinal plants, barks, roots, seed and flowers as well as a nearly equal number of preparations—extracts, powders, ointments and the like. It was, in short, big business, and established the Shakers as America's first reputable manufacturing druggists.

In a recent book, *The Queen of the Shakers*, Arthur Joy lists the plants which were grown on these community farms. Many of the wild plants of the Indian materia medica are noted; others were demanded by settlers familiar with European practice. A partial list:

hops	coltsfoot	sarsaparilla
mullein	milkweed	fleabane
peppermint	thoroughwort	wintergreen
hardhack leaves	tansy	sumac
chicory	rue	balm
thorn apple	pumpkin	bugle
sage	hyssop	elderberries
motherwort	dandelion	skullcap
burdock root	poppy leaves	spearmint
pennyroyal	thyme	catnip
snakeshead	foxglove	marshmallow
horseradish	mint	lavender
lobelia		

In the years that followed, purveyors of drugs less scrupulous than the Shakers perpetrated many medical frauds. This uncaring attitude of some elements of the drug *industry* (not the corner druggist) is nothing new; we find as a preface to a discussion of false drugs by one P'ei-lan, published in China in 1666, a quoted proverb probably *then* not new:

> Sellers of drugs have two eyes;
> Prescribers of drugs have one eye;
> Takers of drugs have no eyes.

Such a viewpoint was not confined to China. In a book of advice to farmers written by one Heresbachius, published in 1601, we find this statement:

> Nature hath appointed remedies in a readiness for all diseases but the craft and imbecility of man for gain (surrounds us with) deuced apothecary shops, in which a man's life is to be sold or bought where for a little spoil they fetch their medicines from Jerusalem and out of Turkey, while in the meantime every poor man hath the right remedies growing in his garden: for if men should make gardens their physicians, the physicians craft would soon decay. You know what your old friend Cato saith "what a deal of physick he fetcheth out of a poor colewort?"

America today

The beginning of the twentieth century saw an almost total repudiation of plant remedies and almost total acceptance of synthetic medicines. The friendly family doctor with his old-fashioned folk remedies and hieroglyphic prescriptions, which surely had a touch of magic, was superseded by the highly trained specialist who kept himself informed on the up-to-the minute details of his branch of medicine.

Here the author wishes to pay tribute to science for the advances in medical, surgical and hospital practice which have lengthened American life span and practically eliminated some previously fatal diseases. Medical reporters dramatized the various discoveries and soon the patient thought he knew as much as his physician. Many of the laymen would ask for a shot of the miracle drug of the day, which might have been good for a specific condition but not necessarily for the total patient. In fact, the miracle drugs frequently produced side effects which were harmful to other parts of the body. Thus, as it became increasingly apparent that the cure was sometimes worse than the sickness, a reappraisal of chemical medicines inevitably began.

In 1962, two widely publicized events led to a further swing away from inorganic dosage. First was the startling and tragic news that deformity in newborns could be traced directly to thalidomide, a chemical used to suppress nausea in pregnant women.

The second important event was the publication of Rachel Carson's book, *Silent Spring*. Newspapers everywhere printed editorial comments, television broadcasts devoted special programs to it, and selections were read into the Congressional Record. On the surface, this book seems to have little connection with our subject, since it attacks the use of pesticides. But the review in the *New York Times*, September 1962, explains a developing viewpoint:

> "In answer to the charge that the balance of nature has been upset, it has been pointed out by some members of the chemical industry that modern medicine is equally upsetting. This sort of defense merely invites a pox on both the biocide and the drug industries. *Silent Spring* offers warnings in this direction too: trivial amounts of one poison often make trivial amounts of another suddenly disastrous; and poisons stored in the body may be tolerated during health, but take effect dramatically as soon as any sickness decreases the body's resistance. It is high time for people to know about these rapid changes in their environment, and to take an effective part in the battle that may shape the future of all life on earth."

As may be supposed, the drug industry did not escape criticism. Pharmaceutical companies (having recently undergone a Congressional investigation on a charge of over-pricing their products) were now accused of promoting synthetic drugs after inadequately testing them, which they then misrepresented and oversold to the public.

But the picture is not one-sided. Responsible elements in the pharmaceutical trade have spent millions in research, including the sending of expeditions into remote places all over the world.

Mr. Erwin H. Ackerknecht, in the UNESCO "Courier" sums it up:

> ". . . It is quite obvious that besides useless substances, as they occur in all pharmacopoeias, even in our own, primitive pharmacopoeias contain a surprising percentage of effective drugs in spite of the magic ideas which govern their use. The

Spanish conquerors of the sixteenth century were sufficiently impressed by the drug lore of the Indians to organize research in this field. Modern science has stood aloof from such studies among the 'superstitious heathen' for at least a century. But lately, pharmaceutical industry has been sufficiently impressed by the potentialities of such studies to spend a considerable amount of money for research on primitive drugs. We have no doubt that from those studies will come further evidence of the amazing and surprising knowledge of effective drugs possessed by primitive peoples."

The return to plant-based drugs has been slow but inevitable. In recent decades, Rauwolfia has been found effective for blood pressure; curare is given in anesthesia; and an extraction from the periwinkle plant, widely used in treating Hodgkin's disease, may arrest leukemia, according to the report of pharmaceutical scientists, at the April 1962 meeting of the American Association for Cancer Research.

The wide interest in folk remedies has been demonstrated to the author, who received literally hundreds of letters from readers of a short chapter on medicinals which appeared in his first book *Using Wayside Plants* (also published by Hearthside Press).

It is hoped that this guide to American medicinal plants will help us understand the herbal remedies of the past, thereby guiding us to better health in the future through the use of Nature's bounties.

CHAPTER III

PREPARING PLANTS FOR MEDICINAL USE

It is medicine, not scenery, for which a sick man must go a-searching.

Seneca
Epistolae—Civ. 18

ONSIDERATION of the use of wild plants as medicine, must include "a few words" on collecting and preparing the plants. The freshness of herbs is related to potency, as is also the time of year when each plant or plant-part is gathered and processed.

Collecting plants

Primarily it should be understood that an armentarium of drugs can not be acquired on one trip nor at one season. The plants whose medicinal values are confined to the root system will usually be most potent in the spring before much growth takes place; the properties of bark will be available when the plant is in an active growing state; buds, which are often highly potent, can only be obtained in the spring; pollen will be obtainable only during a short season; the strength of drugs obtained from leaves and stem tips will probably be best when the plants are just about to come into flower; and seeds of value as medicine can obviously only be obtained when the fruit ripens. Hence, those who wish to secure and prepare their own plant medicines, must get out in the open the year around.

The distillation of medicinal herbs shown in a book by Hieronymus Brunschwig (Brussels 1517).

The collection of plants will have values other than that of healthful tramping in the woods. It will sharpen your senses, for plant gathering requires the use of the eyes for keen observation, and your sense of smell and taste. It is probable that the professional herb-gatherers of the Blue Ridge mountains depend a great deal on finding the plants through smell and the completion of certification by tasting. Thus is sharpened those senses otherwise too often neglected.

Another observation which the searching herbalist is apt to find interesting is the extent to which there is an effect of soil and climate on the potency of drugs. Present day botanical explorers and herbalists of earlier generations, are agreed that specimens of the same plant grown in different localities will vary infinitely in the proportions of the medicinal principles yielded. The ability of plants of any kind to secure mineral properties from the soil or rocks on which they grow is remarkable. As proof, taste the difference in apples from, say, the state of Washington against those from the rocky soils of the Hudson Valley or Vermont. Or consider the different tastes of wines pressed from the same varieties of grapes, but grown on different soils; differences, for instance, such as one will find between some of the merely palatable California wines, as related to many of the flavorful wines from mineral rich soils of New York's Lake district.

Similarly, there are also identifiable differences between plants gathered in the wild, growing in the natural humus of the woods, and those same plants transplanted and grown in a garden with chemical fertilizers.

Basically the successful gathering of herbs is dependent on correct identification of the plant desired. Here one may have to rely on knowing friends or go on the collecting trip armed with a well-keyed floral guide to the region. Professional herb gatherers of the Appalachians and other sections accumulate their knowledge from childhood, while even botanists who work with plants all their lives are puzzled at times by the members of one or another genus; hence the amateur should not feel discouraged in his hunt for, and identification of, some of the herbs he will need. If at all in doubt about the plant, let the decision be negative, until an expert can decide.

Having identified the plant, the collector must then be certain that he knows which part of the plant is used for medicinal purposes. There is small use in collecting whole plants if only the roots are used, nor is conservation served by digging up the roots of a plant when only leaves are needed. Chapter V gives specific information.

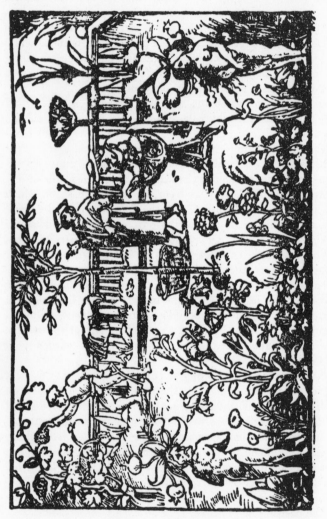

In this woodcut from the title page of Den groten Herbarius (Antwerp, 1533), a doctor directs a woman in the gathering of herbs, while a workman tends a grapevine. In the foreground, at each side, are unrealistic but traditional representations of the supposedly powerful Mandrake.

Preserving plants

Having found and gathered the plant parts indicated, the collector should recall that, in the heat of summer especially, due care should be taken to protect leaves and tops of plants so that they may be put into the dryer in as pristine condition as possible. Crushing fresh foliage containing volatile oils means the loss of valuable properties and ordinary "wilting" is no substitute for careful drying.

Actually the method of drying is a matter of the first importance; the quicker the drying takes place, the more likely one is to conserve the properties. In older days it was the habit to tie the herbs in bunches and hang them in the hot dry attic of the home. This was a good place for a number of reasons: it *was* hot and dry; there was usually a gentle breeze from an open window; there were no direct sun-rays to take the color from the leaves; no moisture to cause harmful mildewing.

In the days of ranch-style and split-level homes, an ideal attic may not be easy to find. In that case one must resort to a more scientific method of preparing plants for storage. This will involve the building of an herb drier as elaborate or expensive as seems possible or justifiable. Ideally, such a drier, to be used out-of-doors in bright sunshine, should include such features as 1) a thin muslin cover to provide shade, 2) a box with a screen wire bottom to permit full circulation of air, 3) a slatted tray on which plants may be laid for drying, 4) a side opening door to permit insertion of the tray, 5) a pipe support for the whole box to permit turning to follow the sun over a long day and 6) a glass lid which may be lowered at night and against showers. Such a box may be made simply and inexpensively and of a size of about 2' x 3'. The specifications for such a drier and the accompanying sketch are given by permission of the *Herb Society of America.*

A simple herb drier

The drier, by Arnold M. Davis, made of ⅞" material, may be constructed by any practical carpenter. A sheet of gray or white muslin is tacked below the glass: this muslin will filter out enough of the light to preserve the color of the leaves. The disposition of the water

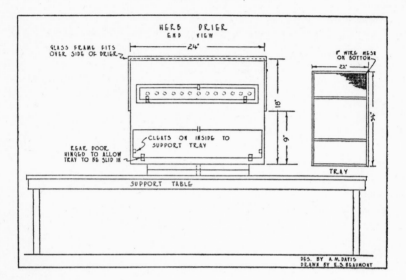

HERB DRIER
END VIEW

GLASS FRAME FITS OVER SIDE OF DRIER

CLEATS ON INSIDE TO SUPPORT TRAY

REAR DOOR HINGED TO ALLOW TRAY TO BE SLID IN

SUPPORT TABLE

WIRE MESH ON BOTTOM

TRAY

DES. BY A. M. DAVIS
DRAWN BY E. S. BEAUMONT

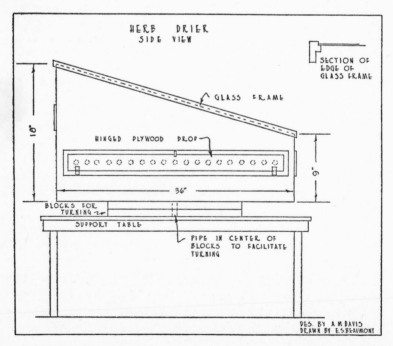

HERB DRIER
SIDE VIEW

SECTION OF EDGE OF GLASS FRAME

GLASS FRAME

HINGED PLYWOOD DROP

BLOCKS FOR TURNING

SUPPORT TABLE

PIPE IN CENTER OF BLOCKS TO FACILITATE TURNING

DES. BY A. M. DAVIS
DRAWN BY E. S. BEAUMONT

which will result from dehydrating of the leaves of the plant is provided by the holes bored in the sides of the drier. These are 1″ holes placed 3″ apart on the four sides of the drier and are covered with hinged plywood drops. When the herbs are first placed in the drier all of the drops are open. As the drying process advances one or more of these slides are closed until the entire circulation of air is excluded.

To get best results with such a drier it should be turned with the sun so that in the morning it will face east and in the late afternoon it will face west. Of course, the most effective time of the day will be high noon when the sun is almost directly overhead and thus generates its greatest heat. If herbs are picked early in the morning and placed in the drier they should be completely dried by afternoon and in good condition for either permanent storage or other processing. This statement would apply to a bright sunny day in the middle of summer. In the early spring and in the late fall, when the sun's rays are not as powerful, the herbs will need a longer period to dry. This is perfectly safe, if the drops are closed at sunset, to exclude moisture. This drier is definitely for the amateur collector or home grower and not a commercial appliance. With a little practice it should give a superior dried herb with a minimum of effort.

Such a drier may be used at any time of year for buds, shoots, leaves, bark or roots. The material should remain on the tray only until it is dry. This will vary from 24 hours for foliage to three, four or more days for fleshy roots.

When plant materials are dry, store them in ground-glass, stoppered, or other airtight containers to prevent moisture and consequent mildew. Do not macerate or otherwise prepare the material for medicinal use at this time, for the secret of maintaining potency seems to be in retaining the chemical components in their "original package." Store bundles of stems or roots in a dry place for a period of extra-drying or curing if there be any doubt that they are not thoroughly dry. Note, too, that plant parts, even seeds, which may *seem* to be dry when gathered might actually quickly mould in tight storage without a specific period of air drying as outlined.

The obvious question at this point is—what do I do with these drug plants after I have them collected, dried and properly stored? Answer—you will find them listed in the Index according to the condition which they are reputed to cure.

Medieval apothecary's shop as shown in a woodcut from
Das Buch des Lebens offered by one Ficinus (Florence 1508).

Compound medicines

Practice among herbalists and the formulae of the present drug trade indicate that the properties of various plants combined are often of greater value than of one isolated specimen. The secret of the Indian medicine men and even of the accredited doctor, is in his "combinations of ingredients" as the advertising phrase has it. And not always the same combinations, by any means.

One of the most up-to-date formularies used by professional pharmacists gives many different combinations for the same medicine. In the work mentioned (Belanger—q.v.) there are, for instance, fifteen formulae for a compound tonic, sixteen formulae for expectorants (cough remedies), nine for laxative compounds, ten for healing ointments, five for liniments, etc. Mostly these medicines have some common ingredients, many of which are derived from the plants mentioned in this book.

Hence, within the limits of safety and judgment, the herbal practitioner must "play it by ear" and experiment and utilize such standard formulae as are medically recognized, or which may have been handed down in family or community. It is not possible nor wise to give in these pages detailed prescriptions for the compounding of complete remedies as this is a book about *plants* and their reputed properties.

Knowledgeable readers probably will know that home medicines usually hinge on the use of infusions of dried herbs, fluid extracts, tinctures and the further doses, salves, liniments, lotions, compounds, etc., which may be made from the basic derivative.

Why are compounds more effective than single drugs? There are those who feel that a combination of plants, each having about the same effect, would increase the active power of the total remedy. Practice has shown that certain materials will guard the stomach or system against any upsetting effects as well as increase the probability of the system's accepting the drug. In particular, plant drugs of a mucilaginous nature will often guard the system against deleterious actions of some plant constituents.

A further reason for compounds is often to make the medicine more acceptable by altering its appearance or taste. Hence, in almost any preparation from the drug store or in home medicines, we find (1) a base or active ingredient, which is the substance assumed to be the curative agent (2) an additive which promotes the operation of the basic ingredient (3) some corrective to disguise the taste or perhaps moderate its activity by dilution or counter action and (4) the element which contains the substances and provides a usable form—such as water (hot or cold), honey, alcohol, oil, wax, etc.

Given these factors, we find that medicinal preparations come in a variety of *types* of prescriptions and for a wide variety of physical anomalies. To aid the reader in understanding the action and use of plant drugs a modest glossary follows.

CHAPTER IV

A GLOSSARY

*Dictionaries are like watches; the worst is better than none,
and the best cannot be expected to go quite true.*

Samuel Johnson
in *Johnsoniana*, Piozzi

VERY field or profession has its specialized vocabulary, hence it is to be expected that a number of words used by the botanical pharmacologist may not ring a bell in the ears of the layman. Also, the early herbalists used words that are no longer current in the medical profession, yet they are necessary in a book dealing with ancient lore. To aid the reader, some 75 of the most common terms are here discussed. For uncommon terms missing from this glossary, the reader is referred to any reliable dictionary.

Abortifacients

Any drugs which cause abortion.

Acrid

Harsh, bitterly pungent to the taste, or irritating to the skin or mucous membranes.

Alteratives

Medicines, often prescribed in the form of a tea, whose effect on the body is gradual, not immediately noticeable.

Amenorrhea

Absence or suppression of the menstrual discharge, from causes other than pregnancy.

Anodynes

Any medicines that allay pain. Most herbs which can be classified as anodynes are narcotic and highly dangerous, therefore little mention of them is made in this work.

Anthelmintics

Medicines for expelling intestinal worms. Plants containing substances which are obnoxious to the worms or which act as cathartics have been used for this purpose. Camomile, tansy and male fern are examples.

Antiperiodics

Substances which can allay or prevent the return of periodic paroxysms such as periodic fevers.

Antipyretics

Any medicines which tend to prevent or allay fevers.

Antiscorbutics

Preparations used to combat scurvy. In these days of generally well-balanced diets, such medicines are not of general interest, as they were a few generations ago. In medicines prescribed for scurvy one would usually find dandelion roots, lemons, and sarsaparilla as ingredients.

Antiseptics

Any plants or chemical products which oppose the growth or cause the destruction of micro-organisms or (in common parlance) germs.

Antispasmodics

Medicines which reduce the involuntary contractions arising from physical or nervous causes.

Aperients

Herbs which are gently laxative.

Aromatics

Plants, drugs, or medicines with a spicy scent and pungent taste. Among the aromatic plants are ginger, sweet flag, the mints, lavenders, and household herbs such as peppers, cloves, nutmeg, caraway, etc. The essential oils in these plants, added to medicines, make them palatable. The fragrances these herbs provide give a definite lift to our consciousness.

Asthma

A disease characterized by difficulty in breathing. Emotional as well as physical causes are known, so it is reasonable to assume that some of the sedative herbs would have an alleviative, if not a curative effect.

Astringents

Substances that contract the tissues and check discharges of blood, mucus, etc. Their use is indicated for hemorrhage, dysentery, and the like. In this class of materials we find plants such as agrimony, oak bark, willow, sage. A sample prescription would include burdock seeds, rose leaves, ginger, raspberry leaves and willow bark. Blackberry brandy, used to check diarrhea, is well known for its astringent quality.

Carminatives

A piece of mint after dinner is a mild carminative; it acts to reduce flatulence, which may be caused by a large meal. Other herbs which, separately or together, are used for this purpose include anise, and caraway, cloves, dill, ginger, and other aromatic spices.

Cathartics

Medicines which relieve constipation; Purgatives. *Laxatives* (q.v.) stimulate and quicken peristaltic action, while cathartics stimulate the secretions of the intestines, often with strong physical manifestations.

Cholagogues

Any medicines which promote the discharge of bile from the system.

Chorea

A nervous disorder characterized by twitchings such as in St. Vitus's dance.

Colds

Says a recent *Family Medical Encyclopedia,* "There is no specific remedy against the viruses of the common cold." It then goes on to list a number of things which may alleviate the symptoms and the misery. Relief to the nasal passages is often of help; the use of expectorants eases the throat, and bed rest is the best remedy of all. In another chapter some plants are mentioned as having been used for "the most common infection that afflicts and annoys mankind."

Constipation

This condition is alleviated by the use, at appropriate intervals, of mild laxatives. See that heading.

Corroborants

A somewhat fancy and perhaps outmoded term for that which is invigorating. Specifically tonics.

Coughs

Coughs, as almost everyone knows, have many causes. When it is determined that a cough is due to malfunctioning of the respiratory system, recourse may be had to simple medicines discussed under *Expectorants.*

Decoctions

Decoctions are medicines made by simmering herbs in water. (Vigorous boiling may destroy the vital properties of the plant).) Decoctions, without an added preservative such as alcohol, should not be kept for long but should be freshly prepared, especially in hot weather. Of course, the solid substances should be strained from decoctions before being used as medicinal drinks.

Demulcents

Medicines which are soothing to the intestinal tract, usually of an oily or mucilaginous nature. Glycerin and olive oil, though quite different from each other, are well known examples.

Deobstruents

Any medicines which have the power to clear the natural ducts in the body.

Detergents

A word which has, through advertising, come to prominence. In medicine it refers to substances (such as soap) which are used to clean wounds, ulcers, and the like.

Diaphoretics

This is synonomous with *Sudorifics,* both words implying the ability to produce sweating. This method of cure, along with sweat baths, has been used for the promotion of specific and general health by many races over many centuries.

Diarrhea

An unnaturally profuse discharge from the intestines. The causes are so various that a continuation of the condition indicates the need for medical advice. In cases of simple and sudden diarrhea, a number of plants have properties capable of alleviation, among which a principle found in the blackberry vine has long been used. Radical attempts to stop a sudden onslaught of diarrhea can be dangerous, since diarrhea may well be the body's safety effort to get rid of acute poisoning.

Diuretics

Medicines tending to increase the secretion and discharge of urine. Some hundreds of years ago it was thought that almost any untoward condition of the body would leave its telltale trace in urine, and early pictures of physicians show them engaged in urinalysis. So, too, we find in all old herbals many drugs mentioned as having diuretic properties. Powders, draughts, mixtures, and beers containing diuretics have all been used, usually to no harm and probably to much good. Among notable herbs with diuretic values are dandelions, juniper berries, lemon juice. Milk is a desirable diluting agent for diuretic extracts, as milk itself is a mild diuretic.

Dropsy

This fairly old-fashioned term, perhaps more properly referred to as *edema*, indicates the excessive accumulation of fluid in the body tissues. It is known to be commonly associated with disorders of the heart, blood vessels, or the kidneys and was formerly treated with digitalis. Today, however, the recommendation would be to let the condition be treated by a physician, who may well administer the herb, digitalis, or other proven remedies. Due note has been made in the chapter which follows of the various plants, in addition to digitalis, which have been recommended for dropsy.

Dysentery

Bowel disorders caused by amoeba, bacteria, worms, or chemical poisons. See *Diarrhea*, above.

Dyspepsia

Indigestion or non-digestion. Certain herbs, listed in the following chapter, have long been known to relieve this condition.

Electuaries

Those who delight in reading old herbals will often find the word "electuary," and wonder at its meaning. It denotes mixtures of dry and powdered medicine in a suitable vehicle such as honey, worked into a mass of such consistency as to be easily taken from a spoon and as easily swallowed. The drug so administered is non-soluble.

Emetics

Agents which cause vomiting. Many of the plants in this book are reputed to be valuable as emetics; naturally some are more so than others. Almost everyone knows that it is not herbs alone which induce vomiting; taste, motion, smell, sight, and physical inducement, as well as emotional upsets, will do the same. It is known that the Romans used emetics in times of feasting to clear the stomach and make room for more food, but at present the use of emetics is confined to persons who suffer from bilious attacks, dysentery, jaundice, and similar digestive disturbances.

Emmenagogues

Medicines which promote the menstrual discharge. One writer suggests that women living in isolated colonies were the first white people to take advantage of the herbal lore of the Indians. The list of aids for the promotion of the menstrual discharge is a long one.

Emollients

Somewhat the same meaning as *Demulcents*, but emollients are materials which soothe the skin rather than the internal membranes.

Emulsifying agents

Any materials which encourage the union of oily or resinous substances with aqueous (watery) materials.

Expectorants

Remedies which assist in enabling the patient to bring up and spit out excessive secretions of phlegm which accumulate in lungs and windpipe. Many plant drugs are valuable for this purpose.

Febrifuges

Synonymous with *Antipyretics*. Any agents which help dissipate a fever.

Fevers

Probably more plants have been noted as an alleviant of fevers than of any other condition. There are so many kinds and causes of fevers that no rules or prescriptions may be given. In fact, in many cases it is not desirable to halt a fever, which in itself may be a curative factor.

Flatulence

Gas in the stomach or bowels. This is an old complaint of mankind, and for centuries herbs of one sort or another have been used in its treatment. Mints and sweet flag are examples of two common ones.

Gonorrhea

The most common and curable venereal disease. The search for universal herbal specifics for gonorrhea and syphilis was a principal drive in much early exploration. Now, at long last, modern medicine has discovered that it is indeed the antibiotics derived from a "low" form of plant life which safely and surely cure if used under careful medical supervision.

Gout

A disease marked by painful inflammation of the joints. At one time, when we knew even less than we do now about the causes and cures of gout, diuretics were prescribed for its relief. Today, medical research has found that uric acid does indeed seem to be at the base of this disease.

Hallucinogen

Any drugs which cause hallucinations. Mescal (peyote) is an example.

Hemorrhage

A doctor would distinguish between hemorrhage and bleeding, and it is well to do so here. A copious loss of blood from accidental or other causes can quickly cause loss of life, and there would be no time for plant hunting.

For cases of the much milder bleeding assumed in the present use of the word hemorrhage, a number of plants are listed to be used.

Some Indian tribes are said to have utilized the dried spores of the puff-ball fungus as a hemostat, the fineness of the dust causing the blood to quickly coagulate. A bandage utilizing wrung-out sphagnum moss will absorb a lot of blood and apparently has some "built-in" germicidal action.

Hemorrhoids

Commonly called piles. In many cases relief, rather than surgery, seems to be all that the doctor prescribes. Many plant products, mostly astringent in nature, are noted in the pages which follow. A modern medical book says, "suppositories and mild skin-anesthetic ointments give quick relief," and it is just this kind of relief that is given by properties of the plants listed later in the book.

Hepatics

Substances which affect the liver harmfully or correctively.

Infusion

The soaking in water of any substance to extract its virtues. This is a most important word in any herbal for, with few exceptions, an infusion provides the simple and quick way of extracting the medicinal principle from dried plants.

To make an infusion, take a small portion of the leaves, stems, roots or what-have-you from the container and reduce them to a powder in a mortar (or something similar). Then, put the recommended amount of the powdered plant into the recommended quantity of water, just as you would make tea. A porcelain or glass pot is recommended. The temperature of the water should be around 112° F. or slightly higher. Stir constantly keeping the mixture hot. After ten minutes or so, remove from heat and strain. The infusion is then ready to drink hot or cold as recommended. A mixture such as this when boiled is a *"decoction"* (q.v.). Actually soaking for an extended period in cold or tepid water will release the active principles of some plants.

Itch

There are so many kinds of itching, caused by everything from poison to nerves, that relief is the first *desideratum*. Extracts from a few plants have been used for such relief.

Laxatives

Usually safe to take in temporary conditions of constipation are some of the plant laxatives mentioned later. Certain plants mentioned under that heading are *Cathartic* in action, and their use must be considered with care.

Menorrhagia

Profuse menstrual bleeding.

Mixture

It is hardly necessary to explain this word, but as concerns herbs it is used to indicate a suspension of mostly insoluble materials in a mucilaginous medium.

Narcotics

Drugs which in moderate doses relieve pain, in excess doses or with continued use are poisonous. Because any narcotic drug must be administered with the greatest of care, no plant narcotics are discussed in this work. In cases where plants of an otherwise useful nature are narcotic or poisonous in some part or stage of growth, suitable cautions are given.

Nervines

Tonics for the nerves. On the morning this paragraph was written Aldous Huxley, on the *Today* television show, said that man, with all his knowledge, just does not know how the brain and the mind work. Huxley has long advocated the use of a species of cactus known as Peyote, in an extracted drug *Mescaline,* as a relaxant. Most notable of plants classified as nervines, and one listed in the *National Formulary*, is valerian, which pharmacological textbooks refer to as a "calmative in nervousness." Other plants with similar values are noted in Chapter VI.

Ointments and Liniments

The difference between salves, ointments and liniments is largely based on the difference in their wax content. Soap; turpentine; plant gums such as camphor or myrrh; oils, such as sassafras, thyme, hemlock or eucalyptole; glycerin, etc. are all mentioned in various formulae for salves.

In the home of the author, for many years, an ointment used against plant poisons, burns and itching is made from an old, handed-down formula which (in proportions not given on the label) contains: white oak bark, black oak bark, red sumac berries, button-snake root, mallow root, borax, and eucalyptole in a base of wax, benne-oil, and petrolatum. Note that the formula contains the astringent qualities of the oaks and sumacs, the healing properties of borax and eucalyptole, and the carrying mediums of oil and Vaseline.

Pills

Medicinal materials held together in dry or wet form by their own or added properties. Medicine which is intended to act quickly should not be made into pill form.

Poisons

See *Narcotics.*

Powders

A few drug plants may be reduced to powder for administration, but authorities do not recommend it. The properties are soon dispersed into the air; the medicine is hard to take; and a drug in this form may not give up its healing qualities in the stomach.

Psoriasis

A skin disorder of unknown cause which is more annoying than dangerous. For this and similar skin irritations and eruptions, a number of plants have been used in American herbal medicine.

Purgatives

Generally synonymous with *Cathartics* (q.v.).

Refrigerants

An old medical term, now rarely used, referring to plant drugs which cool the blood and reduce fever. In this day of looking for causes rather than alleviating the symptoms, a modern doctor would likely be amused at the term.

Rheumatism

A condition characterized by stiffness of the joints or muscles. Evidences of the depredations of rheumatism have been found in the bones of prehistoric man, and it is said that ten per cent of all Americans are afflicted with what used to be called "the misery." It is, therefore, not strange that possibly fifty plants of this book have been prescribed, or that quacks glibly promise cures for rheumatism. In view of the fact that acetylsalicylic acid (aspirin) is one of the current and only known medicines used by doctors for the alleviation of rheumatism, one could suppose that those plants which contain salicylic acid might have been of help. As for the majority of the herbs mentioned, the psychological value of none of them can be discounted.

Rhus poisoning

An itching skin disorder resulting from infection by the oily poison of various members of the *Rhus* family, the common three-leaved poison ivy especially. Special note should be taken that poison ivy appears in slightly variant forms in various parts of the country and under the name of poison oak as well as ivy. A white fruited shrub form of *Rhus* is highly poisonous to some. Also, one may be violently poisoned by the smoke from burning ivy plants or from the slightest contact with the plants. Different people are affected in different ways and by different plants.

Some household and garden chemicals may cause a skin irritation called dermatitis, which is not unlike the manifestations of poison ivy.

Rubefacients

Substances which redden the skin. A number of plants are so described in herbals. Beyond the need of girls for bright pink cheeks to attract the men, one wonders who would want to rub his cheeks with nettles.

Scrofula

Infection and enlargement of the lymph glands. Diseases such as this were once great scourges, hence we find frequent references to cures in the old herbals. It is essentially a form of tuberculosis, no longer common because of sanitation and modern medicine.

Scurvy

A membrane and skin disease, today quite uncommon in Western countries, where the vitamin C of citrus fruits, rose hips, etc., is easily come by.

Sedatives

In the medical climate of the 1960s, sedatives are too well known to require definition. As will be noted later, a number of herbal infusions have sedative properties.

Stimulants

In using this word one must distnguish between *narcotics*, which first stimulate and then depress; *tonics*, which stimulate by raising the general health over a period of time, and true *stimulants* which quicken vital action and digestion, raise body temperature, and increase general awareness, all on a transitory basis. Among the best-known plant stimulants are culinary herbs such as anise, pepper, cinnamon, cloves, dill, ginger, horseradish, nutmeg, peppermint, and sage; while among more commonly known medicinal herbs are elecampane, horehound, hyssop, lavender, lobelia, marjoram, rue, spearmint, and yarrow.

Stomachics

Medicines which excite the action of the stomach by stimulating secretions; something in the nature of a cordial. Drugs which may otherwise be listed as aperient or tonic are in this category, but a number of distinct species are rated of value as stomachics.

Styptics

Medicines which cause contraction of blood vessels. See *Hemorrhage*.

Sudorifics

Herbs which cause copious sweating. Sweating, natural or induced, is necessary to normal or improved health.

Tinctures

Infusion describes a solution of organic material in water, *tincture* refers to a solution in alcohol. Many plants have their properties locked up in oils, resins, or wax which are not soluble in water. Where the plant material is in the form of sugars, salts or gums, warm or cold infusions will dissolve the medicinal substance. In some cases of extraction a weak spirit containing both alcohol and water may be best. Very often the handling of the raw dried herb will expose the oily nature of the plant and indicate to the user the desirability of extracting the qualities with either water or alcohol or a combination.

Tonics

Often, tonics are referred to as "bitters," and they often act as stimulants and alteratives. The combinations of herbs (and/or other medicines) which have been recommended as tonic are legion, and the kind of plant considered to have tonic properties may vary greatly with race, climate, and culture.

Ulcers

A condition of inflammation and destruction of the skin or internal mucous membranes. Most herbals refer only to skin ulcers, for which a number of cures have been recommended.

Vermifuges

See *Anthelmintics*.

Vesicants

Agents which produce blisters or sores. Poison ivy, for instance.

Vulneraries

This word is not in common usage but is found especially in old herbals. In the days of hand-to-hand combat, the need for medicine, of any origin, which might heal wounds was of first importance, and plant drugs which were used for this purpose were called *Vulneraries*.

CHAPTER V

THE MEDICINAL PLANTS DISCUSSED

. . . we have in this country a great variety of good medicinal plants which may be administered to the people with great advantage, if properly adapted to the season, age, and constitution of the patient. . . . If their virtues were well known . . . then those very herbs or roots, I suppose, might continue or increase their reputation.

John Bartram—1751—Philadelphia
in an introduction to a work by Thomas Short

HOSE plants which, in the American scene, seem to be the most useful medically are presented next. Beyond these two hundred plants, almost eighty additional ones are listed in a following chapter. There are at least a thousand other species whose reputed virtues are detailed in other books, and so, arbitrary selection was necessary here.

Although previously mentioned, it is desirable again to point out that many plants have been omitted which, though medicinally valuable, are too poisonous to be considered as home medicines. Others are of questionable value. Nor has it been possible to tell here about the medical flora of the great Southwest or of California, which differ greatly from the common flora of East, South, and Midwest. The reader who lives in California will, however, be pleased to know that a comparison of plants of this book with the botany of that state, shows that above 30% of the genera discussed here are to be found there. In another field the materia medica of native Indians has been

59

barely touched upon, for the practices of each tribe differed so completely.

It is hardly a deep excursion into the science of Botany to point out that all plants belong to families. The knowledge of plant families may seem unimportant to the amateur herbalist and yet it may be helpful to know relationships. For instance if you know that a particular plant belongs to the Mint family you could assume it was aromatic; to the Cashew family, that the plant might be poisonous; to the Composite family, that the flower is daisy-like.

The line illustrations which I have secured or drawn especially for this book, are intended partly for identification but mostly as a reminder of some of the characteristics of leaf and flower. An identification guide would duplicate what is so well done in regional wild flower books, to which the reader is directed.

To provide a measure of uniformity, the nomenclature throughout is that of *Gray's Manual of Botany-Eighth Edition* except where the plants have fallen out of the range of that book; in those cases reliable regional authorities were consulted. Set on separate lines, the botanical name is shown in bold face italics; the family name in caps and small caps; the common name in italics.

ACERACEAE

The maples

Minor astringent properties are found in *A. Spicatum* (the mountain maple), but the family's best known and most healthful product is the maple sugar which is so easily extracted from *A. saccharum* and *A. Negundo*. Sugar, a quick stimulant, is essential to the diet, and an ingredient in many medicines. For those who compound plant medicines from local plants, maple syrup may be the only available source of sugar.

The sap from the well-known sugar maple is, without question, the best, but the sap of the box elder *(A. Negundo)* has a reasonable sugar content. This latter tree has a greater range (Canada to Florida), but has none of the more desirable tree-qualities of the slower growing and beautifully shaped "true" maples. Sap from either tree is available only in the early spring when cold nights and warm days cause the sweet juice to course up and down the tree.

Achillea Millefolium

Compositae

Milfoil, yarrow, old-man's pepper, thousand-leaved, nosebleed, thousand-seal, dog-daisy, knight's milfoil, soldier's wound-wort, devil's plaything, and others

Both scientific and common names reveal a great deal of the story behind plants, and *Achillea* is no exception. Myth has it that Achilles first revealed the uses of the plant to mankind. From the finely-cut, fern-like foliage we get the species name *Millefolium,* or thousand-leaved. Its family name reveals that it is a member of the daisy family, which is easy to see when we examine the tiny florets which make the head of (generally white, sometimes pink) flowers. "Old-man's pepper" refers to its mildly pungent taste and smell, while "nose bleed" goes back to its use both to induce nosebleed, and, because of its astringent quality, to stop mild bleeding.

We are further told that it was known anciently as *Herba militaris,* knight's milfoil, and soldier's wound-wort, all of which suggest that it was used as a ready-to-hand field bandage for battle wounds, although its value for staunching flows of blood is doubtful. Its last name, "devil's plaything," refers to its use in divination. We can well suppose that this was one of the herbs used by the witches in *Macbeth.*

Milfoil was brought to this country probably for medicinal use by early settlers. It is now widely distributed in fields and meadows, coming into bloom in early August, when it may be gathered and dried for later use.

Youngken, in his textbook, lists it as an "aromatic bitter, diaphoretic and emmenagogue." One recipe recommends 1 ounce of the dried herb steeped in a pint of warm water, this infusion to be taken at the rate of a wineglassful several times a day. For colds, it is suggested that dried elder flowers and mint be added to the brew.

Acorus calamus

Araceae

Sweetflag, calamus, sweet root, etc.

If the men who translated the King James version of the Bible knew their plants, we can say that calamus (with four references in the Old Testament) is one of the few healing herbs whose continuous use can be traced from ancient times. Since the roots of calamus were an article of commerce in the Near East four thousands years ago, it is easy to see why we find continual references to sweetflag in early medicinal writings, including several by Theophrastus, who lived in the fourth century B.C. In America, we find references to many uses made of *Acorus* by the Indians, with an indication that it was rated by them to be good for almost anything.

The sweetflag is a rather unusual plant. Resembling the iris, it actually is allied to jack-in-the-pulpit and skunk cabbage, an arum. The flower stalk comes up as a leaf (a scape), and midway in this leaf appears the so-called spadix (see illustration). This spadix and the distinct fragrance of the foliage are its identifying characteristics. Dried foliage was at one time sold to churches for scattering over the floors to provide a "saintly odor," or, more likely, to cover up the smells of unwashed bodies. In fact, one of the charges against the famed Cardinal Wolsey was that of extravagance in buying these "rushes" for his church.

As with other members of the Arum family, the plant grows always in swampy or stream-edge spots throughout the U.S.A. The part used medicinally is the root which should not be peeled, for the vital principles are just under the surface layer. The dried root is powdered and infused one ounce being mixed with a pint of water. The prescribed dose is a wineglassful. The raw root may be chewed as a stomachic having a reputation as a sure way to stop "stomach rumbling." This plant seems to have no poisonous reactions if taken in larger doses.

POLYPODIACEAE

Venus' hair fern, black maiden's hair fern, rock fern

This lovely fern is found not only in America but, in a slightly varied form, in Europe, where it has long been considered a medicinal plant. Here, it grows from Florida to Mexico, north to Virginia and west to Illinois. The most familiar fern to the northerner, maidenhair fern *(A. pedatum)* is said to have properties similar to *A. Capillus-Veneris,* but this is not confirmed. The two can be distinguished by the fact that *A. pedatum* has a somewhat branched frond-stem (or rachis), while *A. Capillus-Veneris* is single stemmed. The latter is a native of generally warm-temperate zones, and, like all members of the family, prefers lime soils with shade and moisture.

Both Latin and English names are revealing. *Adiantum* means unmoistened or water repelling, and Venus is said to have arisen from her watery home with dry hair. Because of this connection with hair, the plant has been used as a hair tonic, but it seems to have little value for such a purpose.

Herbal references indicate that it has long been known as an emmenagogue, but even more generally as an expectorant because of its mucilaginous properties. The plant, fronds and rootstock alike, is dried and used (one authority says), at the rate of 1 ounce of the dried plant to 1 pint of boiling water, and taken as needed.

The French have a cough remedy known as *Sirop de Capillaire,* made by using 5 ounces of the dried plant and 2 ounces of peeled licorice root in 5 pints of boiling water, adding, after 6 hours, 3 pounds of sugar and 1 pint of orange juice for palatability.

AMARYLLIDACEAE

Century plant, American aloe, maguey,
American agave

The century plant is at the center of
the economy of the Mexican country-
dweller. It furnishes him with shelter,
food, drink, and soap, as well as the raw
materials for fiber. It is from *A. ameri-*
cana and some of the many other species
that pulque, tequila and mescal are
made. Medicinally, the juice of the
agaves has been used as a diuretic and especially as an anti-syphilitic.
Martinez, who writes on the medicinal plants of our southern neighbor, devotes a number of pages to agave, and Von Hagen says that
there are 371 specific uses to which it is put in Mexico. The many
cures credited to agave seem to be authentic, but one wonders
whether adequate tests have proven its anti-syphilitic qualities.

Such a reservation should not, however, blind us to the basic
value of this family. In Mexico, the upturned leaves serve as shin-
gles; the juice in every state is usable; and the plant is grown as a
money-crop in vast plantations. We should come to know and appreciate the century plant for other than its strong "architectural" features as a tubbed plant on the lawn, for which it enjoyed wide popularity half a century ago.

ROSACEAE

Common agrimony, cocklebur, sticklewort

Agrimony for many centuries has been one of the "simples" known to country folk for its medicinal values. The confusion of its common names shows the advantage of scientific nomenclature. In this country, where the early settlers compounded their medicine out of the plants of the field, we find that, properly, agrimony is the species *A. gryposepala*. But one can also find (widely distributed from Europe) the somewhat similar *A. Eupatoria*. Reference to various herbals discloses, however, that there is also a "Hemp Agrimony," which is *Eupatorium cannabium*, and a "Water Agrimony," *Bidens tripartita*, also known as Bur Marigold. In general, however, all the species are presumed to have similar properties as well as the leaf formation and a spiked (yellow) flower shown in our illustration. Their locale is usually in the climatic zone of New England and the Middle Atlantic states.

Agrimony is always listed as a "tonic, alterative, astringent, and a deobstruent for liver and spleen." Other plants bear these same qualities, and the absence of Agrimony from official pharmacopoeias indicates that no great potency exists. Yet the writer knows personally people who have described cures of "gravel stone" through the use of Agrimony, and all authorities value infusions of it (with honey) for sore and husky throats. The French drink it as a *tisane* or tea.

Potter, in his modern herbal, gives the dose as 1 ounce of the dried herb to 1 pint of boiling water, sweetened with honey, taken half a cupful at a time as frequently as desired.

GRAMINEAE

Witch-, couch-, quitch-, dog-, Dutch-, quack-grass

To imply to a farmer or gardener that witch-grass has any value would set up a chain of doubt, for this aggressive weed, of European origin, is a prime pest. Once established, it can defy the greatest vigilance, for its underground rhizomes divide and spread and suddenly appear as a mass of wiry grass. But its medicinal properties have long been known and are still recognized in pharmaceutical texts. Its name in medicine is *Triticum,* and in French, *Chiendent officinal,* the latter word implying its use in accepted medical practice.

To readers who are also gardeners, a picture or description of witch-grass is hardly needed. Harvesting and drying the rhizomes and roots in the spring will be no hardship (though a little work). The dried product can be stored until needed for catarrhal conditions of the genito-urinary tract, or for a diuretic. All writers agree on these uses and for related conditions such as kidney diseases, gout, cystisis, rheumatism, and fevers.

Medicine from witch-grass is prepared by making either infusions or decoctions. For the former, 1 ounce of dried roots to 1 pint of boiling water is to be taken at the rate of a wineglassful three or more times per day, as needed.

Some writers say that when cattle are turned out in the spring on fields of quick-grass their health soon improves. The name dog-grass comes from the fact that sick dogs will often seek out and chew the stems of the grass, which causes vomiting, with its consequent curative effect.

Thus the plant which the gardeners rejected, has become a cornerstone of medicine.

LILIACEAE

Star grass, ague root, colicroot, star-wort, true unicorn root, devil's bit

It is interesting to see how often plant folk-names indicate something of their medicinal properties. And again, one finds the Latin name descriptive as *fari-nosa*, or "mealy," to indicate the appearance of the outer covering of the flower buds.

Aletris is not common for it requires special growing conditions. In sandy and grassy open woods it is found from Florida to Texas and north to Maine and Wisconsin. The rather tall stalk of insignificant flowers rises from a flat rosette of typical lily-like foliage.

However, for medicine, it is not the leaves or flowers which interest us but the rhizome and roots. These bitter-tasting underground parts are dried, granulated, the useful element being best extracted with alcohol rather than water. It is to be taken in small doses only; otherwise it may produce nausea. Dosage of the tincture is given as "5 to 10 minims" (or drops).

And what is it to be used for? Potter says "As a female tonic it has but few equals and may be given in all cases of debility." Other writers say that it is a useful uterine sedative; most valuable in its effect on female organs; used in cases of chronic miscarriage; a general tonic, and good for flatulence, colic, rheumatism, hysteria, etc. Surely it should not be overlooked in any consideration of important American medicinal plants.

ALISMACEAE

Water plantain, mad-dog weed

Alisma seems to have been used by the herbalists of many countries, although its poisonous properties necessitate caution in home doctoring. Curiously, its common names have little relation to reality. Although it is said to have been used in Russia as an antidote for hydrophobia, this has never been proved, yet "mad-dog weed" still sticks. In the other case, it is not even closely allied to plantain. The shape of its leaves suggests the plantain foliage, thus providing the common name of water plaintain.

Since it has astringent properties, early herbalists used the juice of the leaves as a diuretic, and for allied urinary diseases. Because the bruised leaves cause irritation to the skin and the general properties are of doubtful value, an eminent herbal authority, Meyer, said that "it seems to have lost its reputation." However, a most recent British herbal lists it as a diuretic and diaphoretic, and prescribes doses of an infusion of 1 ounce to a pint of boiling water in a cupful, taken three or four times a day. French, Japanese, and Russian references to the plant prove that its use has been widespread.

Entirely outside the realm of medicine is the attention paid to *Alisma* by John Ruskin. In a discussion of the architectural principles on which the great cathedrals were built, he used the water plantain as a prime example of the basic symmetry of nature. If the reader finds this plant growing, it will be worth a little study to measure (as Ruskin suggests) the proportionate distances between progressions of leaves and flower stalks. He will find that the relationship of one distance to the other is a relationship approximating the anciently understood and "magical" proportion, used by the Greeks and all great builders and artists, and which we currently incorporate into the artistic principle known as dynamic symmetry. Here one has an excellent example of the interest that can be found in nature and plants quite aside from any utilitarian value.

The water plantain grows widely in the east coast region of North America and is found in suitable locations in the middle tier of states as well. It will always be found growing in shallow water, or on muddy shores, or in ditches.

Allium sativum

Liliaceae

Garlic, clove garlic

Perhaps few plants are as universally known or used for medicinal and culinary purposes as the several members of the genus *Allium,* or onion. All herbals, from whatever country, mention the values of garlic or onion. In parts of the middle and southeastern U.S.A., garlic has "gone wild" and may be collected, and everywhere it may be grown or purchased. However, because of the objectionable odor, garlic eaters are sometimes socially objectionable; even Horace and Shakespeare made such adverse comments.

Despite this, garlic-eating peoples are usually healthy, and many are the medicinal values ascribed to this plant. In World War I the British depended greatly on the antiseptic quality of garlic juice to control the suppuration of wounds. The raw juice was diluted with water and applied on swabs of sterile sphagnum moss. It is claimed that thousands of lives were thus saved.

Garlic (and to a lesser extent wild garlic and the much milder onion) are said to be beneficial in asthma, bronchitis, rheumatism; for coughs, colds, and hoarseness; as a vermifuge; and in the opinion of one authority, in curing poison ivy.

The medical profession is not agreed on its values in hypertension or heart conditions, and some other recommendations are suspect. A specific recommendation is made in Grieve's *Modern Herbal:*

> Syrup of Garlic is an invaluable medicine for asthma, hoarseness, coughs, difficulty of breathing, and most other disorders of the lungs, being of particular virtue in chronic bronchitis, on account of its powers of promoting expectoration. It is made by pouring a quart of water, boiled hot upon a pound of the fresh root, cut into slices, and allowed to stand in a closed vessel for twelve hours, sugar then being added to make of it the consistency of syrup. Vinegar and honey greatly improve this syrup as a medicine. A little caraway and sweet fennel seed bruised and boiled for a short time in the vinegar before it is added to the Garlic, will cover the pungent smell of the latter.

The enthusiastic herbalist should explore the many writings relative to the value of the entire onion family, and the gardener as well should note that the variety, beauty, and ease of culture of the many ornamental Alliums make the family a most desirable one.

Betulaceae

Common alder, red alder, speckled alder, green alder

Nicholas Culpeper wrote in 1653 that "the leaves (of alder) put under the bare feet galled with traveling, are a great refreshing to them" and again "leaves gathered while the morning dew is on them, and brought into a chamber troubled with fleas, will gather them thereonto, which being suddenly cast out, will rid the chamber of those troublesome bedfellows." If these were all the virtues of alder, the plant would not have much pertinence today.

The alder of which he wrote was the European species *A. glutinosa,* but the medicinal properties of alder are common to the several forms including the American one of these notes.

Because alder contains a considerable quantity of tannin, astringency is a principal property. Potter says that "the bark is used in a decoction as a gargle for sore throats. The leaves are glutinous and were used to cure inflammations."

Alder wood resists decay under water, and it is said that much of Venice is built on alder piling. The twigs, bark, and catkins are a source of a black dye that has been known and used for centuries. Used alone, it dyes wool a reddish color and, used with copperas, produces a good black. Young shoots produce colors from yellow to cinnamon, while the leaves will produce a dye for leather.

The common alder grows best when its feet can find water, and is generally distributed throughout North America. Botanists indicate that there is considerable variability even within a given species, presumably due to the cumulative effect of terrain and climate, but for medicinal purposes it can be assumed that *A. rugosa* and its variations all have about the same value.

Althaea officinalis

Marshmallow, mortification root, sweet weed

As with so many of our "native" wild plants this is an escape or introduction. The story of how many European plants have become a part of American flora is interesting. It involves intentional introduction, and accidents such as seeds coming as part of straw packing or (especially with sea-side plants) as part of a ship's ballast. Possibly the marshmallow, being a plant of salt marshes, entered in this latter way. It is now found only on banks of tidal rivers and brackish streams.

In this plant we have the source of the original, non-synthetic, mucilaginous marshmallow paste. The roots are harvested in autumn, well dried, and the brown corky layer removed. The whitish inner root yields the substance used in marshmallow manufacture, the name of the confection coming from the plant.

It also has other values, for at least eight of the authorities consulted agree on the medicinal properties of marshmallow root. Primarily a demulcent and emollient, it is a popular ingredient of cough remedies, for bronchitis, etc. "In painful complaints of the urinary organs and cystitis it exerts a relaxing effect upon the passages as well as acting as a mild curative. The powdered or crushed roots make a good poultice, which may be relied upon to remove the most obstinate inflammation and prevent mortification."

An infusion of 1 ounce of leaves to 1 pint of boiling water, taken frequently, is the recommended internal dosage. Because of its mild yet healing qualities, it is recommended for teething babies.

Malvaceae

Hollyhock

Much that is said in the discussion of
marshmallow root (q.v.) is applicable to
the garden hollyhock, an introduction
to American gardens from the Far East,
and one which is so common that it
might fairly be mentioned as an American plant. The properties of hollyhock
are, then, like that of its cousin, demulcent, emolient, and according to some
authorities—diuretic. The plant part
used (at times) of the hollyhock is the
flower, from which the outer calyx is
removed, the flowers then being dried
in trays with plenty of air circulation. They will be a dark purplish
black, and may be used medicinally or (in another connection) as a
coloring matter. Youngken also says that the roots are a legitimate
substitute for the more properly used root of the marshmallow, either
root being high in mucilage.

For most of us, the medicinal importance of the hollyhock is not
great, but to ornament a blank wall there is no plant quite its equal!

Perhaps it has all been best said by a poet, Abraham Cowley,
whom Mrs. Leyel quotes:

> The hollyhock distains the common size
> Of herbs, and like a tree do's proudly rise;
> Proud she appears, but try her, and you'll find
> No plant more mild, or friendly to mankind.
> She gently all obstructions do's unbind.

AMARANTHACEAE

Pig weed (Pigweed)

Although no one member of this family is of great medicinal value, a number of them have occasional or reputed uses which the reader should know about, so we will consider the family as a whole. To the gardener, the amaranth may be the stiff, dwarfish red cockscomb, the plumed prince's feather, or the weed often growing up with the plants, pigweed. Other members of the family are known as tumbleweed, redroot, beetroot, while one related form, *Achyranthes repens*, is known as forty-knot. In most of these plants there is a mild, astringent, medicinal principle. Meyer, the American authority, indicates its use in cases of diarrhea, or for mouth and throat irritations; one cupful of an infusion made in the proportion of a teaspoon of the dried leaves to a cup of boiling water is his suggestion.

The greatest medicinal value seems to be ascribed to the cultivated prince's feather *(A. hypochondriacus)*, for Potter (1956) says "highly recommended" in cases of menorrhagia, diarrhea, and dysentery.

In discussing the amaranth, it is interesting to note that the Doctrine of Signatures records it as being a hemostat because of the strong red color of every part of the plant. Better minds ruled against this, however. We find that the "Father of Medicine," Galen, is quoted by Gerard as saying that "there can be no certainty gathered from the colours, touching the virtues of simple and compound medicines."

Although the amaranth in one or another of its forms has been on a list of medicinal plants for many years, the values are relatively slight, and the properties indicated are more easily found in many other plants.

<small>UMBELLIFERAE</small>

Angelica, Alexanders, masterwort

In the northern tier of states and
down midway into the coastal plain,
Angelica is found in rich, moist thickets
and bottomlands. Somewhat resembling
its cousin, celery, it is a rank biennial
(to 5-6 feet high), and has purplish
stems. The crushed plant has an odd,
strong, but not unpleasant odor, and a
sweetish taste. Collectors should make
certain identification of this plant, for
other members of the family are highly
poisonous. This native species is not the
same (though with similar properties)
as the angelica of Europe and of garden cultivation *(Angelica arch-
angelica)* whose stalks have been candied and used as a confection.

One could easily guess that, with such "angelic" names, the plant
has been highly esteemed. There is a considerable body of literature
on the folklore and religious beliefs associated with angelica. How
much it is credited with medicinal value due to its association with
religion is hard to say. However, according to reliable authority, it
does have stimulating, aromatic, and carminative properties, and
formerly had official recognition. As with other members of this
family, the active principles are highly concentrated in the fruits
(seeds), although the stalk and leaves and, in the garden variety,
the roots may be used.

In addition to the uses suggested above, Meyer rates it as an expectorant, and indicates that it relieves flatulent colic and heartburn.
Also, as a diuretic it is "serviceable in promoting elimination through
the urine and the skin." He gives as a dose a simple infusion of a
teaspoon of seeds to a cup of boiling water, of which several cupfuls
per day may be taken.

It may interest some of our readers to note that angelica is an ingredient of vermouth and chartreuse and even (says the *Herbalist*),
as a substitute for, or addition to, juniper berries in gin.

Compositae

Garden chamomile; English-, Roman-, true-, chamomile; earth apple, corn feverfew, barnyard daisy, turkey weed, may weed

Because of the apple-like smell of the leaves, the Greeks named it *kamai* (on the ground) *melon* (apple), from which comes almost directly our English "chamomile." The Greeks, as did the Egyptians before them, valued this herb, and it remains today one of the standard herbal medicines of country-folk in many parts of the world.

There are related species of *Anthemis* which, while similar and having somewhat the same effect, are not considered truly a substitute. The plant of this sketch is a low growing, pleasantly strong-scented, downy, and mat-like perennial whose flowers are remarkably daisy-like with white petals and yellow center. This species is an escape from cultivation, and may be found near present or formerly inhabited areas. However, it is also quite often found in gardens, where many authorities say that its presence will prevent disease in other cultivated plants.

The closely related genus, *Matricaria Chamomilla* is often confused with *Anthemis*. Roughly speaking, English people think of the low, mat-like *Anthemis* as chamomile, while the Germanic peoples know and use similarly the taller growing *Matricaria*, which is separately discussed in this book.

For internal medicinal use, the flower heads of *Anthemis* are dried and used in infusions, decoctions, as extracts or pure oils or in poultices. The infusion is made with an ounce of dried flowers to a pint of boiling water, taken either warm or cold. This produces the well-known chamomile tea, long known as soothing, sedative, and completely harmless; doses may be as large as desired. Stronger infusions may be introduced as an ingredient to a hot bath with soothing effect.

Since the uses of chamomile are so varied, it seems best to list them:

1. Youngken in his pharmacological textbook gives the active principle of chamomile as "anthemic acid" and lists it as an aromatic bitter. This brings it into the class of stomachic and tonic. An antispasmodic, one writer says it will immediately stop delirium tremens.

2. It is often recommended in cases of hysteria, as a nervine, and by some as an emmenagogue.

3. Poultices of moist dried flowers are recommended for use in all inflammations and abcesses, and, through similar application, for earache and toothache.

4. Used as a hair wash, it is said to act as a "blond dye."

5. An infusion used to wash hands and face before walking in the woods will ward off insects.

An analysis of all that has been written about chamomile would indicate that here is the "general medicine" *par excellence* which is not only efficacious but perfectly safe.

One correspondent of the writer, having cut her hand on a rusty nail, reports that an old German woman recommended soaking the hand in a chamomile infusion; "My hand was healed in a few days, and in the years that have followed I have found these blossoms infallible wherever I have used them. In recent months it cured my foot when badly poisoned by lye. Soaking in a warm infusion is very restful for tired feet, and takes the soreness from callouses. It is also an excellent remedy for ivy poison." Such a plant should be a part of every garden. Not only will it provide medicine, but its pleasant fragrance will pervade the air, and it will help other plants stay healthy. Also, it is an excellent ground cover.

Apium graveolens

UMBELLIFERAE

Celery, smallage, small ache

A discussion of celery may seem strange in a book about wild plants, but in isolated areas celery does grow wild. These wildings—only a few steps from the fine cultivated stalks of celery—are part of that great parsley family which includes so many poisonous plants.

For that reason, a note of caution is necessary here, to point out that essentially celery *is* a poisonous plant. We know that celery is improved in flavor if it can be first subjected to frost, thus removing the acrid principles just as (in the same family) parsnips are hardly fit to eat until they have spent the winter in the ground. Some people are allergic to celery, and for them the real harm comes from poison which is given off by the leaves under conditions of considerable moisture. This poison may produce a rash not unlike poison ivy. Gardeners—beware!

This has not, however, prevented celery from being a choice salad plant from the earliest times. It is said that the Romans enjoyed it and wove crowns of the leaves for dinner guests, while John Evelyn, in his interesting book on salads in the seventeenth century, gave celery high recommendation.

The druggist knows only the "fruit" or celery seed, which his guides list as a "stimulant and condiment." Herbalists rate it as more important than that, however, and ascribe such virtues to it as nervine, antispasmodic, diuretic, and carminative. Almost every reference includes mention of celery as being of great value in rheumatism but, many plants are thus credited and the claims must be taken with a grain of salt. Rheumatism is an almost universal complaint for which modern medicine has found alleviation, not cure. Because the disease comes and goes with or without treatment, it is easy for the sufferer to imagine that celery or almost any other plant has been of value.

APOCYNACEAE

Dogbane, Indian hemp, bitterroot

Dogbane grows throughout the United States as well as in Europe. It is a perennial plant attaining five to six feet in height on sandy soils, often along streams. It has a branching habit, whitish flowers, and all parts of the plant exude a milky juice. Another species *(A. cannabinum)* of dogbane bears the same common name and (with minor variation) has the same medicinal properties. The many popular names of these plants all bear testimony to the interest in and use made of them by the early settlers who perforce explored any medical knowledge of plants which came from the Indians or was passed along from their Elizabethan heritage. Such names as—American ipecac, catchfly, honeytrap, milkweed, silk weed, black Indian hemp, choctaw-root, rheumatism-weed suggest some use or connection. The Indians, especially in California, have used the plant as sources of fiber to make twine, nets, and even clothing, and it would not be difficult for the nature lover through experiment, to discover how strong and stable the fibers are.

Medicinally the part of the *Apocynum* used is the large milky roots and/or rhizomes, which are dried and powdered. For a hundred years this drug was officially accepted, but in the trade has now been superseded by other materials. Because of its powerful effects and digitalis-like action, it should be listed as a poison although its use by the Indian medicine man for many centuries shows that, handled with knowledge and care, it had great value. In large doses the drug is emetic, and in medium doses a cardiac stimulant. In mild doses it is a general alterative, tonic, and cathartic.

As to what may be a mild dose, there is not much agreement, and it is always wise to proceed with caution. Meyer gives a dose as one teaspoonful of the dried root in a pint of boiling water taken 2 to 3 tablespoonfuls six times daily. One other writer gives "1 grain of the powdered root" as a dose.

Apocynum cannabinum

A<small>POCYNACEAE</small>

Dogbane, Indian hemp, rheumatism weed, Indian physic

It seems wise to include in these pages some discussion of certain rather dangerous plants which are generally known as "medicinal." While dogbane is not as poisonous as water hemlock and other plants, it should certainly be classed as too dangerous for use by all but experienced medical practitioners. Suitable cautions are noted in all discussions of *Apocynum*.

Dogbane is a rather tall-growing, branching, perennial herb found widely in open fields or borders of woods almost everywhere in the U.S.A. The stems, when broken, exude a milky juice, and are very fibrous. Rope woven from the dried fibers, giving rise to the name Indian hemp.

The rhizome and root are dried, and, according to Meyer, infused at the rate of a teaspoonful of the powdered root to a pint of boiling water, taken at the rate of a teaspoonful of liquid three to eight times per day.

Dogbane acts like the digitalis group of heart stimulants. It is considered very powerful, and, in anything but small doses, produces violent vomiting. Youngken lists it as a "Cardiac stimulant in threatened cardiac failure, and diuretic in dropsy," and that about sums up, authoritatively, the comments of others.

One can imagine from the name that it was known to the Indians. Without question it does possess medicinal values, but every caution should be taken in its use.

ARALIACEAE

*American-, wild-, Virginian-sarsaparilla,
sweetroot, small spikeweed, spikenard,
rabbit's food*

The adjectives used as a preface to
the name sarsaparilla should serve to
warn that this is not the true sarsaparilla
of the soda-fountain labels. However,
both the true sarsaparilla and the plant
of this sketch *are* American plants; one
finds no mention of any sarsaparilla in
old and European herbals. The name itself is a combination of two Spanish
words (*zarza*, bush, and *parrilla*, little
vine). The commonly known aromatic drug, sarsaparilla, is extracted from any of several species of *Smilax*, found in various parts
of South America, but here in North America, early settlers found a
plant with a similar taste, and hence arose the common names noted.
The Indians treasured sarsaparilla, for a pioneer New England botanist, Manassah Cutler, says that, during their wars or hunting expeditions, the Indians subsisted for long periods on its roots.

Differing from other members of the genus, the wild sarsaparilla is
a small, low plant consisting of a stem scarcely rising out of the
ground, with a single long-stalked leaf and an even shorter flower
stalk with an umbel of white flowers. It grows in woodlands, and the
part used is the long, horizontal and thickish roots.

Aralia nudicaulis has been used in recent years as an ingredient of
root beer and, as with *A. racemosa*, for inclusion in cough syrups.

Medicinally, we find mention of *A. nudicaulis* as aromatic diaphoretic, stimulant, and alterative. The dried roots would be infused
at the rate of a teaspoonful to a cup of boiling water and used either
as a pleasant stimulating drink or as an addition to other preparations.

ARALIACEAE

Spikenard, pettymorrell, wild licorice, old man's root, pigeon weed, Indian root, spignet, life of man, Indian spikenard

Here is a shrubby, herbaceous plant which grows in nearly all of the eastern United States, usually in rich woods. It has a much-branched stem from 3 to 6 feet high, with large, saw-toothed leaflets, and white flowers followed by brownish berries which eventually turn dark purple. The part used is the large rhizome or root which both smells and tastes aromatic and has been used as a substitute for its close relative, *A. nudicaulis.*

We find that, as with most plants which are aromatic, *A. racemosa* is listed as tonic and stimulant. Spikenard is also slightly expectorant in its effect, and thus we find it an ingredient in cough syrups, with white pine, cherry bark, etc. In all references, we find also that it is listed as an alterative and that it is a blood purifier. However true these statements may be, at least it is a pleasant and harmless herbal drug and, as indicated by some of its names, a plant used by the Indians.

An infusion is made of the dried powdered rhizome at the rate of ½ ounce of root to a pint of boiling water, in doses of a wineglassful as needed.

COMPOSITAE

*Burdock, great burdock, beggar's but-
tons, lappa, stick button, clotbur, horse-
burr; plus a host of other local names
including "burr," "dock," "rhubarb,"
etc.*

Possibly one of the first plants with
which little children become acquainted
is the burdock, whose "seeds" with their
sticky burrs literally force themselves
upon the passerby. There are several
species of *Arctium* (including *A. minus*,
a smaller growing form). *Arctium* is a
biennial rhubarb-like plant growing on
our roadsides. It is interesting to note
that all of the four species listed in
Gray are introductions from Europe,
yet burdock is found almost everywhere
in the eastern United States.

The dried first-year root has been
used in the pharmaceutical trade for
years. Although it is not presently "offi-
cial," it is generally considered a diaphoretic, diuretic, and alterative.

Arctium lappa—top
Arctium minus—below

Potter says that it is "one of the finest blood purifiers in the herbal
system, and should be used in such cases alone or with other remedies. Both root and seed may be taken as a decoction of 1 ounce to
1½ pints of water, simmered down to 1 pint, in doses of a wineglassful 3 or 4 times daily."

Other recommendations are to use the leaves in poultices for the
relief of bruises, tumors and other swellings, and some authorities
mention it as an antidote for snake bites. Around any plant which has
been used for as many centuries as has burdock, many stories and
claims have arisen, including an interesting one by Culpeper:
"Venus challenges this herb for her own, and by its leaf or seed you
may draw the womb which way you please, either upwards by applying it to the crown of the head, in case it falls out; or downwards in
fits of the mother, applying it to the soles of the feet; or if you would
stay it in place, apply it to the navel, and that is one good way to
stay the child in it."

Arctostaphylos Uva-ursi

Uva-ursi, mealy plum vine, mealyberry, bearberry, red bearberry, bear's grape, bear's billberry, bear's whortleberry, foxberry, rockberry, crowberry, hog-cranberry, upland cranberry, mountain cranberry, mountain box, barren myrtle, universe vine, brawlins, sagachomi, kinnikinnick

Often, the smaller the plant, the longer the name, the more common names, and the more there is written about it. Bearberry, the common name most familiar to the author, is a spreading evergreen plant, hardly over three inches tall. It is happiest in a sandy, sunny, starved condition. Native not only to the North American continent, it also is well known in Europe, and medicinal uses of it have been noted as early as the thirteenth century.

Pick and carefully dry leaves in late summer, care being taken to take them in mid-day, without moisture on the leaves, and to use only perfect foliage.

These dried leaves (in the National Formulary under the name *Uva-ursi*) are useful as a diuretic and mild disinfectant of the urinary tract. It is administered in home treatments as an infusion made at the rate of 1 ounce of the leaves to a pint of boiling water, sometimes in connection with other materials, such as marshmallow root. The claims made for Uva-ursi is that it has a specific action on the urinary organs, and is especially useful in cases of gravel, ulceration of kidneys or bladder, catarrh, gleet, leucorrhea, menorrhagia.

Thomas Meehan, the great nineteenth century American botanist and plantsman (whose son taught me to know and love plants) says that another way of taking Uva-ursi medicinally is to soak the dried, powdered leaves in brandy, taking a little of this in a cup of hot water. But he doesn't give quantities. He does, however, tell how the plant may be transplanted (it is notoriously difficult to move). He suggests that one should, on finding a clump, draw the young stem up through a hole in a flower pot, fill with soil, and leave for a year for roots to develop. Then the stem may be severed and the bearberry transplanted to the garden.

ARACEAE

Jack-in-the-pulpit, Indian turnip, cuckoo plant, wild turnip, wake robin, etc.

Possibly the first wilding with which one becomes acquainted as a child is the interestingly-formed spathe which, in this family, acts as the flower stalk. Here, under a protecting hood, stands Jack, the preacher, later to be dressed in a stalk of brilliant crimson berries. Jack is probably preaching against the danger that is present at his feet; the roots of the plant are quite poisonous if chewed fresh. However, they have medicinal qualities when dug, dried, and powdered. The properties ascribed in *Arisaema* are those of a carminative and expectorant. Harris says that it possesses "the property of stimulating excretions of the skin and lungs, is irritant, and diaphoretic . . . the powder of the fresh roots is used for aphthous sore throat of children." It is said that the tubers grated and boiled in milk provide a medicine for coughs and pulmonary consumption.

Indians used the grated dried root as an external application for headache. The action of the sweat on the powder acted as a counter-irritant, and caused such pain as to cover up the headache.

This plant has potent powers and it should be used with care. A dose is suggested as 10 grains of the powdered dry root taken twice daily, with honey or sugar syrup to reduce the unpleasant acrid effects.

Arisaema is a very widely distributed member of the Arum family in the United States and Canada, and can usually be found growing in boggy places. It is easily distinguished in spring by the "pulpit" discovered under the three leaflets on a tallish stem.

ARISTOLOCHIACEAE

Virginia snakeroot, serpentaria, pelican flower, sangrel, birthwort, snakeweed (Texas snakeroot—see below)

Growing in rich woodlands throughout the United States, eastward to about Kansas and up to Connecticut, this low perennial herb was listed until recently as an official drug by the *U.S. Pharmacopoeia.*

A. reticulata (the Texas snakeroot) which is found from Louisiana to Texas, is a close relative of *A. serpentaria,* and both have been used medicinally. Of particular interest are the brownish-colored flowers which grow in a pipelike shape from the bottom of the stems. A cousin of these species is well known horticulturally as the large-leaved vine, Dutchman's pipe.

The Latin and English names of snakeroot both suggest that it has been used as a cure for snakebite, but there seems to be no reportable evidence of any values along this line. Rather, one finds that its properties are diaphoretic, stimulant and tonic. The thickened rhizomes and roots (dried and powdered) are the parts used. Large doses produce vomiting, pains, and general digestive upset, but, taken in mild infusions, it is reported to be valuable as a general tonic, for low fevers, and whenever an aromatic bitter would be valuable.

It is interesting to note that throughout the world there are a number of other species of *Aristolochia,* or a related genus, which are employed in local medicines. One Egyptian species is used to stupefy snakes, while in South America several forms are known as snake-bite cures. It may be that our American forms of the plant have achieved names and reputations by association rather than by their capacity for cure.

C OMPOSITAE

*Wormwood, absinthe, madderwort, mug-
wort, mingwort, old woman*

Many of the plants of this book, while
now native, are introductions from
Europe, often having been brought here
for medicinal purposes. The wormwood
is one of these plants, but it has not
found the entire country congenial territory. It may be seen only along the
roadsides, and in pastures in the northern tier of states, westward to the plains.

This herb belongs to the daisy family
and grows up to three feet high, with
odorous, grayish-green, fine-cut leaves.
The leaves and flowering tops are gathered and dried in August and
September. They are used commercially as flavoring for the liquor
absinthe; with other herbs, as a constituent of vermouth; and somewhat, in times past, for flavoring beer. Botanically it is closely related to *A. dracunculus,* known to all good cooks as tarragon.

Although wormwood has been generally recommended for many
purposes, it should be noted that in concentrated form the volatile
oil is a violent narcotic poison. As a drug, wormwood has disappeared from the pharmacopoeias, but it is still considered as an aromatic bitter, diaphoretic, and flavoring agent, with the properties of
a febrifuge, anthelmintic, and antiseptic.

In home medicine, wormwood is taken as an infusion of the
crushed tops in a cup of boiling water, a tablespoonful at a time during the day. Grieve's herbal says that "a light infusion of the tops of
the plants, used fresh, is excellent for all disorders of the stomach,
creating an appetite, promoting digestion and preventing sickness
after meals, but producing a contrary effect if used too strong."

Because of the strong smell of the foliage, wormwood was used in
medieval times as a "strewing herb" for churches and public places,
and, in chance encounters, this biting perfume is delightful. No herb
garden should be without a plant or two. Value is ascribed to it as a
repellent for moths and as a flea-chaser. In short, wormwood is an
ancient and reputable herb with many uses, but one which should
not be taken without knowledge of its poisonous qualities.

Asarum canadense

ARISTOLOCHIACEAE

Wild ginger, Canada snakeroot, Indian ginger, colic root, false coltsfoot, catfoot, etc.

That a piece of ginger (which comes from the tropics) will relieve stomach-ache is known to almost everyone. But here in America we have a plant which, because of its taste and properties, has much the same value as the true, commercial ginger.

Wild ginger is found in moist woods, from Maine to Minnesota, south to Georgia and Ohio. It is a low-growing, stemless herb, easily distinguishable by its heart-shaped leaves borne in pairs, and its tiny bell-shaped flowers. The thickened root, or rhizome, is dug in the spring, dried, and used in powdered form as an aromatic bitter and carminative.

Some writers go further and claim for it values as a diuretic, diaphoretic, emmenagogue and as a substitute for the plant drug serpentaria (q.v.). It is said that in North Carolina the leaves *are* used as a substitute for ginger.

Meyer gives a dose as a teaspoonful of the root to a pint of boiling water, a wineglassful taken as often as needed. An infusion of more strength may well be useful in inducing copious sweating when such a circumstance is desired. Its use as a component of other valuable, but less pleasant, drugs is also indicated.

It is quite likely that this was one of the well known medicinal plants of the Indians.

Asclepias tuberosa
Asclepias incarnata
Asclepias syriaca

ASCLEPIADACEAE

(1) Butterfly weed, orange milkweed, pleurisy root, flux root, Indian-nosy, silkweed, etc.

(2) White Indian hemp, swamp milk-weed, water nerve root, rose-colored silkweed, etc.

(3) Milkweed, silkweed, common milk-weed

Departing from the usual decision to discuss separately different members of one family, it seems better to lump these three milkweeds and see the family as such. This family shares a common characteristic of stems which exude a milky juice when broken (hence the name). Most nature lovers are familiar with one or another of the twenty-five species found throughout the United States.

The unusual and often beautiful flowers are followed by birdlike pods filled with downlike seeds. Fernald and Kinsey in their book on edible wild plants lump the entire species together, saying that the young shoots are as edible as asparagus or a spring green, and the author knows many people who gather the sprouts for this purpose. But aside from food value, craft, and ornamental uses, the three members of the family each has some special medicinal values which are notable and a paragraph on each is indicated.

A. tuberosa—Growing wild in a clump of roses on the author's lawn are several plants of the butterfly weed. If

A. tuberosa—above
A. incarnata—center
A. syriaca—below

any plant ever did *not* deserve to be called a weed it is this most beautiful and brilliantly colored flower which nearly refuses to grow under cultivation. It grows in dry, sandy, open soils in the eastern half of the country, where its red-orange flowers on 10″ high stalks adorn the summer landscape. Thick roots are dried and used in carefully small doses as a diaphoretic, diuretic, expectorant and alterative. Its common name indicates that it has been used in pleurisy.

A. incarnata—The swamp milkweed is a stronger growing plant than the previous species. It grows in wet spots and on shores to a height of around 3 feet, with flesh-pink-to-lavender flowers in July. Growing thickly, it offers a fine source for the succulent, edible spring shoots. With a few exceptions it is found everywhere in the United States. The thickened roots are the parts used medicinally, and writers agree on their value as an emetic and cathartic. The plant has been recommended in rheumatic, asthmatic, and catarrhal infections, and as a vermifuge. It is also said to be a good stomachic and a quick diuretic, and may be taken as an infusion, either hot or cold, made by using ½ ounce of powdered root to a pint of boiling water.

A. syriaca—The name here indicates a supposed origin in Syria and it is, according to Gray, an introduced plant, now more or less common in the eastern United States. It will be found growing in thickets and on roadsides where its 4 to 5 foot stems bear, in summer, a dull-purplish flower head. The shoots are thick and excellent for eating, as was well known to the Indians.

In general the uses of the root of *A. syriaca* are much the same as for other members of the family, but it should be noted that this species contains more than a fit share of a poisonous crystalline substance called asclepione.

In studying these three plants, one sees that this genera is one of the most useful as well as one of the loveliest of all wild plants. It is extremely variable in habitat, growth, and color. The author has found many interesting references to milkweed uses. One man, writing recently to the *Rural New Yorker*, tells how, as a boy, he cured warts on his neck by the application of milkweed juice, and, his reports that he found a similar reference to such a use in an edition of the same paper in 1871. A correspondent writes the author to give careful details on the successful treatment of a bad case of ringworm on a grandson's head through repeated applications of the milky exudation of *Asclepias*.

Altogether a wonderful and interesting family.

BERBERIDACEAE

Common barberry, jaunders berry, pip-peridge bush

Medicinally the barberry falls within the field of the "Doctrine of Signatures" in that, the wood of the stems being so vividly yellow, it was obvious to all that it would cure jaundice—the yellow disease. One of its common names derives from this belief. Yet, however ridiculous this "Doctrine" may have been, there seems to have been some truth in the association, for a most modern herbal from England says of barberry:

"Tonic, purgative, and antiseptic. Used in all cases of *jaundice,* liver complaints, general debility, and biliousness. It regulates the digestive powers, being a mild purgative, and removes constipation. . . . The berries make a pleasant acid drink of great utility in diarrhea, fevers, etc."

The root, the root-bark, and the berries are used. Several writers recommend a dose of ¼ to ½ teaspoonful of the powdered bark taken as an infusion three to four times daily, while the juice of the berries makes a pleasant and healthful acid drink.

The berries in the fall make an excellent jelly or pickle, beautiful in color, and fine with meat dishes. Fernie says that the jelly is an excellent relief for catarrhal infections, and that the plain juice, with a little sugar, is a healing gargle.

This purely European plant has established itself throughout the northeastern tier of states and it is easily found, in spite of the fact that the first legislation *against* the barberry was passed in 1670, and the plant has been fought and grubbed out ever since. The common (not Japanese) barberry *does* harbor the spores of a wheat rust which really makes it an enemy in the wheat-growing states.

Betula lenta

BETULACEAE

Black birch, sweet birch, cherry birch, river birch, spice birch

It is said that *birch* is derived from the ancient Sanskrit *bhurga*, meaning "that which is written upon." The birch family is a very widespread one and a tree of many uses. The various species have similar values, but this discussion is concerned only with *B. lenta*, which is most highly recommended.

The black birch has black to reddish brown bark, brownish smooth twigs, toothed and pointed oval leaves, and grows largely in the less fertile, colder and more elevated sections of the eastern United States.

Oil of sweet birch is produced commercially, the supply coming from Connecticut and Tennessee, according to Youngken. He says that "The bark and twigs are gathered from the trees from May to late September, chopped or ground and placed in retorts with water which are kept warm overnight by a low fire beneath them. The following day the oil is distilled. . . . Methyl salicylate, the active principle constituting oil of sweet birch . . . is formed" in the process. Thus is produced an aromatic flavoring agent and an anti-rheumatic. Salicylic acid is a major ingredient of aspirin, and one supposes that the action of birch oil in rheumatism is much the same as aspirin, which is so often prescribed for it.

Additionally, the oil thus extracted is practically indistinguishable from oil of wintergreen and is much used in the candy trade. Among the Indians where sugar maples were not used for the purpose, the sweet sap of the birch trees was collected as a source of sweetening, and as well was used as a basis for a fermented beer.

In home use the dried bark or leaves have been used as an excitant, diaphoretic, astringent, antiseptic, carminative, and antipyretic. An infusion may be made at the rate of a teaspoonful to a cup of boiling water.

BORAGINACEAE

*Borage, star-flower, beebread, burrage,
(false) bugloss*

The lovely, blue-flowered borage, an
introduction from Europe, is found
growing occasionally in waste places in
the northern tier of states. It is also cultivated quite widely in gardens. The
nodding heads of star-like flowers grow
from a cluster of hairy, obovate leaves,
altogether not much over a foot high.

The leaves are dried when the plant
is to be used medicinally, while the
fresh, green leaves, which taste like cucumber, are pleasant in salads. The
crushed leaves are a well-known ingredient of claret cup, and one
may make a refreshing drink by combining them with lemon and
sugar.

The constituents of borage are mucilage, potassium nitrate, and
calcium oxalate with other natural salts. The properties listed for it
are refrigerant, demulcent, emollient, and diaphoretic. Recommended
dose is 1 ounce of leaves infused in 1 pint of boiling water and taken
in wineglass doses.

All writers since Roman times mention its exhilarating effect, and
some ancient writers even say that it will cure mental illness. Another use of the leaves is as a poultice in inflammatory swellings,
this presumably being due to their mucilaginous quality and to the
healing power of the salts.

A good reason for growing borage in the garden is to use the leaves
as a pleasant cucumber-like nibble; to enjoy the blue of the flowers;
and to attract the honey bees who seem to prefer borage above any
surrounding flowers and who, alone, have the proper apparatus to
secure the honey and fertilize the flowers. There is much more that
might be said about borage, but one can only urge that the reader
buy a package of seed and grow this plant in his garden, for both
health and pleasure.

Calvatia gigantea

GASTROMYCETES

Puffball, giant puffball

The puffball is a widely distributed fungus which is found most usually after warm rains in late summer. Children (and, regrettably many adults) know it only as something attractive to kick around or to squeeze when ripe, to make it "puff." However, when young, it is one of the most desirable of all edible fungi, delicious sliced and fried in butter.

There is another species of a quite large puffball, *Lycoperdon cyathiforme*, and several small species, together with some lesser known and unimportant members of the family which are not "balls" and therefore of interest only to the botanist. But the three or four species of useful puffballs, whether large or small, may be described as a globose or depressed ball, furrowed at the base, and white inside and out when young. This bulk of moist, white spores changes gradually to yellow, and then to brownish or black, and later, when quite dry, they are discharged by the bursting of the skin. So tiny are these spores that an ordinarily large puffball contains around seven trillion of them. One can imagine that if all of these spores developed, the world would be paved with puffballs.

It is just before this time of bursting that the medicinal interest begins. These spores have long been valued as a hemostat (blood clotting agent) known around the world. Early herbals, such as that of Gerard, mention this use. Although the Indians generally feared fungi, they did know that spores of puffballs dusted on a bleeding wound would quickly stop the flow of blood. Correspondents of the author have used the spores to arrest nosebleeds.

Just one caution. This powder (sometimes used in fireworks) should not be used near an open fire, as it ignites very quickly. In another vein it may be noted that the smoke from the burning powder acts as a narcotic, and has often been used to stupefy bees when gathering honey or working with the hives.

What the future may reveal about puffballs it is hard to say, for, just as this book goes to press, a news release concerning them comes from Washington. Experimental research at the University of Oklahoma has shown that a principle called Calvacin has been isolated, which has been found to be active against cancer in mice. Clinical trials with humans are to be started soon.

CRUCIFERAE

Shepherd's purse, shovel-weed, St. James' wort, case weed, pick purse, mother's heart, clappedepouch, pepper and shot, etc.

A recent magazine article says, "This is a good example of one of the useful plants just pleading not to be ignored and to be gathered by all passers-by and used as medicine. . . ." And this view is reflected in all of the many writings about shepherd's purse.

Here we have a naturalized, annual weed found throughout most of the United States. It grows from a rosette, from 6 to 18 inches, high, according to the soil. The leaves are toothed, and the distinguishing feature of the plant is a little purse-shaped seedpod from which came its name. When broken, the foliage (like so many of the *Cruciferae*) has a peculiar and unpleasant odor, and a somewhat biting taste. In some sections, the fresh young plants are used as a spring green. The seeds themselves are much liked by small birds, and could well be collected for feeding stations.

The plant's medicinal virtues are few but significant. Jacob says this:

"The plant is bitter and pungent with astringent properties, antiscorbutic, expectorant, diuretic, emmenagogue, and deobstruent. . . . The juice placed on cotton and inserted in the nostrils will arrest hemorrhage."

In fact, it is this styptic quality which is generally attested to. During World War I *Capsella* was used in Germany as a styptic instead of other plant materials which could not be imported. One recipe for a styptic solution is to boil 3 ounces of the entire herb in 2 pints of water, taking 2 teaspoonfuls every four hours, or to use such fresh solutions for external bleeding.

One does not, of course, find reference to the use of shepherd's purse by the Indians or in early colonial medicine because it had not become naturalized. Neither does it appear to have been listed in American pharmacopoeias, but the general agreement as to its styptic values makes it necessary to regard it as a useful medicinal plant.

Cassia marilandica

LEGUMINOSAE

Wild senna, Maryland cassia, American senna, locust plant

Beginning at about the latitude of Pennsylvania, south to Florida and west to Texas, one will find this woody herb growing up to 6 feet tall, with alternate leaves, and leaflets as shown in the sketch. The flowers are bright yellow. Used for medicinal purposes, the leaves were listed for many years in the *U.S. Pharmacopoeia*. Youngken says that the leaves contain the same principle found in the East Indian senna sold in drugstores, but in lesser amounts.

Many readers have heard of Senna as a leading purgative, and for such a use this wild American form seems to be equally valuable. The recommended dose is a teaspoonful steeped in boiling water for half an hour, taken a little at a time during the day, or half a cupful at night.

This plant was used as a cathartic by the Indians, who also made poultices from the moist, bruised roots for sores, and a decoction from the root for fevers.

There are few references to senna in the early European herbals because the *Cassia* of the drug trade came largely from Arabia, India and similar climatic and cultural centers which, in the centuries of herbal compilation, had little communication with the "West." Similarly, Europeans knew little of American Indian medicine at that time. How different from these days of a "small world" and instant communication, when knowledge in any scientific field becomes general in a matter of days rather than centuries.

BERBERIDACEAE

Blue cohosh, papoose root, squaw root,
blue ginseng, leontice, blueberry root

Looking quite unlike the barberry, to
which family it belongs, this is a stemless herb growing around 15 inches
high, found in rich woods in the temperate, eastern part of the country. In
the spring there rises up a stemlike support for a leaf cluster, in the center of
which appear a few insignificant, yellow flowers. The "blue" in the
common name comes from a bluish bloom on the foliage and the
later blue berries which follow the flowers.

The part used medicinally is the thick, crooked rhizome, from
which grows a mat of roots. The rhizome is dug and dried, and an
infusion of an ounce of the powdered root is used in a pint of boiling
water, taken at the rate of 2 or 3 ounces, three or four times daily.

Not now appearing in approved drugs for the trade, *Caulophyllum*
has been used for more than a century and probably long before
that by the Indians, from whom our knowledge of it has come. The
name squaw root indicates a possible value, for its principal recommendations are for various female conditions. For instance, a general comment is to the effect that its use stimulates uterine contractions, thus hastening childbirth. It is likewise said to induce menstruation, and to have antispasmodic properties.

Jacobs, in addition to making the above statements, also reports
claims for "diaphoretic and other remedial properties. It is a demulcent, antispasmodic, sudorific, emmenagogue, and diuretic. . . .
A favorite remedy in chronic uterine diseases, rheumatism, dropsy,
colic, cramps, etc." He cautions "the dust is extremely irritating, and
it causes contraction of both voluntary and involuntary muscular
fibers. Its spasmodic action on general muscles is somewhat chorea-
like; it causes joint pains."

The weight of evidence recommending blue cohosh gives it much
more merit than its exclusion from the pharmacopoeia would indicate.

Ceanothus americanus

New Jersey tea, wild snowball, red root

This is a low shrub growing about 3 feet high, with downy leaves, and white flowers coming in June and July. It grows in dry, open woods or on gravelly banks throughout most of the United States. Its name comes from the fact that it was used during the American Revolution as a substitute for the taxed tea from England.

For medicine, the bark of the root is dried and ground and infused at the rate of a teaspoonful to a cup of boiling water, drunk a little at a time, up to two cupfuls per day (says Meyer).

We find *Ceanothus* listed among the medicinal plants of the Cherokee and Navajo Indians, and one species is used in Mexico. This species has also been used in Canada to produce a cinnamon-colored dye for wool, for the roots contain a great deal of red coloring matter.

Ceanothus is mentioned as an astringent, antispasmodic, anti-syphilitic, expectorant and sedative. It has been prescribed in cases of asthma, bronchitis, whooping cough, and dysentery as well as for use as an injection in gonorrhea, gleet and leucorrhea. For sores in the mouth, it is said to be an excellent wash, due to the astringent properties of the bark.

GENTIANACEAE

Centaury, feverwort, bitter herb, red centaury, Christ's ladder

Culpeper, in *Complete Herbal,* written in 1653, in a sentence says about all that is important about centaury (also known as *Erythraea Centaurium*) "the herb is so safe that you cannot fail in making use of it, only giving it inward for inward diseases. It is very wholesome but not very toothsome."

Care must be taken to distinguish this member of the Gentian family from other commonly called centauries which are members of the family of Composites or Daisies. It is a plant of European origin which is found widely in the United States, growing in damp and waste spaces, meadows, and hedge rows, to a height of 6 to 18 inches, according to locale. The flowers are pink-purple, leaves opposite-lancelate. The plant may be collected when coming into flower in July, dried, and used in infusions at the rate of 1 ounce of herb to 1 pint of boiling water, taken a wineglassful at a time.

A review of all the literature on *Centaurium* finds agreement that there are no specifically valuable properties worth noting, except as simple bitters having value in aiding digestion, stimulating the system, and (perhaps through suggestion) providing a tonic effect to the system. A slightly biting smell of the leaves is lost when dried, but returns as a bitter taste as medicine.

Several sources recommend the use of centaury with barberry as an excellent remedy for jaundice and like complaints involving the liver.

Geoffrey Grigson tells us that among the Irish, centaury is a blessed herb brought into the house for good luck between the Annunciation and the Assumption of the Blessed Virgin Mary, and that on the Isle of Man it is named "Steps of Christ," since it was said to have grown where Christ trod on the way to Calvary.

The name Centaury seems to have come down from the Greek plant having been named for Chiron, a medically skilled centaur of ancient mythology.

Parmeliaceae

Iceland moss, Iceland lichen, cetraria

As the only member of the family of lichens to be discussed in this book, it is wise to note here the interesting physiological make-up of all lichens. We have here a plant, showing itself in a wide variety of forms everywhere in the world, yet a plant which is composed of a fungus growth whose parts are intertwined in one or another species of algae. In this combination (a symbiosis), each component is able to secure food or moisture from the other, the fungal element deriving food from the green algae, and the algae benefiting by moisture obtained from the fungus.

Just two of the many forms of lichen.

Medicinally, lichens were apparently known to the Egyptians, and in the fifteenth century when the "Doctrine of Signatures" was so highly regarded, the many odd shapes and colors of lichens provided many imaginative suggestions for cures. The hairlike filaments of *Usnea* were "good for stimulating the hair"; yellow lichens would cure jaundice; lung shaped *Lobaria* was helpful in lung conditions; while lichens found growing on skulls were valued in epilepsy. But such extravagant and absurd claims were soon proved groundless, and about the only lichen which today appears in reliable herbals is the one noted here, Iceland moss.

Iceland moss contains a large amount of starchy matter known as lichenin, which is soluble in boiling water and which gelatinizes on cooling. It is said that the taking of this in jelly form improves the appetite and digestion. Excessive use may induce looseness of the bowels, but otherwise it is harmless. The use of an Iceland moss decoction is recommended in chronic catarrh and bronchitis, its demulcent action relieving coughing. An ounce of the well-washed moss is boiled in a pint of water. The resulting liquid may be used (with suitable flavoring) as a jelly or, warm, as a medicine.

One other lichen related to the above which is useful to the drug trade is *Roccella*. It (with other species) produces a drug called Cudbear, long used as a coloring agent for drugs, and in the preparation of litmus paper.

PAPAVERACEAE

Celandine, greater-, garden-, common-celandine, tetterwort, wart-weed, felon-wort, swallow wort, Grecian may (note: lesser celandine is a species of *Ranunculus*)

It is a rather curious circumstance that all writers agree that one rarely finds celandine growing far from dwellings, and then usually on waste places, dumps, etc. But this is actually a plant which has followed civilization from its home in Eurasia, and always amid plenty of tales of its medicinal usefulness. Looking quite unlike a poppy, to which family it belongs, it has yellowish, gray-green leaves and fragile, yellow flowers. The most distinguishing feature is the orange juice which flows quickly when any part of the plant is broken. This juice is unpleasantly flavored and extremely acrid, and contains at least one principle which is poisonous, to the extent that the reliable Mrs. Quelch says, "as a purgative [the action of the juice] is so violent it had better be left alone, at least as a home medicine, though a fluid extract may be obtained, and can be taken safely if the prescribed doses are not exceeded."

Actually, the plant was named by the Greeks, and mentioned by Roman writers, with recommendations to use the juice for removal of corneal opacities. And in time of the "Doctrine of Signatures" the yellow-orange juice quite naturally suggested it for jaundice or liver complaints, not only to be taken internally, but, by one suggestion, leaves of celandine to be put in the shoes to cure jaundice.

But several of the names indicate a possible use for the juice as a remedy for "tetters" (such diseases as ringworm, eczema, herpes) and for the cure of warts. There does seem to be a caustic quality in the juice (or the roots even more than in the upper parts), and this could be of value for skin conditions. One further notes that there are a number of recommendations for applying the freshly oozing juice to corns, applying daily until cured.

For internal use, remembering its somewhat poisonous nature, Potter gives a dose as an infusion of 1 ounce of the herb to 1 pint of boiling water, taken in wineglassfuls. It would thus be a purgative and diuretic.

SCROPHULARIACEAE

Balmony, turtle-head, shellflower, salt-rheum weed, bitter herb, hummingbird tree, snake-mouth

Here is one plant which does not appear in the older herbals as it is a true American perennial plant. It is found usually, and rather sparingly, along stream edges and in other wet, shady places in Canada and throughout the United States, growing about two feet high. The descriptive names come from the similarity of the appearance of the half-opened flowers to the head of a turtle or snake, while other names describe its taste or values. It is said to have been an important Indian medicine, but research does not disclose what tribe used it. From the standpoint of finding it, one should be aware that the foliage and flower color is highly variable, Gray noting eight or nine differences.

The chemical properties of balmony are extracted either by tincture or infusion. The best statement of its use in medicine is that in Grieve's herbal:

"The whole, fresh plant is chopped, pounded to a pulp, and weighed, and a tincture is prepared with alcohol. The decoction is made with 2 ounces of the fresh herb to the pint (a dose being 1 to 2 ounces of the decoction). . . . The leaves have anti-bilious, anthelmintic, tonic and detergent properties, with a peculiar action on the liver. . . . As an ointment it is recommended for inflamed tumours, irritating ulcers, inflamed breasts, piles, etc."

Speaking of its value in liver conditions, and under the heading of curiosa, we find one authority saying that balmony is a "remedy for the left lobe of the liver."

To those of our readers who are garden-minded, this plant will best be known as turtlehead. In some of the other American species it is a good plant for the perennial border, sometimes offered as *Penstemon barbatus,* to which latter family it is very closely allied.

CHENOPODIACEAE

Wormseed, Mexican tea, Jerusalem tea, Jesuit tea, Spanish tea, ambrosia, stick weed, goosefoot, stinking weed, epazote (Mexican)

Although most of the introduced wild plants have come to us from Europe, some, such as *Chenopodium,* have come from south of the border. It is a plant noted in Mexican herbals, and some suggest that it came from Chile, perhaps by a long process of migration as was the case with the potato and tomato. Depending on locale, this may be an annual or perennial, with small greenish flowers growing about 3 feet high. It will be found in waste places and along roadsides throughout much of the United States. It should at once be noted that the plant is basically *poisonous,* and, although in Mexico it is noted for other purposes, the little, glossy, black seeds as an anthelmintic would be the only safe use in home medicine.

In official medicine, the oil is extracted by distillation from the whole plant and is known as Chenopodium Oil, given as a single dose for adults at the rate of 1 cc. per dose. In home medicine, a teaspoonful of the seeds may be mixed with honey, to be given twice in one day and followed with a good laxative. One authority says to use "powdered seeds given in doses of 15-60 gr. . . . at bedtime and in the morning before food, for two or three days, followed by some cathartic."

Other uses, detailed in several herbals are those of a tonic and antispasmodic, for nervous affections. In Mexico it seems to have been prescribed in ammenorrhea and for painful and profuse menstruation. As a poison, it is basically a narcotic affecting the brain, spinal cord, and stomach, and should therefore be treated with the respect due any otherwise useful poison.

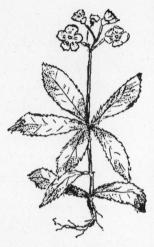

PYROLACEAE

Pipsissewa, wintergreen, waxflower, princess pine, king's cure, ground holly, love-in-winter, rheumatism weed, ratsbane, dragon's tongue, pyrole, etc.

This plant offers possibility of confusion because of interrelationsihp of names. First let it be said that this is a plant of other countries the name coming from the Greek, *Cheima*-winter and *philein*-to love, indicating its evergreen nature. But in the past it has borne a scientific designation as a Pyrola, or True Wintergreen to which it is closely related, but quite different in appearance and usage. Also we have another member of the genus, *C. maculata*, called the spotted wintergreen, which, although having similar properties, is not considered a true substitute for the subject of these notes. Hence, when gathering this plant look for pipsissewa rather than wintergreen or spotted wintergreen.

Dr. Barton, writing in 1804, says that the name pipsissewa is Indian—and a pleasantly tripping one at that. Probably all of the Indians made as much use of the plant as, we are told quite definitely, the Pequot and Narragansett tribes did.

The place to find this plant is always in deep, coniferous woods throughout the United States. Look for sharply pointed green leaves on a plant only 5 inches or so in height. Waxy white flowers appear in early summer, and the leaves are sweet-smelling when fresh. The dried leaves may be made into an infusion at the rate of 1 ounce to 1 pint of boiling water, taken in wineglass doses.

The literature on pipsissewa is in agreement on its value as a diuretic, astringent, tonic, and alterative. It is used in cystitis, gonorrhea and as a mild disinfectant to the urinary tract. The name king's cure indicates its past use in scrofula. For nearly a hundred years an "official" drug, it has now given place to the inorganic medicines. Several writers point out that its action as a diuretic is similar to that of *Arctostaphylos Uva-ursi* (q.v.) but that side effects are fewer. For commercial purposes, it is gathered and prepared for market by the herb-gatherers of North Carolina and other mountain areas.

OLEACEAE

*Fringe tree, snowdrop tree, old man's
beard, white fringe, flowering ash, poison ash, graybeard tree, shavings, snow-
flowers*

To make a pun, one might say that
this plant is on the fringe of the plants
of this book, for, although fringe tree
bark has for long been listed in the
homeopathic pharmacopoeia, its medi-
cinal value is subject to question by the medical and ordinary herbal
professions.

The fringe tree may be described as a large shrub or small tree as
its maximum height is about 25 feet, with shrublike growth. It is a
native of moist woods and stream banks from New Jersey to Texas.
When in bloom, it is easily seen, for the snowy petals are long and
narrow and in great masses look like snow, or an "old man's
beard." The bark of the root or, in some cases, the fresh bark of the
smallish trunks or the root are the parts used medicinally.

It will be noticed that one name is poison ash, and this seems
appropriate. Jacobs says that an overdose of a tincture of the root
bark "causes frontal headache, a bruised sore sensation of the eye-
balls, nausea, bitter eructions and retching, followed by pressure to
stool, vomiting, black evacuations of the bowels, slow pulse, cold
perspiration, and great general weakness." Caution is therefore indicated.

As to the reputed virtues of the bark of the fringe tree, it is mentioned as a tonic, diuretic, aperient, narcotic, alterative, febrifuge,
and astringent. If an infusion rather than a tincture is to be used, it
should be made at the rate of 1 ounce of dried bark to 1 pint of
boiling water, taken a tablespoonful at a time. Because of astringent
properties, this same infusion might be used as a lotion for wounds
and ulcers.

If, in addition to being interested in herbal remedies, the reader is
also a gardener, the fringe tree can be recommended for use as one of
the finest and most interesting of the large background shrubs—a
truly good American contribution to the landscape.

Chondrus crispus

GIGARTINACEAE

Irish moss, carrageen, chondrus

Considering the thousands of miles of coastline in America, it would hardly be proper to omit mention of the medicinal values to be found in products of the sea. These values have been learned empirically by peoples who live close to the ocean waters (English, Scandinavian, Japanese as examples), but are not always so well known to the inland folk. It is, obviously, impossible to discuss here all of the plant products which thrive in or near salt water, but a general statement would certainly include the fact that in products of the sea there is usually a concentration of iodine, together with other salts, all of them vital to health. Now that transportation to the rocky coasts of New England is so easy and popular, it might be of interest to discuss here the Irish moss, which is found along the shores from Cape Cod northward.

First let it be said that this is not a moss, but a seaweed, found growing attached to rocks in shallow water. After a storm it may be found on the beaches, either fresh (purplish in color) or partly bleached (whitish). Commercially, it is gathered from the rocks, washed and bleached and sold; in 1959 over 11,000,000 pounds were harvested.

Such vast quantities were consumed largely in the food trade, where its mucilaginous nature makes it useful as a blender, or gel, for chocolate milk, frosting mixes, pie fillings etc. But for medicinal purposes the values are as a demulcent and nutrient; in the form of its mucilage as an emollient, demulcent, and emulsifying agent; and as a vehicle in various skin lotions and jellies. One home remedy recommends that it be combined with the juice of a cucumber for kitchen burns. It is highly recommended in chronic coughs, bronchitis, etc. (combined with other herbs), in irritating diseases of the bladder and kidneys, and is presently sold in drugstores as the principal ingredient of an intestinal lubricant.

COMPOSITAE

Chicory, succory, blue sailors, blue dandelion, wild endive

Of extremely wide distribution, chicory is another wild plant of America which has been introduced from Europe. It is closely related to the dandelion, and often in the spring it is easy to confuse the clumps of the two as they appear on lawns or in fields. But in bloom, when the two- (or more) foot stalks bear lovely blue or soft pink blooms, there is no dandelion resemblance.

A plant of ancient usage, the name has been traced back through Arab medical language to Greek and Egyptian, and mention of the use of chicory is found in Roman writings. One finds that it was greatly appreciated as a spring green by south Europeans, who understood its value as a tonic after the lack of green food in winter. In France (and in our own South, subject to French influence) the roots are dug, dried, ground, and added to coffee, not as an adulterant but for its distinctive flavor.

To many, chicory is known as the blanched winter vegetable of the markets sold as endive or witloof chicory, but to Lawn Addicts, it may be a weed which utterly defies pulling up, as its roots go very deep.

No great medicinal values are ascribed to chicory, although it is mentioned in herbals as a diuretic, laxative, and tonic. And it seems to be generally recommended for jaundice and liver complaints, to be taken freely as a decoction, made at the rate of 1 ounce of dried powdered root to a pint of water.

Meyer says that a tea made from the roots "may be taken whenever the stomach has been upset."

RANUNCULACEAE

Black snakeroot, black cohosh, bugbane (cim-bugs; fugo-drive away), rattle root, rattle weed, squawroot, macrotys, papoose root, rattlesnake root, and many others

Again in this plant one has trouble with common names. There is a "blue" cohosh also called papoose root, and another squawroot, *Caulophyllum thalictroides* (q.v.). In these names we also detect connections with the Indian pharmacopoeia, and this in confirmed by the writing of Dr. Barton in 1798 who says, "it having been used by our Indians . . . (who) set a high value on it." It is a true American plant which has been introduced into Europe for medicinal and ornamental purposes. It raises a lovely, feathery, wand-like, 3-4 foot stalk of flowers, fine for the back of the flower border.

Cimicifuga grows over most of the eastern and middle U.S.A.; being at home in rich open woods. At the end of its growing season, the rhizomes and roots are dug, dried, and later powdered for medical purposes. An official drug for nearly a hundred years, it may be given as an extract, tincture, or infusion. For the latter, two teaspoons of the root to a pint of boiling water is suggested.

Youngken's pharmacological textbook says *"Cimicifuga* is employed as an anti-rheumatic and as a remedy for chorea, dysmenorrhoea, neuralgia and tinnitus aurium (buzzing in the ears)." Other writers include its use in various spasmodic affections, epilepsy, as an astringent, diuretic, and alterative.

Potter, for instance, says, "In small doses useful in children's diarrhoea. In paroxysms of consumption it gives relief by allaying the cough, reducing rapidity of pulse, and inducing perspiration. . . . In whooping cough its action is highly spoken of. . . . Said to be a specific in St. Vitus's Dance of children." Overdoses produce nausea and vomiting. Although without any confirming statistics, it is reputed to be an insecticide, and a snakebite and bee-sting cure.

With all of these virtues, it is not hard to see why it would be a valuable addition to the medicine "cabinet" of the Indian squaw, who, quite likely as much as the "medicine man," was responsible for the health of native American families.

CLETHRACEAE

*White alder, summer sweet, sweet pep-
per bush, pepper-bush*

In moist and sandy places from
Maine to Texas, one finds *Clethra* one
of the spiciest and most delightfully fragrant of flowers. It blooms on 6 to 8
foot shrubs, over a long, late, summer
period. Not important as a medicinal
plant (its leaves and flowers are rated
to be a diphoretic and excitant), it is
nevertheless a good source of honey in
many sections, and, as such, provides
the excuse to include in these pages a
short discussion of the importance of
honey.

Known to possibly a million purchasers and two million readers
in this country is the book by Dr. D. C. Jarvis, *Folk Medicine*, in
which the values of honey and vinegar and other natural plant medicines are discussed. Just to reproduce the headings in his chapter
on honey suggests the many values of this most wonderful of
medicines:

Honey in infant feeding	To control muscle cramps
Honey and bed-wetting	Honey for burns
Honey in producing sleep	Honey in athletic nutrition
An old-fashioned cough remedy	Honey handled best by kidneys

A technical description of honey would tell only that it contains
the easily digested sugars (dextrose and laevulose), mucilage, vola-
ile oil, wax, and formic acid. Yet there is much more to the story
than that, for the fact that honey does not ferment or spoil indicates
its value as a bactericide.

On the subject of *bees*, a number of instances are known of persons who have found relief from rheumatism in the extremities
through the controlled stinging by bees. This is done by means of
lively bees being placed over the affected areas in an inverted tum-
bler, and irritated to make them sting. Again we hear of a bee tea,
made by pouring boiling water on the worker bees and drinking the
"infusion" for the relief of difficult passage of urine.

Cnicus benedictys

COMPOSITAE

Blessed thistle, holy thistle, bitter thistle, spotted carduus

A number of the thistles are reputed to have medicinal properties, and the values of this species have been passed along with the advance of civilization, from Southern Europe, to England, and thence to America. For the plant, as found here and there in the East and South of this country, came to us with the immigrants. It is a much-branched plant, with alternate, lance-shaped leaves, and bears small heads of yellow-appearing flowers, from May to August.

The bitter-tasting leaves are used as an infusion. Meyer's recipe is a teaspoonful to a cup of water, to be taken in sips during the day. Few writers consulted value greatly the blessed thistle, but all list it as tonic, diaphoretic, and, in large doses, emetic.

In earlier times it seems to have had a wide reputation, and the "blessed" name attached to it shows belief in its beneficent effect. Culpeper, writing in 1653 in the middle of the Reformation period, makes a rather snide comment about the name:

"It is called . . . Blessed Thistle, or Holy Thistle. I suppose the name was put upon it by some that had little holiness themselves."

Geoffrey Grigson, discussing this religious aspect of herbal-writing, interestingly says about Gerard's comment anent the related, Our Lady's Thistle:

"he goes on to a silent display of Protestantism and no Popery. . . . He must have known the legend very well (that the white veins were marked by the Virgin's milk, when she suckled the child), and he must have known that this sacred Milk Thistle was held to increase the flow of milk. But not a word. There must be no superstition."

But yet in that time there *was* plenty of superstition, for each plant was under the sign of a planet, as when Culpeper says of *Cnicus:*

"It strengthens the attractive faculty of men and clarifies the blood, because (it is) ruled by Mars." Well, maybe so.

LILIACEAE

*Lily-of-the-valley, convallaria, May lily,
Our Lady's tears*

It may seem strange to include such
an obvious garden flower, but Gray's
Botany says, "in the wild it is abundantly spread from cultivation—introduced and naturalized from Europe."
And our pharmacological authority,
Youngken, says "cardiac tonic." Until
recently, it has been considered an official drug, and there is a long history of
its value not only as a substitute for
Digitalis but in a number of other situations. This fragrant garden
flower has followed man from one garden to another for many centuries, and was mentioned as early as the fourth century.

In medicine, the whole plant may be used, especially the rhizome
and roots, but the carefully dried tops (including flower stalks) are
also quite potent. It is usually administered as a tincture, but an infusion may be made with ½ ounce of the herb to 1 pint of boiling
water, taken in doses of a tablespoonful. Grieve's herbal says:

"valued as a cardiac tonic and diuretic, the action of the drug
closely resembles that of Digitalis, though it is less powerful; it is
used as a substitute and strongly recommended in valvular heart disease, also in cases of cardiac debility and dropsy. It slows the dis-
turbed action of a weak irritable heart, whilst at the same time increasing its power. It is a perfectly safe remedy. No harm has been
known to occur from taking it in full and frequent doses, it being
preferable in this respect to Digitalis. . . ."

Yet with this laudatory statement some caution is advised, as lily-
of-the-valley is said to be quite poisonous if eaten fresh.

The mucilaginous nature of the plant juices suggests that lily-of-
the-valley might be healing in external conditions, and one indeed
does find a suggestion that "a poultice of the roots takes away the
marks of bruises." Culpeper, writing in the seventeenth century,
even says that "The distilled water of the flowers is very effectual and
is recommended to take freckles, spots, and sunburn from the face
and other parts of the body."

We thus see that there are unsuspected virtues in this lovely flower.

RANUNCULACEAE

Gold-thread, mouth root, canker root, yellow root, tisavoyanne

We are using here the scientific name, *C. groenlandica*, of Fernald, as that is the authority used throughout this work, but the gold-thread is most often listed as *C. trifolia*. Whatever the botanists may decide, the truth is that all medical texts agree on certain values of the plant. In different species its properties are common to medicine in Asia, India, and Japan.

Gold-thread is found in the United States growing in sphagnous swamps and moist woods down through New England, into the southern mountains, and over into the middle tier of states. It is easily identified by its yellow, thread-like roots, which, in many countries, have been as highly valued for their dye as for their medicinal properties. The tiny, evergreen, strawberrylike foliage is sparse and grows only about 5 inches high, bearing a white starlike flower in late spring and summer. A Department of Agriculture bulletin (#77) says that the root (or the whole plant) is collected and dried in autumn, and that, commercially, it is in reasonably constant demand. The medicinal properties are best extracted in a tincture, but a simple infusion may be made by using a third of a teaspoon of the dried roots to a cup of boiling water, steeping for half an hour, and taken a tablespoon at a time every three hours.

Gold-thread has several uses. It is a pure, nonastringent, bitter tonic, and, as such, has values in dyspepsia and similar conditions. Every mention of *Coptis* indicates its value as a remedy for the mouth condition known as thrush, which occurs in young children, and for other ulcerations and sores in the mouth.

Another commonly reported use of *Coptis*, with closely related *Hydrastis* (Golden Seal), is in the cure of dipsomania, or the drink habit.

CORNACEAE

Flowering dogwood, dog tree, false box,
Florida cornel, Indian arrow wood, box-
wood, bitter redberry, cornel, and (Indian names) *Mon-ha-can-ni-min-schi,*
Hat-ta-wa-no-min-schi

A purely American plant, the familiar
flowering dogwood is found quite generally through the United States growing in acid soils and in mixed and semi-
shady locations. Aside from its eco-
nomic values, it is surely one of the finest of flowering trees. It was
unquestionably used medicinally by the Indians. Also, it is a hard,
dense wood, and, as the name "arrow-wood" suggests, it was probably used for making arrows, and for similar purposes.

Although discarded from the *U.S. Pharmacopoeia* seventy-five
years ago, the bark has many reputed values, especially as a substitute for quinine or Peruvian bark in the treatment of intermittent
fevers. Setting aside this use as being doubtful and not of current
importance, one notes that the dried bark rates as a bitter tonic,
astringent, febrifuge, and antiperiodic. The principles which make it
valuable may be extracted with either water or alcohol, a simple infusion being made with a teaspoonful of dried bark or dried root
bark to a cup of boiling water, half a cupful hot or cold taken on
retiring. The astringent qualities have caused it to be used in the
treatment of sore mouth and as a poultice in external inflammations.
All writers on dogwood note that the fresh bark acts as a strong
cathartic.

It is said that the Indians used split stems of the hard wood as a
toothbrush, and one assumes that the astringent quality helped to
harden the gums at the same time.

One of the very creditable statements about dogwood is that its
flowering provided the Indians with a reliable indication of the date
on which corn was to be planted, blooming when all danger of frost
was past. Our modern weather prognosticators quite likely could do
no better.

Cytisus scoparius
(formerly Genista scoparius)

LEGUMINOSAE

Broom, Scotch broom, broom tops, link, banal, hay-weed

Although it is usually found in sandy coastal areas, there are so many references to medicinal values of broom that it is included for those who can collect it. It may at times be found elsewhere, escaped from cultivation or planted in gardens.

Broom is a three-foot shrub composed of narrow, leafless green branches which, in June, bear yellow, pealike flowers. The common name suggests how easily one might make a hearth-broom from the gathered stems, and it has been used in this way for centuries.

There are many references to its use in the oldest of herbals, and always for its properties as a purgative and diuretic. The fresh green tops, are picked just before flowering, when they contain the maximum of active principles. As an official medicinal herb, the tops are dried and powdered, but they may be given as a simple infusion of 1 ounce of dried tops to a pint of boiling water, taken frequently, a wineglassful at a time.

One of the active principles which is separated into crystals is a drug, Sparteine sulphate, which "is used as a cardiac depressant to quiet an overactive heart, in functional palpitation, etc." Such a drug is not, however, a home remedy.

There are a number of references to an infusion of broom with dandelion roots, as a beneficial medicine in bladder and kidney infections and in chronic dropsy. A recipe in Grieve's herbal is:

"One ounce Broomtops and ½ ounce Dandelion roots are boiled in one pint of water down to half a pint, adding toward the last, ½ ounce bruised Juniper berries. When cold, the decoction is strained and a small quantity of cayenne added. A wineglassful is taken three or four times a day."

In all of this it should be noted that in large doses it is emetic and poisonous, and that it seems to be especially poisonous to animals.

Solanaceae

Jimson weed, Jamestown weed, datura, stramonium, apple of Peru, thorn apple, stinkweed, devil's trumpet, angel's trumpet

Datura, although poisonous, is often mentioned as a valuable medicine. There is some disagreement about its origin, but it is now found everywhere. The wild plant usually grows around barnyards and in waste but fertile places. It has long been an official drug; it was used in ancient India, whence, presumably, came its name *Datura.* Used as a poison, it stupefied or killed prisoners.

Every part of the plant seems to be dangerous, especially the green seeds which, having harmed children attracted by them, give the plant such a bad name.

The leaves, the parts used medicinally, are collected just as the plant is in flower, and dried.

An anodyne, narcotic, and antispasmodic, jimson weed is sometimes substituted for belladonna *(Atropa belladonna).* Its greatest value seems to have been in treatment of the spasmodic coughing of asthma, for which its smoke may be inhaled. But even this, if overdone, may cause violent reactions. Jacobs says that it has been used as a "sedative, debilitant, hypnotic, mydriatic, and is reputed to be useful in nervous affections . . . the leaves are applied to boils and ulcers."

Meyer adds, "Although it may have valuable uses in the hands of a skilled herbalist, it is unsuited to domestic use and should not be employed in home medication."

Digitalis purpurea

Foxglove, fairy thimbles, thimbles, folk's glove, and many other local names

Without exception, references to foxglove state that *Digitalis* should be used as medication only under the direction of a physician. Not a true native wilding, and not yet widely found on roadsides, foxglove is popular in gardens everywhere for its delightful flowers. It is also known as an important medicine, therefore, mention is made of its properties to satisfy curiosity, and to provide adequate cautions.

It seems curious that the true properties of this plant should not have been discovered until well into the eighteenth century. Early herbalists suggested only external use, and not until 1775 did an English doctor learn of its value from a country woman who used it. From then on its benefits were scientifically explored.

Digitalis is used in neuralgia, insanity, febrile diseases, acute inflammatory complaints, palpitations of the heart, and asthma and as a cardiac stimulant and diuretic.

For medical use, the leaves are picked from the second-year growth, just before the plant comes into flower. In some places in the United States the leaves are grown commercially on herb farms. What is not always realized is that the action of Digitalis is slow at first, and the effects are cumulative. Grieves summarizes:

"[*Digitalis*] is liable to accumulate in the system and to manifest its presence all at once by its poisonous action, indicated by the pulse becoming irregular, the bloodpressure low and gastro-intestinal irritation setting in. The constant use of Digitalis, also, by increasing the activity of the heart, leads to hypertrophy of that organ."

DIOSCOREACEAE

Yam, wild yam root, colic root, China root, devil's bones, dioscorea, rheumatism-root

In spite of the name yam, this plant is not of the same family as our edible sweet potato or yam, which is found in the family of the morning-glories. There are, to be sure, certain resemblances, such as heart-shaped leaves, a climbing habit, and underground tubers, but there is no close botanical relationship. An herbaceous plant found in thickets, open woods and in damp soils, *Dioscorea* grows in the United States west to Kansas. It is collected commercially in the herb-gathering sections of the southland.

For medicinal use, the branched and crooked roots are dug, in autumn, dried and powdered. A decoction is prepared by adding 1 ounce to a pint of water. A dose is one half of the mixture, since it acts readily. Reportedly, the roots lose their potency after a year and new roots should be gathered annually.

The wild yam root is not an official medicine, but its principal reputation is as a cure for bilious colic and as a diuretic and expectorant. In addition to these values, Jacobs says that it is also for:

"spasms, cramps, flatulence, after-pains, and affections of the liver. The roots and rhizomes are antispasmodic, diaphoretic, uterine tonic, expectorant, anti-rheumatic, intestinal stimulant, and emetic. It is also a remedy for intestinal irritations. It has proved to be a valuable remedy for cholera-morbus, spasm of the diaphragm, spasmodic asthma, dysmenorrhoea and kindred afflictions."

Grieves further says that it is especially valuable for the nausea of pregnant women and for cases of spasmodic hiccough.

Diospyros virginiana

EBENACEAE

Persimmon, winter plum, date-plum, possum-wood, simmon

. The common persimmon is found all over the United States except in the northern tier of states, and in subtropical zones. It grows in dry fields, old woods, and clearings, and is a small tree rather than a shrub. Its spring flowers are followed by plum-like, green berries which remain very puckery to the taste until the frost or complete ripeness turns them into a yellow (to reddish), delicious, soft, and luscious fruit. Those who know the delights of eating the cultivated and related Japanese persimmons will recognize this as its American counterpart.

The Latin name, *Diospyros,* means "Fruit of Jove" or "Heavenly plant." This name may have come from the delightful quality of the fruit or, more probably, because a European species of *Diospyros* is said to have caused oblivion, thus transporting one to heaven, the land of Jove.

The medicinal values of persimmon are not too great. However, the obvious astringent properties found in the fruit are also present in the bark, which has been used by country people although not so noted in the pharmacopoeias. The bark is astringent, styptic, and, due to the tannin content, very bitter. It is used in diarrhea, dysentery, uterine hemorrhages, and as a bitter tonic. The outer bark is mentioned as corroborant, antiseptic, and as a febrifuge. The inner bark is extremely bitter and a very good astringent tonic, useful in sore throats, fevers, dysentery, and diarrhea.

The ripe fruit has been used in making a beer or brandy distillation. They are subastringent, nutrient, antiseptic, and, possibly, anthelmintic. The unripe fruit, combined with alum, may be helpful in an ulcerated sore throat and also as an internal astringent, just as is the bark.

POLYPODIACEAE

*Male fern, knotty brake, male shield
fern, sweet brake, shield root, marginal
shield fern, European aspidium* (Aspidium filix-mas *of some classifiers*)

This plant has definite medicinal
value, one which has been recognized
for centuries, and one which entitles it
to its present place in the U.S. *Pharmacopoeia*. Properties found in the rhizome of this fern are definitely deadly
to intestinal worms, and it is therefore
valuable as an anthelmintic, taeniacide or worm medicine. Containing a poison, the drug must be used with certain cautions.

The male-fern is found growing everywhere in the United States
and Europe. For medicinal purposes the useful species include not
only *D. filix-mas* but also the similar marginal shield fern or evergreen wood fern, *D. marginalis*. The roots of the fern are dug in the
autumn and carefully cleaned of all the root hairs, old leaf bases, and
dirt, and then split and dried carefully at a temperature of seventy
degrees. The best extraction of the oleoresin is obtained through the
use of ether. Meyer says that infusions may be made and taken a
little at a time. Better medical practice indicates the use of an ethereal
extract given at night in capsule form at the rate of a single dose of
one drachm, to be followed by a purgative *other than castor oil*. A
cathartic should be taken some time before the dose is administered,
and complete fasting should be observed for one or two days. Such
a treatment should affect a cure in one dose. However, all instructions must be carefully followed to avoid poisoning. Also, the roots
lose their potency after a year.

The seeds (spores) of this fern are so tiny as to be almost invisible,
and the "Doctrine of Signatures" states that use of the fern will confer invisibility. Hence, in *Henry IV* Act II, Scene 1, "We have the
receipt of fern seed; we walk invisible."

Equisetaceae

Horsetail, scouring rush, joint weed, bull pipes, shavebrush, bottlebrush, pewterwort, devil's-guts, field or common horsetail

There are a number of varieties and forms of *E. arvense*, and possibly a dozen species, of *Equisetum*, some taller, thicker or otherwise diversified. According to most botanists flowering plants began with this genus. Horsetails are generally considered primitive plants; they represent a flowering plant which is directly related to the quite different flora of the Carboniferous age. In Gray's *Botany*, *Equisetaceae* is the first listed family.

Horsetail contains some unknown factor which is poisonous to animals, and this indicates caution in using it medicinally. Actually, there is no great evidence of the value of *Equisetum* in home medicine, and it is not mentioned in pharmaceutical texts. The statement made in Grieve's *A Modern Herbal* may best represent the possible values:

"The barren stems only are used medicinally, . . . used either fresh or dried. . . . Diuretic and astringent. Horsetail has been found beneficial in dropsy, gravel and kidney affections . . . Besides . . . a strong decoction acts as an emmenagogue . . . The decoction applied externally will stop the bleeding of wounds."

Even assuming these values, the author prefers to use some of the other recommended plants for such purposes.

Yet horsetails (any of the species) do have a value in the home, for the names "scouring-rush" and "pewterwort" indicate the presence of silica, which makes horsetails of value for scouring pots and pans, and *Equisetum* can be so used by campers. The useful part of the plant is the leafless, spore-bearing "flowering-stalk" which appears before the feathery-foliage growth.

Compositae

Canadian fleabane, horseweed, hogweed, butterweed, pride weed, colt's tail

Fleabane is a purely American plant which was taken to Europe around 1640 and became so well known that mention of it appears in seventeenth century herbals. It is presently included in herbals from both France and Mexico, though it does not seem to have appeared in the official pharmacopoeias.

The name fleabane might indicate some value as an insecticide, but Culpeper says it was given because the seeds are as small as fleas. A tall weed, it sends up unbranched stems from three to six feet high when in flower. It small flower heads have white to greenish, unattractive, daisylike blooms. Fleabane grows in waste places throughout the United States and over much of the temperate zone.

Medicinally, it is a pungent tonic, astringent, and diuretic, claimed to be efficient in diarrhea, gravel, diabetes, scalding urine, and in hemorrhages of the bowels, uterus, and of wounds. It may be taken as an infusion made by a teaspoonful of the dried powdered plant in a teacup of boiling water, a wineglassful as a dose. The whole plant is used, to be gathered when in bloom, and carefully dried.

Several writers indicate that the extracted oil is similar to oil of turpentine, but less irritating. It is recommended for pimples, and Parkinson said long ago that "bound to the forehead is a great helpe to cure one of the frensie."

There are a number of other species of *Erigeron*, all of which are said to possess the same medicinal properties, though in lesser degree. To put the plant in perspective, it would appear that its use and recommendation over three centuries afford it a reputable place in our list of medicinally valuable plants, even though orthodox medical men have not chosen to take much notice of it.

Eriodictyon californicum

HYDROPHYLLACEAE

Yerba Santa, mountain balm, consumptive's weed, gum bush, bear's weed, holy herb

The flora of the west coast of the United States is in many ways distinct from that of the major part of our country. It is (regrettably) impossible to include a great number of plants which have been used medicinally by Indians and early settlers of those areas. Yerba Santa, one of the best known of these Western plants, still bears the Spanish name given to it by the padres, who learned of its value from the Indians.

This "holy herb," an evergreen shrub with lance-shaped leaves, grows on dry hillsides in lower California. The plant has a resinous exudation of the leaves and stems. Considered in reputable reference works, it seems to be chiefly valuable as an expectorant, used for bronchial and laryngeal troubles and for chronic pulmonary conditions. Combined with *Grindelia* q.v., it is recommended for asthma and hay fever. Special note is taken of its value as an aromatic syrup, used as a vehicle for bitter-tasting quinine (which, as "Jesuit's bark," was also associated with the Spanish priesthood). The part of the plant used is the leaves, and the extraction is best made with alcohol. In asthma, it is said that an excellent method is to smoke cigarettes made from the dried leaves.

CELASTRACEAE

Wahoo, burning bush, arrow wood, Indian arrow wood, spindle tree, skewer wood

This ten-foot shrub grows throughout the middle and eastern United States, a native of this country and cultivated elsewhere. It has an excellent habit and beautiful fall foliage, interesting four-sided green branches, and purplish flowers and fruit. There are several other members of the family, including the vining bittersweet with its orange-red fruit, so often gathered for decoration.

Although the family is beautiful, it is also poisonous. The leaves of the vining bittersweet are said to be poisonous to horses, and those of *E. atropurpureus* to sheep and other animals. But, as with so many poison plants, it is useful in small doses. The bark of the root (stem bark is sometimes used) is mentioned as a tonic, hydragogue, cathartic, diuretic, laxative and, in official medicine, as a cholagogue.

All authorities indicate the necessity for caution in the use of this drug. The recipe in Grieve's herbal suggests that a decoction be made of the dried roots at the rate of one ounce to a pint of water, boiled slowly and taken only a small wineglassful two or three times daily. An even weaker decoction is suggested by Meyer.

The related *Euonymus europaeus* is called louse-berries because the small fruits were baked, powdered, and sprinkled on the hair of small children to kill head-lice; the same value is known for the other American species, *E. americanus*.

Eupatorium perfoliatum

CompositaE

Boneset, thoroughwort, feverwort, Indian sage, agueweed, vegetable antimony, sweating plant

Boneset is a plant of swamps, marshes and low grounds, found commonly throughout the United States. It grows to 3 to 4 feet, erect, with hairy, opposite leaves which seem to be perforated by the stem, and bears large heads of white flowers. The name, which seems to refer to its value in helping bones to set, actually came from the plant's value in treating colds and the flu, which, in early days, were called "breakbone fevers."

Our knowledge of its benefits came from the Indians, for Dr. Barton, in 1798, reported that "this medicine is used by our Indians in intermittent fevers," and this use is confirmed by other contemporary writers. Its present day value is attested to by country people; one correspondent wrote the author:

"A bowl of boneset tea was often taken at night to break up a cold, which it usually did, it surely is bitter enough so it should do something."

The virtues mentioned for boneset by Jacobs are:

"It is a tonic stimulant, promoting digestion, strengthening the viscera and restoring the tone of the system; it is a valuable sudorific, alterative, antiseptic, cathartic, emetic, febrifuge, corroborant, diuretic, astringent, deobstruent and stimulant. The warm infusion is used as an emetic, sudorific, and diaphoretic in fevers and constipation. Also used in rheumatism, typhoid fever, pneumonia, catarrh, dropsy, influenza, excellent for colds, fevers, dyspepsia, jaundice, debility of the system, etc."

What more could one want than this? Boneset has been found in official listings for nearly a century and a half and could well be rated a basic medicine in the American herbal list.

For use, the upper leaves and flowering tops are dried, and infusions made at the rate of an ounce of the dried herb to a pint of boiling water, taken in doses of a wineglassful. Take hot to induce perspiration, for colds, and (in stronger doses) as an emetic.

COMPOSITAE

Gravel root, joepye, jopi root, queen of the meadow, trumpet weed, kidney root, purple boneset, Indian gravel root, motherwort, niggerweed, quillwort, hemp weed, purple thoroughwort

This native of all but the most southern parts of the country grows in damp soils, rich but waste places, old fields, etc. About six feet tall, it is distinguished by its purplish to white head of flowers in August. The Latin name *Eupatorium*, is said to have come from Mithridates Eupator, a king of Pontus, the first to use the plant medicinally. "Joe pye" is said to be the name of an American Indian who cured typhus fever with extractions of the root.

The rhizome is used medicinally. Decoctions or infusions have been prescribed for dropsy, strangury, gravel, and other urinary disorders. It is mentioned also as "especially valuable as a diuretic" with astringent and alterative properties, and as a nervine or tonic.

The roots smell like old hay and have a slightly bitter, aromatic taste. One writer gives a dose as "two to four fluid ounces of the decoction taken three or four times a day." It may be considered an auxiliary to other tonics, emetics, and diuretics. While not poisonous, overdoses cause nausea, pains in the stomach and bowels, increased heart action, and a run-down feeling. This species of *Eupatorium* is closely related (as the common names indicate) to the better known boneset, and these plants have been considered interchangeable.

Fragaria vesca

ROSACEAE

Wild strawberries—the common, American, European, field, or native strawberry

There are several species and varieties of the strawberry but for medical purposes the differences are unimportant. An infusion of the leaves or roots (1 ounce of dried leaves to a pint of boiling water) is said to be a mild astringent and diuretic, valuable especially for diarrhea in children and for disorders of the urinary organs. Contrariwise, the fruit eaten in quantity is likely to have a mildly laxative action. For some, it is poisonous to the extent that it may cause digestive disturbances or a skin rash, similar to smallpox in appearance.

Grieve's herbal recommends strawberries as a dentifrice and cosmetic. The juice of the fresh fruit is retained for a few minutes on the teeth which are then cleaned with warm water containing a pinch of bicarbonate of soda. Cosmetically, a cut strawberry rubbed over the face after washing will whiten the skin and remove a slight sunburn. One assumes that the more acid the berries, the more efficacious the remedy.

Aside from the medicinal values, we agree with one ancient writer who said, "The Berries themselves are excellent food to refresh and comfort the fainting spirits, and to quench thirst" and, we add, the wild ones most of all.

Oleaceae

American white ash

This is about the only plant in this book known by a single name. The white ash is a sturdy tree common to much of the United States, and is easily identified through its compound leaves with small flowers coming in panicles from the axils of the preceding year's leaves. Familywise, the ash is related to the olive, the privet and the lilac.

Medicinally, the value of the ash is not so great as other plants, at least not the American species. But Italy annually sends to the United States thousands of pounds of a substance called manna, the exudation of the bark of *Fraxinus ornus*, and about the best laxative known for children.

The active principle in manna is called mannite, or mannitol, which, in lesser proportions, is also found in the American white ash and in other species. From this we may deduce that the American ash has similar laxative values. Some writers recommend the use of an extract of the bark, while others prefer an infusion or decoction of the leaves.

One writer, for instance, says that "the bark is tonic, cathartic, diuretic, febrifuge, diaphoretic, astringent, anti-arthritic, and alterative. It is said to be mildly laxative and has been used as an adjuvant to other laxatives and to disguise their taste. It has been prescribed for vertigo, headache followed by fever. . . ."

In the middle Atlantic states the leaves of some ash species are valued as a cure for snake bites, but one wonders if this is not the remnant of an Elizabethan tale, for we find Gerard quoting from an earlier source, "The leaves of this tree are of so great a vertue against serpents, as that the serpents dare not be so bolde as to touch the morning and evening shadows of the tree . . ."

The ash tree was, says Grigson, sacred in Europe and Britain, and many powers were ascribed to it, including the curing of warts and the ruptures of children. To accomplish this, a young ash was split open and the naked, ruptured baby passed through the opening. The ash was then bound up and as the ash healed, so did the rupture of the child.

Ericaceae

Teaberry, boxberry, partridgeberry, wintergreen, checkerberry, pigeon berry, clink, and a host of other local names; called by Canadians, tea of Canada

A shrubby, low-growing (5-6 inches) evergreen, found most often in association with other members of the same family such as laurel and rhododendron, the teaberry has single white flowers in early July followed by red berries in fall and winter. These mealy and spicy berries are one of the rewards of a tramp through the woods at Christmas time, in the eastern United States.

The medicinal property is in the leaves, which contain "oil of wintergreen," extracted through distillation. Before the discovery of the synthetic methyl-salicylate, or the substitution of a similar oil from the sweet birch *Betula lenta* (in some ways better than the product of *Gaultheria*) the demand for the plant as medicine was much greater than at present.

The methyl-salicylate from *Gaultheria*, or whatever source, is a valuable tonic, stimulant, astringent and aromatic, and the extracted oil is used in the treatment of rheumatism. But because of the equipment necessary to extract the oil, it could hardly be considered a "home remedy." Potter suggests that an infusion of the leaves (1 ounce to 1 pint boiling water) be employed in diarrhea and as an infant's carminative.

For all practical purposes, the best use of oil of wintergreen is as a flavoring agent to cover up undesirable tastes. However valuable it may be in certain conditions, the nature of the pure oil is such that, if taken in continued large doses, it can cause inflammation of the stomach, vomiting, high pulse and other symptoms including (says one writer) "stupidity."

GERANIACEAE

Crane's-bill, alum root, wild geranium, wild crane's-bill, stork's-bill, dove's foot, chocolate flower, spotted crane's-bill, and other, more local names

This is an erect, hairy perennial about 18 inches tall, with divided leaves and rosy-purple flowers. It grows in rich woods in the eastern United States from Canada to Georgia. The pointed, upright seed cases are distinctive, as are the evanescent flowers.

Medicinally, the leaves may be gathered and dried to use in an infusion as a mild astringent. The part used in the drug trade is the knobby rhizomes, which, when dried, produce a purplish-brown powder, whence comes the name "chocolate flower." Having a high tannin content, this powder is a valuable astringent, given in average doses of 15 grains in cases of dysentery, diarrhea, and cholera. Infusions of the leaves are said to be useful as a gargle for sore throat and for ulcerated mouth.

The percentage of tannin in all parts of the plant is very high, and extracts of this may be used in home tanning on an experimental basis. The leaves and roots should be collected just before the plant flowers, when the tannin content is at its highest.

One note of caution. Because of the plant's highly astringent nature, extracts or decoctions of crane's-bill may cause constipation if used for an extended period.

LABIATAE

Ground ivy, gill-over-the-ground, ale hoof, cat's-foot, haymaids, robin-run-in-the-hedge, creeping Charlie (or Jenny), run-away-robin syn. Nepeta Glechoma

Like so many "wild" plants, this European one was introduced by the early settlers, and escaped widely. A ground-hugging perennial vine, its long, trailing stems root at intervals and bear downy, ivy-shaped leaves of dark green. In rich soil its growth is as strong as its pungency, and it can be considered a weed. Pretty, purplish-blue flowers appear on short upright branches through the summer.

The common name ale hoof, seemingly so strange, relates to the medieval use of the plant, before the discovery of the value of hops, to impart the desired bitter flavor to beer, to prevent it from turning sour, and to clear it. This use ended four hundred years ago, but the name remains.

Its properties are astringent, diuretic, and tonic, and it is considered valuable for coughs accompanied by much phlegm. Either the fresh or dried plant may be used for an infusion, made with a teaspoonful of leaves to a cup of boiling water, drunk a cupful or more per day. It is surely not harmful and possibly helpful.

The pungency of the crushed foliage quickly affects the head, and it is said that the juice of the herb, snuffed up the nose, will cure headaches when all other efforts have failed.

Grieves says of *Glechoma* in part:

"The expressed juice may also be advantageously used for bruises and 'black eyes.' It is also employed as an antiscorbutic, for which it has a long-standing reputation. Combined with Yarrow or Chamomile Flowers it is said to make an excellent poultice for abcesses, gatherings and tumours."

Another writer quotes a gypsy friend:

"And us people, if so be as we're hurt with a cut or a sprain, makes an ointment of ground ivy along with chickweed."

Compositae

*Cud weed, catfoot, life everlasting, silver
leaf, rabbit tobacco, cotton weed, etc.*

This weed is found in almost any part
of the States. It grows in dry and usually infertile fields and lawns, and produces white, cottony flowers in August.
Medicinally, the entire plant is dried, an
infusion of it made at the rate of a teaspoon of the dried plant to a cup of boiling water.

Cud weed is a member of the daisy
family, of wide distribution, and usu-
ally rated to have healing qualities. In India and China, this and another species are regarded as antimalarial. Reputedly, it can drive
away moths and other insects. In Mexico and France, several species
are mentioned as valuable in bronchitis and other conditions.

We hear from Culpeper that "Pliny saith, the juice of the herb
taken in wine and milk is a sovereign remedy against the mumps and
quinsy . . . whosoever shall so take it shall never be troubled with
that disease again." And the name cud weed comes from an old
statement that the plant when fed to cattle will help restore the
ruminating faculty.

A more reputable source for the value of *Gnaphalium*, Youngken
notes that it contains a volatile oil and a bitter principle with tannin
and other constituents that is used "in domestic medicine, for pulmonary and intestinal catarrh and for diarrhea and locally as a
fomentation for bruises." He also mentions that similar values may
be found in pearly everlasting *Anaphalis margaritacea* which is botanically a very close relative.

In some of the references the assignment "vulnerary" is given to
these plants, for without doubt, their astringent quality aids healing
externally as well as internally. Thus we see that a little and unimportant weed may have unsuspected values.

Gossypium herbaceum

Malvaceae

Cotton, common, upland, or sea-island cotton

Many species and varieties of cotton have an unknown origin, the most common being the so-called upland cotton of our southern states. From Virginia southward, cotton, originally a wild plant, has ecaped cultivation to a great extent. A textbook of pharmacy discusses the value of the expressed cottonseed oil for culinary and medical use (in the preparation of liniments); the value of the purified cotton wool as an absorbent and protective dressing; and use of the cotton for filtering. The freshly gathered, dried root bark, known to druggists as *Gossypii radicis cortex*, is also used. Grieves herbal gives its preparation: "Boil 4 oz. of the inner bark of the root in 1 quart of water down to 1 pint: dose, 1 full wineglass (4 oz.) every thirty minutes" (presumably until the quart is used).

All reliable authorities agree that this is a valuable medicine as an emmenagogue, and especially good as an oxytocic or abortifacient. For the latter purpose it is recommended, "in place of ergot, being not so powerful but safer, it was used largely in this way by the slaves in the south." Another writer says, "Used in cases of difficult or obstructed menstruation. It seems especially useful in sexual lassitude." In another reference note is made of the fact that a preparation of cotton seed increases the milk of nursing mothers; a strong decoction of the root is said to check hemorrhages.

SMALL CAPS: Compositae

Compositae

Gum plant, scaly grindelia, rosin weed

Grindelia is the most important medicinal plant of California and the Southwest discussed here. Study of the medicines of California Indians shows this plant was not introduced into the commercial drug trade until the late nineteenth century; it was therefore unknown to early herbalists.

The drug Grindelia is derived from at least three species *(G. camporum, G. squarrosa, G. humilis)*, but all are similar perennial herbs that grow about 2 feet high and are terminated by heads of yellow-rayed flowers. The leaves are pale green, leathery, and rather rigid. They are coarse, sticky plants, characterized by white, gummy exudations upon the buds and flower heads. Grindelia may be found on plains and dry hillsides west of the Mississippi.

An infused or decocted extract of *Grindelia,* acts as an expectorant and sedative, with an action resembling atropine. Its principal use has been in bronchial catarrh where there is a tendency to asthma. It has also been of value in whooping cough. Most references mention the possible use of *Grindelia* for relief from ivy poisoning. Recommendations are noted for cystitis and catarrh of the bladder.

Meyer gives as dosage one cupful a day, a mouthful at a time, of an infusion made with a teaspoonful of the leaves and flowering tops cut finely. The herb is harvested and dried in July, when it is just coming into flower; the upper third of the plant which contains the sticky bud is used.

HAMAMELIDACEAE

Witch hazel, snapping hazel, spotted alder, winterbloom, striped alder

Although this plant is an official drug, there is no complete agreement as to its uses and efficacy, yet the fact that annual production in this country of Hamamelis Water (witch hazel) may reach a million gallons, would seem to indicate that the public wants to use it, efficacious or not.

Witch hazel is an American plant growing in moist, light woods, everywhere except in the far West. A large shrub (15 feet), almost indistinguishable from the unrelated hazel-nut bushes, it is a notable and useful landscape shrub; the flowers appear in October and November (except in the spring-flowering form).

The use of witch hazel was taught us by the Indians, who applied the leaves to tumors and swellings. Many other cures have been credited to it. Technically the constituents of Hamamelis are tannin, gallic acids, a bitter principle, and volatile oils. These, acting together, are strongly astringent and hemostatic. Thus we find witch hazel an ingredient of remedies for piles. Grieves, for instance, writes:

"A tea made of the leaves or bark may be taken freely with advantage, being good for bleeding of the stomach . . . and an injection of this tea is excellent for inwardly bleeding piles, the relief being marvelous and the cure speedy. An ointment made of 1 part fluid extract of bark to 2 parts of simple ointment is also used as a local application. . . . In cases of bites of insects and mosquitoes a pad of cotton-wool, moistened with the extract and applied to the spot will soon cause the pain and swelling to subside."

A number of writers also refer to witch hazel extract (as sold commercially) in cases of varicose veins, applied in the form of wet lint bandages. There are, in short, many uses of witch hazel in conditions where an astringent is desired, and the home herbal shelf should surely include a quantity of the dried leaves of this important American medicinal plant.

Labiatae

Mock pennyroyal, pudding grass, penny-royal of America, squaw mint, stinking balm, tickweed

A purely American plant, common throughout most of the States, and growing in dry and sterile soils. It is a branched annual, about one foot in height with small ovate leaves and tiny flowers in the leaf axils. Although the pungency of the leaves and the values and properties of the two plants are similar, this American pennyroyal should not be confused with European penny-royal, *Mentha pulegium*.

A small commercial demand for pennyroyal causes it to be collected in North Carolina, Virginia, and Ohio. It is gathered in the summer and slowly dried and stored, as with all herbs, in airtight containers. It is usually prepared as an infusion of 1 teaspoonful to a cup of boiling water, taken during the day, a mouthful at a time. It is a stimulant, carminative, and em-menagogue, and is especially useful in flatulence, as is true with other members of the mint family.

Additional reported uses are for headaches, nausea, constipation, nervous weakness and prostration, and as an abortifacient. The Indians used the herb for suppressed menstruation. The expressed oils (and likely the fresh leaves as well), when applied to the body will repel mosquitoes and other insects. Meyer says that it is especially valuable for promoting perspiration, a large dose being taken at bed-time, after the feet have been bathed in hot water.

In the case of this plant, the names do tell the truth:

Hedeoma—from Greek *hedys:* sweet, and *osme:* scent
puleogioides—like *Mentha pulegium*
mock pennyroyal—not, as was noted, the true pennyroyal
squaw mint—used by the Indian squaws
stinking balm—It is strongly scented and, to some people, stinking

C<small>OMPOSITAE</small>

*Sunflower, girasol, maiz de Texas
(Texas corn), tourne-soleil, marigold of
Peru, common sunflower*

The common sunflower is an American plant which has been widely cultivated, much improved, and may be found, wild or cultivated, anywhere in the U.S.A.

In *Plants of North Carolina* Jacobs notes that "the leaves are astringent; the seeds are diuretic and yield a fixed oil. . . . The roots were used for snakebite and as a dye. The sunflower is used in cough, pulmonary affections, dysentery, inflammation of the bladder and kidneys, and as an antimalarial."

One recipe for the use of sunflower seeds as medicine is: Boil 2 ounces of the seed in a quart of water. Boil down to a little less than a pint and strain. Add 6 ounces of gin and 6 ounces of sugar. May be taken three or four times daily in doses of 1 to 2 teaspoonfuls for pulmonary affections and coughs. In the same way the seeds, browned in the oven and then used for an infusion, are said to provide relief in cases of whooping cough.

There is a considerable body of literature relating to the many economic values of sunflowers. Simply as a food for man, for chickens, or for wild birds, it is much in demand. Used as food, it is highly regarded in every part of the globe, as it is very rich (21%) in oil.

That the Indians knew the great value of sunflowers we discover from references such as this from the "Journal of Lewis and Clark" for the month of July 1805.

"The Indians of the Missouri, more especially those who do not cultivate maize, make great use of the seed of this plant for bread, or in thickening their soup. They first parch and then pound it between two stones, until it is reduced to a fine meal. Sometimes they add a sufficient proportion of marrow-grease to reduce it to the consistency of common dough and eat it in that manner. We . . . thought this a very palatable dish."

RANUNCULACEAE

(Syn. Hepatica americana) *Liverleaf, hepatica, noble liverwort, herb trinity, May flower, mouse ears, crystal wort, etc.*

One would expect that a plant named "wort" which often signals an herb with medicinal values, and with "liver" added, would be a valuable me-dicinal herb; but for once the name is misleading. Actually we have here a plant named from the appearance of the foliage, which is liver-shaped. This is noted also in the Latin name from *hepaticus*, pertain-ing to the liver.

It has been described as an "innocent herb," as infusions may be taken freely without much fear of overdose. One can imagine that its prescription in cases of liver complaint are a hangover from the days of the "Doctrine of Signatures," when the shape or color of a plant suggested its medicinal values. The author has, for instance, this note about liverwort from a correspondent:

"One neighbor who had been ill for some time had no relief from her physician's remedies, and her family had been told by the physician that she couldn't possibly live for more than a very few days, was given some of this tea to drink every little while and it wasn't long before she was better and lived for years. She always said that it was the kidneywort which saved her life."

Despite such a story, there is nothing to indicate any important me-dicinal constituents of the plant; it appeared in the U.S. *Pharmaco-poeia* only from 1830-1870. Hepatica may best be listed as a tonic and mild astringent to be given freely in infusions. One suggestion is for a water distilled from the plant to be used for sunburns and freckles, but even this doesn't appear to have great merit.

Hepaticas grow best in the colder, wooded areas of the eastern states. It is a low-growing, perennial herb with long-stalked, leathery, smooth leaves, dark green above, about 2 inches in diameter, with three lobes. The flowers are single, white to purplish, the differences between the species being small and of botanical interest only. In sum, a nice wild plant to get to know, but not important.

Hydrangea aborescens

Seven-barks, common or wild hydrangea

This is a shrub of the moist, rich woodlands, from New York south to Florida and west to Missouri. A good landscape plant, it is often found in home gardens. It has broad, ovate leaves, with heads of white to greenish flowers growing on stems arising from the base to a height of 3 to 4 feet. The plant is related to the blue, less hardy, but more ornamental Japanese hydrangeas of East Coast areas.

The part used in medicine is the thickened root or rhizome, which, botanically, is interesting in itself. The name seven barks comes from the variously colored layers of root bark which can be peeled off one after another. When the fresh root is dug, it should at once be cut or crushed, to be used later for infusions or decoctions. A simple infusion is made with a teaspoonful of the root to a cup of boiling water, taken mouthfuls at a time through the day.

There are a number of references to the use of *Hydrangea* root by the Indians, especially the Cherokee tribe, for calculous diseases. While, one authority says, it does not cure stone in the bladder, it removes gravelly deposits and relieves the pain of their emission. It is listed, therefore, as a diuretic, lithotropic, and antilithic, while the leaves themselves are deemed to be tonic and slightly cathartic in their action. It is said to have been used in sections where brick factories are located to assist in removing brick dust deposits from the bladder.

Youngken points out that the hydrangea contains a substance called rutin (found also in rue and buckwheat) which is valuable in "decreasing capillary fragility and reducing the incidence of recurrent hemorrhages." The isolating of this element is not, however, a home process.

RANUNCULACEAE

Golden seal, turmeric, orange root, yellow puccoon, eye balm, ground raspberry, jaundice root, Indian paint, yellow root, Warnera, etc.

One can be quite certain that a plant having many common names is highly regarded and much used. Golden seal became known to us through the Cherokee Indians, and it remained on the list of official drugs until recently. Its exclusion from the pharmacopoeia may have been due to its increasing scarcity, for the plant in its wild state was largely exterminated by professional collectors. Formerly it was widely distributed in rich woods, and later was grown commercially in Ohio.

The yellow root (which has been used as a dye, as has the very closely related Yellow-root, or *Xanthoriza*, growing under similar conditions), sends up a collection of single leaf stalks, terminated by a petalless flower which turns into an inedible raspberrylike fruit.

Youngken says that "*Hydrastis* is an 'alterative' to mucous membranes and a bitter tonic. It is sometimes employed in gastro-intestinal and nasal catarrh, in inflammation of the mucous membrane of the vagina, uterus, and urethra." For home medicine, the root is dried and powdered. This powder is dissolved in boiling water (1 teaspoon to a pint) for use as a tonic. It may be snuffed for catarrh, or taken as a vaginal douche. The Indians are said to have used it on ulcers and for arrow wounds. One reference notes its value in a wide assortment of conditions such as dyspepsia, erysipelas, remittent, intermittent, and typhoid fevers, torpor of the liver, ophthalmia, ulceration of the mouth, and spermatorrhea.

A recent writer says: "It would be more used than it is, if its good qualities were better known. It may be given alone or in combination with other suitable medicines. It promotes digestion, improves the appetite, and acts as a general stimulant to the system. In convalescence it is highly beneficial."

Hypericum perforatum

Guttiferae

*St. John's wort, God's wonderplant,
devil's scourge, llamath weed, goat
weed, grace of God, hundred holes, herb
John, rosin rose, terrestial sun, amber
touch and heal, and other local names*

A European plant, St. John's wort was early brought to the States, and is now widely distributed in roadsides and neglected fields. It is notable for its sun-bright yellow flowers and the unusual **LEAF** **DETAIL** leaves, with small black dots on the edges, and numerous, transparent, round oil glands immersed in the surface. The name *perforatum* is due to the number of small hole-like dots in the leaf. It is perennial and grows generally from 1½ to 2 feet high. An infusion may be prepared (1 ounce to 1 pint boiling water) and taken in wineglass doses. The oil found in the glands may be extracted in olive oil and used as a base for an ointment. It is reputed to be astringent, nervine, and aromatic. Useful in coughs, colds, and all lung diseases, it also is highly esteemed in disorders of the urinary passages. The ointment is serviceable for bruises, scratches and insect bites. In spite of all this, however, we do not find it in any of the official lists of drugs, and the most reputable herbal writers give it scant recommendation.

Indeed, we have here, according to Geoffrey Grigson, "Magically, in white magic, rather than black, one of the most famous of European plants (and) one of the chief herbs of St. John the Baptist." The birthday of St. John is at the summer solstice, an important day in pre-Christian times. Some think that the flowers of this sun-bright plant were associated with celebrations of this day, and that this association continued when the celebrations came under the auspices of St. John. Beyond the sun connection is the fact that the oil glands produce a red fluid which is "St. John's blood" adding to the magical, if not medicinal, value of the plant. Many are the folk tales about the values of St. John's wort. In Ireland, the plant was especially venerated because of its connection with St. Colum Cille, while in other parts the red juice from the glandular dots was called "Mary's Sweat." In Britain and on the Continent, plants of the herb were hung over doorways, and otherwise used in exorcisms.

AQUIFOLIACEAE

Ilex Cassine, *Dahoon holly, cassine,*
yaupon, black vomit

Because of botanical confusion, it
must be stated that *this* southern coastal
holly is the one so named by Walter,
and, on best evidence, is the plant used
by southern Indians as their "Black
Drink" for purification (vomiting) ceremonies. Some mention is made of other
medicinal properties, but actually the
emetic qualities of this, like other hollies, is its principal value.

Ilex verticillata

Ilex glabra, *Inkberry, gall-berry*

This low-growing, shrubby evergreen with black berries grows
from Coastal Maine to Florida. It acts as an emetic even in small
doses.

Ilex verticillata, *Winterberry, black alder, prinos, feverbush, red-*
berried alder

This is the "deciduous holly" gathered during December in
swamps from Canada to Georgia, and used as a red decorative berry
at Christmas. It gets the name black alder from the darkening of the
leaves in fall, and the blackish stems.

Medicinally, this species has been used more than those mentioned
above, and there is still a small commercial demand for the dried
bark. A hundred years ago, Good, in his *Family Flora,* said that "it
is perhaps as well known among country people as any of the indigenous medicinal plants of the United States." But certain of his and
other recommendations of the time have proven fallacious. The berries, like other hollies are emetic and the bark astringent. In this
latter capacity the Indians were said to have made use of winterberry, thus the knowledge of its values in our own nonofficial materia
medica. If one accepts the unverified recommendations, a decoction
of winterberry may be used as an astringent in diarrhea, in intermittent fevers, and as a tonic in general debility.

Impatiens capensis

Balsaminaceae

Balsam, jewelweed, touch-me-not, snap-weed, "celandine," lady's earrings, quick-in-the-hand

Two principal species grow very widely in wet places throughout the United States, one, *I. capensis*, more generally known as *I. biflora*, and a second, *I. pallida*. The plant is a succulent, often tall-growing annual. The seeds are fired from the capsule in summer, and, it is this rather unusual method of seed distribution which has provided inspiration for some of the common names. The spurred flowers are followed by a capsular fruit which bursts elastically into spirally coiled valves, thus expelling the seeds.

But *Impatiens* is listed here because of its reputation as an antidote for ivy poisoning. (To the writer it is a wonder of nature that Impatiens grows not too far from poison ivy; both plants like the same moist conditions). It must be understood that what works for one person may not help another, for the reactions to ivy and its cures are very personal.

A friend of the author, a former camp counselor, tells how he boiled down masses of jewelweed and applied this to ivy-infected campers with excellent results. Potter says that a salve similarly prepared from plants boiled with lard is an excellent application for piles, and that the raw juice will remove warts and corns and cure ringworm.

John Josselyn who, in 1672 wrote what one could describe as the first American Herbal, *New England Rarities;* makes considerable note of the many values of this plant whose name he did not know. He says that it was considered by the Colonists a "sovereign remedy for bruises of what kind soever."

But the juice of jewelweed is *not* recommended for internal use. While not considered poisonous to man, it *is* reputed to be harmful to stock. References to its use in cases of jaundice and liver complaints, would seem to indicate a doubtful procedure.

For the author, the knowledge of the possible value of the juice rubbed on immediately after contact with common poison ivy would be recommendation enough.

Compositae

*Elecampane, scabwort, elf dock, horse-
heal, wild sunflower, velvet dock, inula*

This is not a plant of American origin, but, since its introduction, it has
spread along the coast and over to the
middle states. Inula is a tall-growing (4
to 5 feet) perennial of the daisy family,
and is erect, striking, and handsome,
with downy foliage, bold leaves, and
large flowers which bloom from July to
September. The part used in is the thickened root, which is gathered in the second year in the late fall. The dried
crushed root is to be steeped (1 teaspoonful to a cup of boiling water)
a little taken at a time, a cupful or so each day. Overdoses should be
avoided.

Actually elecampane is most often noted as an ingredient in compound medicines, and seems rarely to be recommended alone. Youngken says, "Its active constituent, helenin, has been employed as an
antiseptic and bactericide in pulmonary diseases," thus confirming
the reputation of the drug for use in tuberculosis. It has also been
used for centuries for the treatment of pulmonary diseases in horses,
giving it its common name, "horseheal." Beyond this, one finds mention of inula as a tonic, gentle stimulant, and as a diaphoretic, diuretic, expectorant, emmenagogue, and aromatic.

The reader will find much of interest on this plant in Grieve's
herbal or in *The Englishman's Flora*, by Grigson.

One story relates to the common name elf-dock:

"Elecampane entered into many Anglo-Saxon recipes, half magical.
In one complex prescription, prayers were sung over the helenium;
it was marked with a knife, and the roots were dug up next evening,
after the medicine-man had been careful not to say a word to anything of an awful kind or any man (i.e. elf, goblin, fairy) he chanced
to meet on the way. The elecampane root was then laid under the
altar for the night, and eventually mixed with Betony and with lichen
from a crucifix. The medicine was swallowed against elf-sickness or
elf-disease."

Iris versicolor

IRIDACEAE

Blue flag, poison flag, flag lily, liver lily, snake lily, marsh iris, American fleur-de-lis

The very beautiful blue flag iris is a plant of wet, swampy locations and grows from Canada to Florida and west to Arkansas. Similar in foliage appearance to the sweet flag *(Acorus calamus)*, from which it should be carefully distinguished, it has erect stems to 3 feet high, and lovely purplish-blue flowers which appear from May to July.

The medicinal part of the plant is the rootstock or rhizome, which is collected in autumn and dried. Any part of the plant taken internally, especially when fresh, is actively poisonous. And extra caution in using this plant is advised due to its similarity, as noted, to the quite edible sweet flag. But, as with so many plants, it is the poisonous quality under controlled dosage which is valuable, and we find that *Iris versicolor* was an official drug for over a hundred years.

Blue flag is an American plant, whose medicinal properties were known and passed to colonists by the Indians. Bartram, in his *Travels,* tells us that it was favored by the Indians as a powerful cathartic; and he intimates that its wide distribution was largely due to the estimation in which they held it for medicinal purposes.

As a simple home medicine, Meyer gives a dose as one teaspoonful of the root to a pint of boiling water, the infusion to be taken cold, 2 or 3 tablespoonfuls, six times a day. The action of such an infusion, or of the more scientifically prepared extracts, are diuretic, alterative, emetic, purgative, and cathartic according to the dosage and circumstance.

One writer suggests that the dried root of blue flag may be powdered and used as a substitute for orris root (normally from root of *Iris germanica*) as an ingredient of tooth powder. In another connection it is noted that the flowers yield a fine blue infusion which may be used to test for acids and alkalies, in place of litmus paper. Blue flag is a valuable plant as well as one to be treated with caution.

JUGLANDACEAE

*White walnut, butternut, filnut, lemon-
nut, Also (with much the same properties)* Juglans nigra—*Blackwalnut*

Both of these species of walnuts are
native to a large section of the rich
woods of the eastern and midwestern
United States. Those who walk the
woods in fall value both plants for the rich rewards of edible butter-
nuts and black walnuts—amply discussed in *Using Wayside Plants*.

The walnuts are straight trees up to a hundred feet, with compound leaves running to 20 inches in length. The genus is widely
distributed throughout the world. One or another form of the genus
has been treasured from ancient times, the name *Juglans* itself coming from *jovis*—Jupiter, and *glans*—acorn, or "royal nut of Jupiter."

One hundred and fifty years ago in our country, Dr. Barton wrote
that "the extract of the . . . butternut-walnut . . . appears to me to be
one of our most valuable native cathartics. It is well adapted to the
treatment of dysentery, in which, however, it appears to be operative
merely as a laxative. A decoction of the inner (root) bark of the
tree has been very advantageously used."

For home use, the bark of the butternut root is collected in autumn
and, after drying, may be powdered. Meyer calls a dose a teaspoonful
to a cup of boiling water, taken a mouthful at a time through the
day.

Dorland's *Medical Dictionary* reports that the crushed green hulls
of walnuts have long been used against fungus infections such as
ringworm. This, plus the illegal use of the same green hulls by fisher-
men to immobilize their prey, has led to pharmacological research
in Missouri (*Science*, Nov. 17, 1961), which confirms the depressant
quality of the crude green hulls, and indicates the need for further
scientific investigation.

Meanwhile, the use of walnut hulls goes on in empiric medicine.
One writer advocates the use of the juice of the husk, boiled with
honey, as an excellent gargle. The oil extracted from ripe nuts is
said to be especially good for colic, and possibly as a cure for tape-
worms. It is also recommended for skin diseases of various kinds.
Without doubt, as research continues, we will hear more about the
medically approved values of the several species of *Juglans*.

Juniperus communis

Pinaceae

Common juniper, ground juniper, juniper bush, horse savin

Growing usually on dry hillsides, one finds this evergreen shrub growing from New Mexico to Alaska and eastward to the Atlantic. As differentiated from many other evergreen plants, the ground juniper is distinguished by its very prickly foliage. The tiny, sharp leaves are arranged in whorls of three. The fruit is globular, blue, and the size of a small pea. Only the ripe, second-year fruits are used in medicine.

A hundred years ago it was said of juniper that it was "one of the most valuable, important and universal articles of the Materia Medica," and the fact that it still remains a part of the druggists' stock proves this statement. While there are a number of related values, it is officially known as a stimulant and powerful diuretic, combined with other material having similar values. Jacob lists a number of conditions for which juniper is valuable: scorbutic diseases, dropsy, kidney diseases, skin diseases, leucorrhea, gleet, and gonorrhea. It is said that country people in Europe eat, now and then, a handful of the berries as a mild diuretic or laxative.

In home practice, an infusion may be made of the ripe berries by crushing an ounce of the berries in a pint of boiling water, taken over a period of 24 hours. On a doctor's prescription, the "oil of juniper" would be prepared by the druggist for a number of chronic genito-urinary disorders—throughout literature, much mention is made of its value in such conditions.

In England, dropsical patients are sometimes ordered to take "Holland Gin." The juniper berry has been used as a flavoring for that form of alcohol for many years, the name "gin" coming to us from the French *genievre*. One of the old-country names of juniper was "Bastard-killer," for the berries were swallowed to produce abortion and to assist in childbirth. Whether this knowledge came from or to the American Indians, it is hard to say, but Shoshone Indians believe that a tea from the berries, taken on 3 successive days, is efficacious as a birth control medicine.

LABIATAE

Motherwort, lion's ear, lion's tail, throw-wort

Youngken says of motherwort that it is used "by the laity, in the form of a deccoction or infusion for amenorrhea. A stimulant and bitter tonic."

This sums up this member of the mint family which came here from Europe and is now widely distributed. Like other mints, its stems are square, the leaves cut-lobed, with pale purple whorls of flowers in the leaf axils. It grows up to 5 feet in height. The leaves have a rather rank smell and a bitter taste. One peculiarity noted long ago is its apparent happiness growing in waste places, for Gerard said in the sixteenth century that "it joieth among rubbish, in stonie and other barren and rough places."

Its scientific name, *L. cardiaca*, might indicate that it was of value in heart conditions, but such a reputation has been discounted. Today it is regarded by all writers chiefly as an emmenagogue. It is this value which gave it the name of motherwort (i.e. womb plant), for it was valued in the Middle Ages "for them as are in hard travell with childe."

Elsewhere it is recommended as a simple tonic, useful in recovery from fevers when other tonics are inadmissible. An ounce of the dried herb to a pint of water makes an infusion which may be taken a little at a time. Culpepper writes that there is "no better herb to take melancholy vapours from the heart, to strengthen it, and make merry, cheerful, blithe soul than this herb."

In conclusion, this plant has very little to offer from the purely pharmacological point of view, but, as a common household herb, has many reputed virtues. One notes an old saying:

"Drink Motherwort and live to be a source of continuous astonishment and of grief to waiting heirs."

Lobelia inflata

CAMPANULACEAE

Indian tobacco, pukeweed, asthma weed, vomitwort, field lobelia, bladder pod, gagroot

Probably no other wild plant has been the subject of as much dispute as has *Lobelia inflata.* Although actual litigation is a century and a half behind us, agreement on the value of this plant is still not general. The most recent and reliable book in the library of the author says—"Indian tobacco . . . is regarded as one of the most valuable remedies ever discovered." Yet Meyer, in *The Herbalist,* says that "Lobelia is too dangerous for internal use by the unskilled." We find Lobelia mentioned in the *National Formulary,* and Youngken describes it as an expectorant in asthma and chronic bronchitis. Although it is also mentioned often as an emetic, some say that it is totally unsuited for this purpose (though effective) because of the distressing nausea which it causes.

Based on all of the evidence, it is the judgment of the author that the use of even a mild infusion of *Lobelia* (or the chewing of the seeds as sometimes recommended) should be avoided except under the guidance of a competent physician. Its acceptance by the medical profession in asthma and whooping cough is due in part to its sedative and depressant qualities. It also contains a number of alkaloids, especially the poisonous, acrid alkaloid, lobeline.

It seems quite probable that Indian tobacco was known medicinally to the first Americans and was certainly known and used by the early settlers. It was brought into great prominence as a general specific by Samuel Thomson, whose story is told in Chapter II. Sued for the death of a patient after administering this drug, he was not found guilty and later went on to promote the use, not only of this plant, but of many others, and to establish, as was noted, the "Patent medicine" fad which has far from disappeared from our scene.

This species of *Lobelia* (there are several others which have been recommended medicinally) is an annual growing in open fields east of the Mississippi. It grows up to 3 feet in height and has small, inconspicuous pinkish flowers. Leaves and tops are used.

LYCOPODIACEAE

Running or trailing evergreen, ground-pine, ground cedar, Christmas green, creeping Jenny, club moss, snake moss, wolf's claws, lamb's tail, foxtail, hog's bed, stag's horn, vegetable sulphur

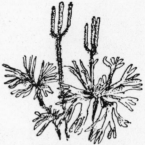

One or another species of *lycopodium* is found around the world. In this country it grows in moist woods, and boggy localities. The lycopods are mosslike, low-growing (3 to 6 inches), creeping plants. The appearance of the close-set leaves gives rise to the name "ground pine." The fruiting head bears spores rather than seeds, and these powderlike spores became the lycopodium powder of medicine.

In actual practice there is not too much to recommend *Lycopodium* in home medicine, but it has long been a substance on the list of recognized drugs. In the drug trade it has been used as a protective dusting for abraded surfaces, and to prevent adhesion of pills. In microscopy, it has been used as a standard for measuring comparative size of substances.

The spores are extremely explosive, and in times past were used in the theatre to produce lightning effects. They also have an extremely water-repellent character; if the hand is powdered with them and dipped in water, it will not become wet. It is reputed that a decoction will, among other things, kill lice, and, quite unrelatedly, improve bad wine.

As an internal medicine there is more hearsay than evidence. Both in Europe and here in the States it has been considered a diuretic, emmenagogue, and antispasmodic. One writer calls it "useful in female disorders," and it is reputed to have value as a stimulant to sexual desire. An infusion is given as 1 ounce to 1 pint of boiling water, taken in tablespoon doses, frequently repeated.

Assessing all of the writings on this spore powder, it seems to be most useful as a dusting powder to be used in eczema and erysipelas, for excoriated surfaces, and to prevent chafing in infants.

Malva rotundifolia

MALVACEAE

Blue mallows, cheeses, common mallow, fairy cheese

In Gray's *Manual of Botany* none of the eight species of *Malva* are listed as American plants, but have been introduced from Europe. All mallows have substantially the same medicinal qualities, as do also the Marshmallows and hollyhocks. Almost a thousand species in this family are known, everyone of which contains the mucilaginous property, none being unwholesome or poisonous. In fact the little seed pods are known as cheeses and are considered safe and proper food for the doll parties of childhood.

It is the demulcent property of the mallows which is medicinally valuable and for which it has been used from ancient times. Theophrastus mentions it in several places; Hippocrates gives specific instructions for its administration, and Pliny even went so far as to say that "Whosoever shall take a spoonful of the mallows shall that day be free from all diseases that shall come to him."

For pharmaceutical purposes, the part used is the root of the larger-growing species, but the mucilaginous property of *M. rotundifolia* is found in its leaves. An infusion is made of a teaspoon of the leaves to a cup of boiling water, taken several cupfuls each day.

Though perhaps not the general specific of ancient times, it is useful for loosening coughs and relieving sore throats, especially with honey. Internally, it relieves irritations of bowels, kidneys and urinary organs and may be added to enemas for its emollient qualities. Grieves suggests that a poultice made of any of the mallows will "remove obstinate inflammation . . . The fresh leaves, steeped in hot water and applied to the affected parts as poultices, reduce inflammation, and bruised and rubbed upon any place stung by wasps or bees take away the pain, inflammation and swelling."

LABIATAE

*Horehound, hoarhound, white hore-
hound (as distinguished from* black,
another genus)

The Latin name, according to the best
authority, comes from the Hebrew name
for the plant, "Marrob," meaning a bitter juice. Its ancient connection with the
Jews is further shown by the fact that
this is one of the five bitter herbs required to be eaten at the Passover feast.
It was known and used by the Romans
and it has always been considered a
good, and sometimes magical, herb.

This plant came to the United States from Europe, and has been
naturalized on roadsides and waste places very widely. It is a hardy
perennial, about 2 feet in height, distinguished by its ovate, veined
leaves with whitish, woolly hairs underneath. The axillary flowers are
small and white. The leaves and flowering tops are dried for medi-
icnal use.

Probably on no plant in this book are all writers so much agreed
as to medicinal values. Perhaps no herbal remedy is so generally
well-known as horehound. The drugstore which does not have horehound drops for sale as a cough remedy and expectorant is rare. It
is also said to be tonic in its effect and slightly diuretic; both valuable characteristics for a cough or a cold.

As a home medicine, it may be taken as an infusion at the rate of
an ounce of dried plant to a pint of boiling water, taken frequently
in wineglass doses.

Many ancient, additional values are cited for horehound, such as a
cure for snakebite, a fly repellent, vermifuge, and as an ointment for
wounds and itches. But these are hand-me-down and questionable
uses, compared to its known value in all pulmonary ailments.

One writer recommends a preparation for use in colds and coughs
which uses horehound and other herbs as follows: One half ounce
each of horehound, rue, hyssop, licorice root, and marshmallow root
boiled down to a pint and a half from a quart of water, strained and
given in half-teaspoon doses every two hours.

Compositae

Wild chamomile, German chamomile, mayweed

After reading this refer back to the species, *Anthemis nobilis,* since both of these species are known as chamomile, both have about the same appearance, both are aromatics, both are escapes from cultivation, and are confused with each other in much of the literature. *Matricaria chamomilla* may be distinguished from *Anthemis* in that it is an annual rather than a perennial, has coarser leaves, grouped rather than solitary flower heads, and some minor structural differences.

Matricaria has the fragrance of pineapple and, for this reason, is the flavoring used by the Spanish in their sherry known as *Manzanilla* (little apples). The French consider this one of the best ingredients of their healthful *tisanes* (teas) while the Germans have long considered it a valuable medicine.

An aromatic bitter and formerly an official drug, it is carminative, sedative, and tonic. An infusion is made of a half ounce to a pint of boiling water. A dose of a teaspoon at a time is considered especially valuable, and completely harmless, for children. Thus administered, it is good in cases of general debility, poor digestion, and convalescence, as its tonic properties stimulate the appetite.

An authority on economic plants, Albert F. Hill, in an article in the *Herbarist,* points out that an extract of the flowers is much used in beauty preparations as a wash for blonde or light red hair. "The tonic properties of the chamomile are beneficial and the dark amber liquid seems to bring out the natural color of the hair."

In the literature, an infusion of *Matricaria* is reputed to cut short an attack of delirium tremens, and to cure nightmares. One writer Francatelli, suggests that a tea made from flower heads, slightly sweetened, is an excellent drink for aged persons. Again, there is the suggestion that a hot fomentation will relieve inflammatory and neuralgic pains.

Thus, whether one finds *Matricaria* growing in the wild or in the garden, it is an herb well worth using and, is perfectly safe.

LEGUMINOSAE

Melilot, yellow sweet clover, sweet lucerne, moonseed, King's clover, etc.

Introduced from Europe and widely distributed in the States, this wild, sweet, yellow clover may be found in waste places, in hedgerows, and similar spots. It is notably distinguishable from alfalfa by its yellow rather than blue color. The name, which comes from *mel*, honey, and *lotus*, a leguminous plant, indicates that bees favor it (and other members of the same family) and that it is closely related to the well-known clovers.

Although bearing the specific name, *officinalis*, it is not now in the pharmacopoeia of this country. But it is mentioned in many herbals with the qualification that it "is supposed to do so and so." Scientific investigation does not disclose many medicinal properties in melilot. About all that is worthy of notice is the presence of coumarin, the same substance found and used so widely in the vanilla (tonka) bean. Coumarin imparts to the drying plant a delightful fragrance, which has probably (along with a somewhat bitter taste) suggested medicinal values.

For use in infusions and salves, the entire plant is collected and dried in May. The effects of melilot are said to be those of a carminative, a mild expectorant, a diuretic, and an aromatic. The leaves and flowers, boiled in water, have been used for all kinds of ulcers, inflammations, and burns, while it has otherwise been made into a salve for ulcers and open sores.

Some experiments with extracts of dicoumarin, prepared from melilot, have been undertaken to discover possible anticoagulant values in thrombosis and embolism, but results are inconclusive.

There is not too much evidence to support medicinal claims for this member of the clover family. Culpeper makes a point:

"The head often washed with the distilled water of the herb and flowers . . . is effectual for those that have suddenly lost their senses, as also to strengthen the memory, comfort the head and brain, and to preserve them from pains and apoplexy."

LABIATAE

Common balm, lemon balm, honey plant, dropsy plant, cureall, citronele

Balm (anciently *bamm*) is common to gardens and runs somewhat wild in much of the United States. It is a persistent perennial, the tops dying down completely in winter, but growing up quickly, a foot in height, with fragrant foliage which is light green, serrated and wrinkled. When crushed, the leaves smell and taste like lemon, and from them is produced a volatile oil used in perfumes and cosmetics.

Medicinally an infusion (1 ounce of herb, dried or fresh, to a pint of water) is recommended as a carminative, diaphoretic, and febrifuge. Many suggestions are made for it in delayed menstruation. It is valuable, too, in headaches and as a hot drink at night to fight insomnia.

Actually, *Melissa* has been used for centuries, and references are found in Roman writings (although the "balm of Gilead" mentioned in the Bible is quite another plant).

Some centuries ago, a general specific known as Carmelite Water combined the balm with nutmeg, angelica root, and lemon-peel; it was highly regarded for nervous headache and neuralgic affections.

This is also one of those plants which, when well dried, make an excellent constituent of a fragrant potpourri. Infused fresh, with lemon and sugar added, it makes a pleasing summer drink.

There are, in the literature, a number of references to balm as an aid to longevity, with specific examples of centenarians who were devotees of this plant as medicine. In some cases balm was taken as "Carmelite Water" or with honey, which, claims *Folk Medicine*, may alone have caused long life.

Many then are the good things said of balm. None is nicer than these words from John Evelyn, the seventeenth century diarist:

"Balm is sovereign for the brain, strengthening the memory and powerfully chasing away melancholy."

Could any plant be better than that?

MENISPERMACEAE

Moonseed, yellow parilla, Texas or yellow sarsaparilla, vine maple

Moonseed, a shortish climbing vine springing from a thickened root which often grows to a length of 6 feet has ovate leaves, with greenish flowers, followed by blue-black fruits like small grapes. It grows from Canada to the Carolinas and west to the Mississippi, always in rich soils, in thickets and light woodlands, usually in cool regions or high elevations.

Infusions or tinctures of the fresh or dried root, at the rate of a teaspoonful to a cup of boiling water, are useful, says Meyer.

It appears in literature chiefly as an alterative. However, Youngken says that it is best as a simple bitter, and that "its value as an alterative is in doubt." Others say that it excels in value the true sarsaparilla in treatment of scrofula, blood disorders, and cutaneous diseases generally. It is also useful as a tonic and nervine.

Caution in the use of the plant, is suggested. An overdose may result in excessive vomiting and purging, or headache, dryness of throat, and general aching. These reactions are caused by the presence of an alkaloid, menispine.

To what extent its similarities to true sarsaparilla have caused *Menispermum* to receive the name and the accreditation of that plant it is hard to say, but one can imagine that the bitter taste has placed this among the medicinals, as plant similarities have done in so many cases.

Mentha piperita

Peppermint, brandy mint, lamb mint, curled mint, balm mint

Peppermint candy is edible proof of the common acceptance of this herb, which is not only delightful in flavor but a stimulating aromatic and carminative. The commercial demand for the extracted volatile oil of mint is so great, that in a town named Mentha, Michigan the growing of this herb is the principal industry.

Peppermint, like most American mints, is an introduction; botanically it is considered a hybrid between spearmint and watermint. It grows wild, as do all members of the family, on the banks of brooks and in wet meadows, and on rich moist farm lands when cultivated.

Oil of peppermint is the most extensively used of all the volatile oils, both for medicine and for other commercial purposes. It has a very strong, antispasmodic action, making it valuable for relieving pains arising in the alimentary canal. It is also valuable for sudden pains, for cramps in the abdomen, and useful in diarrhea. We generally know it as an ingredient of compound medicines. It is useful not only for its effect, but tends to make disagreeable medicines palatable, and is perfectly harmless.

Peppermint has been listed for 140 years in the U.S. *Pharmacopoeia*, and has been a generally-used remedy from the time of the Egyptians.

At home, an infusion of the leaves and flowering tops is brewed, a teaspoonful to a cup of water, and taken cold as needed for the relief of flatulence, headache, and heartburn. (The druggist uses the extracted oil.) The bruised fresh leaves are said to have a slightly anesthetic effect, and may be rubbed into the skin to relieve local pains and headache. Because it can allay nausea, peppermint is suggested as a protection against seasickness. There are many uses for peppermint, of course, in cooking and in industry, in addition to its safe and valuable place in medicine.

LABIATAE

Spearmint, common garden mint, lady's or mackerel mint, lamb mint

Common as mints are throughout the parts of the United States near civilization and water, there are actually few species native to this country, most of them having been introduced by immigrants from Europe. None of the mints are harmful, but some are not tasty. Spearmint, which is so well known as a flavoring in chewing gum, has a distinctive flavor quite unlike that of peppermint.

Our household and medical supplies come from cultivations of the plant in Michigan, Indiana, and California. Vast quantities are grown for the extraction of volatile oils which contain carminative and flavoring properties.

In general, the mints are similar in appearance and habitat and are often confused. Spearmint, named by some writers *M. viridis* or *M. crispa*, is visibly different from peppermint, notably in its lighter color and less-hairy leaves. To most people "the taste test is surely best." Mints have carminative properties. When they are used solely for stomach disturbances, an infusion of 1 ounce of dried foliage to a pint of boiling water is taken in doses of a wineglassful, until relief is obtained. It may be made more acceptable to children by the addition of a little sweetening.

One writer suggests that a decoction of mint leaves may be used to wash children suffering from scabs and blotches, and, also, to relieve chapped hands.

The long history of mint and the references in the Bible to it and to rue, anise and cumin as tithing contributions indicates that in those times they were mediums of exchange, greatly valued. Mint was also used by the ancients to scent the bath, and as a restorative.

Menyanthes trifoliata

GENTIANACEAE

Buckbean, marsh trefoil, bogbean, bog myrtle, bitterworm, marsh clover, water shamrock, bitter root, bog hop

Across the northern part of our country one finds this plant in bogs, quagmires, and pond margins, and it is equally at home in Europe and Asia. From a thick rhizome grows long, petioled, trifoliate leaves, and later in May and June, a separately stemmed flower stalk with white or reddish blooms appears. The fruit is a seed resembling a bean. The leaves are collected from late April to June, dried, and when infused or otherwise prepared, used as a simple bitter tonic.

One writer claims that it is the most serviceable of all known herbal tonics, and its recognition as a pharmaceutical ingredient in this country since 1820 indicates its worth. For home use, an infusion may be made of 1 ounce of dried plant, to 1 pint of boiling water, taken in wineglass doses, frequently repeated. However, it should be noted that too large a dose may act as a purgative.

As with so many bitter drugs of this nature, much is claimed for buckbean by various writers. It is recommended for use in scurvy, rheumatism, jaundice, dyspepsia, hepatitis, worms; as an emetic, alterative, stomachic, anthelmintic, febrifuge, diuretic, cathartic, and for scrofula and dropsy. A tincture of the plant is said to be valuable in obstinate skin conditions and as a substitute for gentian, to which it is closely related.

Although doubtful, there is even a recommendation for the use of a tincture for "clearing obstructions of the sight" and in cases of paralysis of the retina. Linnaeus noted that in Lapland the roots are sometimes fed to cattle, and that the powdered roots when mixed with flour, have been used for human food. It is also said that in the absence of other suitable bitters, buckbean has been used to flavor beer.

Rubiaceae

Partridge-berry, squaw vine, two-eyed checkerberry, deer berry, winter clover, running box

This American plant, the only species of its genus, is found on dry or moist knolls in wooded areas. Ground-hugging and vine-like, with evergreen leaves, it is notable for the bright red berries which color the snowless winter woods. The fruit is tasteless, however, and is mainly used to brighten a terrarium.

As may be guessed from the name "squaw vine," this is an Indian remedy, used by the women in a number of tribes (Cherokee, and Iroquois, among others) to ease parturition. It is mentioned by Cotton Mather, the eminent theologian of the early eighteenth century, and by Dr. Barton at the end of the same century.

In addition to its function at a parturient, all writers mention its effectiveness as a diuretic and astringent, and its use in dropsy, diarrhea, amenorrhea, dysmenorrhea, menorrhagia, etc. A dose is given as a decoction of 2 ounces of the dried plant in 1 pint of water, taken in wineglass doses. Mrs. Leyel recommends that it be administered daily in the last month of pregnancy and in larger doses as confinement nears an end until it is over. She says, further, that in some cases it is combined for this purpose with raspberry leaves, and that the total effect is to keep up the strength of the patient.

In general, aside from these medicinal values, one would agree with Mrs. Blanchan who notes that in "autumn and winter partridge-berry is surely one of the loveliest sights in the woods."

Morus rubra

MORACEAE

Red mulberry, red morus

In many parts of the United States, generally in richer woods, one will find the red mulberry, a true native. It has sometimes been planted as an ornamental tree, as has the white mulberry, a tree imported from China to feed silkworms. The mulberry is a pleasant lawn tree with warm-colored bark, shiny leaves, and an abundance of fruit. Unfortunately, whether red or white, the mulberry tree is a nuisance because of its brittle limbs, messy falling fruit, and low, spreading growth.

The soft, bland and sweetish fruit, eaten in quantity, acts as a laxative. Undoubtedly, as the books say, the fruit, when squeezed, makes a cooling drink "adapted to febrile cases."

Beyond that, one finds considerable mention that a decoction made of the outer bark is a good vermifuge, while the inner bark provides a syrup or tincture which, depending on dosage, is a laxative or purgative for children.

One of the most interesting things about the mulberry is that it is the home of silkworms. Why the worms choose this tree is not known. Undoubtedly the introduction of the Chinese white mulberry can be traced to many unsuccessful attempts to introduce silkworm culture to the Western World.

As the tree generally grows in warm climates, it is notable that it is one of the last to leaf out in the spring. One writer suggests that gardeners can regard the leafing time of the mulberries as a signal that the danger of frost damage to tender plants is over.

The name of the genus, *Morus*, comes from the Greek *Moron;* one wonders philologically if the present use of the word "moron" has any relation to the undesirable qualities of this tree.

Myricaceae

Bayberry, myrtle, wax myrtle, candle-berry, tallow-shrub, M. pennsylvanica *is* M.c. var. latifolia

Throughout coastal North America, down into Mexico, and in many parts of Europe, one of the most useful and widely known medicinal plants is the bayberry. Our pilgrim fathers used the wax in the berries to manufacture fragrant candles. One medical authority observes that this is possibly the most valuable of all wild plants for medicinal use, and many claims are made for its curative properties.

The part used is the bark, preferably the root bark, which, stripped in small pieces early in the fall, is dried and powdered. An infusion of this powdered bark (1 ounce of bark to a pint of boiling water) is drunk warm.

The most outstanding property of this natural drug is its astringency. It has been much used against diarrhea and dysentery. Most authorities also note its use in the treatment of jaundice. In larger doses, it is an emetic. The powdered bark, taken as snuff, is said to be excellent for catarrh and nasal congestions. And the same astringent quality of the bark is also useful in ulcers. Another suggestion is for an infusion as an astringent wash for sore and bleeding gums.

The characteristics indicated above are derived from tannin, and acrid and astringent resins which bayberry contains. A pleasantly aromatic odor and a spritely, medicinal taste add to its popularity. What's more could one ask for than a drug which has known medicinal value, a lively taste and a pleasant smell?

Bayberry grows in brackish swamps and sandy coastal areas, but is found inland where these conditions are approximated and where the soil is slightly acid.

The range of *M. cerifera* is from New Jersey to Florida, while the closely related *M. pennsylvanica* is found from Nova Scotia south to the Great Lakes, and in Indiana. Forms with similar medicinal properties are mentioned in Mexican works as growing in the eastern coastal regions of Vera Cruz and Yucatan.

MYRICACEAE

Sweet gale, bog-myrtle, Dutch myrtle, meadow fern and

Comptonia peregrina var. asplenifolia

MYRICACEAE

Sweet fern

These two plants will be discussed together as they are both in the *Myrica* family. Also, both bear nutlets rather than waxy berries (as does bayberry, to which they are closely related). The sweet fern is easily distinguished by its deeply cut, fernlike foliage, in contrast with the shorter, narrow, notched leaf of sweet gale, shown in the illustration on the right. The true sweet fern is worth knowing for the spicy fragrance of its crushed foliage.

Myrica   Comptonia

This family is found along the eastern coast and in suitable spots as far west as Illinois. The tiny nutlets are a possible source of food for someone walking through the sterile fields where *myrica* grows. In addition to its food value, a number of persons have testified that the myricas cure poison ivy. Such personal certifications have come from Vermont, Maine and Massachusetts. One correspondent says that she has cured "severe poison ivy on my young son with poultices of sweet fern tea." A druggist who knows something of the medicinal practice of the Gay Head Indians says that they depend on sweet fern for this purpose, boiling down a quantity of foliage and applying the juice and/or poultice to the affected part. Sweet fern is also used to scent linen closets, as a repellent for moths in the woolens chest, and, dried, as a substitute for tea.

A correspondent suggests that smoking cigarettes made of sweet fern, when one is "out fishin'," is a sure mosquito repellent. The sweet fern, especially, can be transplanted and makes an excellent low landscape plant, its feathery foliage softening the harder notes of most stiff growing evergreens. A supply of the dried leaves is stocked in late fall; the leaves are gathered just after they have been wilted by a frost, then dried over a stove, and stored tightly.

Nasturtium officinale
syn. Radicula Nasturtium-aquaticum

CRUCIFERAE

Watercress, sisymbrium

The familiar watercress of field and market is not found in medical reference books, but nevertheless has medicinal value. It was introduced to America from Europe, where its values have been known for several millenia. And we find a comment by the historian Xenophon, who advised the Persians to feed watercress to their children if they wished to improve their growth.

Watercress is a member of the pungent mustard family (getting its name from *nasus tortus*—twisted nose—alluding to the pungent smell of the plant. Watercress is peculiar in that it must live in cold and flowing water. It grows best in the spring, although now cultivated for year-round use in the mountains of West Virginia. One should not be fooled by the Latin name *Nasturtium*. Watercress has no relation at all to the genus *Tropaeoleum*, which, because of its pungent, edible leaves, was given the common name "nasturtium."

Although in this day of well-balanced diets the need for protection against scrofula is no longer present, we should note that watercress contains substantial quantities of Vitamins A, B, C and B_2 as well as iron, copper, magnesium and much calcium. Children with weak bones and soft teeth should eat it for the quantities of lime it contains, while diabetics will want to eat it because of its low carbohydrate content and its iron in greater quantity than in spinach.

One commentator says, "its high sulphur content leads homeopaths and osteopaths to prescribe nine-grain cress tablets for eczema, while its unusual Vitamin A content makes it particularly good for night blindness."

Only one caution: When taking watercress from streams in the country, be certain to wash it well; country streams may be polluted.

LABIATAE

Catnip, catnep, nep, catmint

This plant came to us from Europe, and is now widely distributed in gardens or escaped. In all European languages its name includes "cat." Its old Latin generic name was *Cataria*, while the present one, *Nepeta* is said to be the name of an ancient Tuscan town. As cats were ancient pets, we can imagine the generations of cats which have been "crazy" about catnip. When the plant is dry (or when growing plants are broken), cats will make every effort to roll in the leaves, and may literally destroy the plant in their ecstasy. However, they do not seem to bother *growing* plants if the volatile oil is not distributed in the air in planting, handling or cultivating.

But for those plants which escape the cats there are medicinal u es, chiefly as a carminative and stimulant. The part used is the leafy, flowering tops, gathered in August. Because of the volatile nature of catnip, a simple and quick infusion should be made, 1 ounce to a pint of boiling water for adults, taken in doses of 2 tablespoonfuls (2 teaspoonfuls for children), for the relief of colic, stomach pains, and flatulence.

The hot tea made of catnip quickly produces perspiration (as do infusions of other members of the mint family) and thus its use is indicated in colds.

Other statements about catnip worth noting include these:

Rats dislike the plant particularly and will not approach it even when driven by hunger.

If the root of catnip is chewed, it will make the quietest person fierce and quarrelsome.

Culpeper says that the juice, drunk in wine, is good for bruises.

An old saying has it that "If you set it, the cats will eat it, If you sow it, the cats don't know it."

The young tops, made into a conserve, have "been found serviceable for a nightmare."

Nymphaceae

Fragrant water lily, pond lily, bonnets, toad lily

What nature-lover does not know and love the fragrant, white pond lily that is found nearly everywhere in ponds and quiet shallow waters?? Many tropical water lilies are larger and more brilliant, but none have any greater fragrance or perfection of flower.

An analysis of the chemistry of the thickened root shows that it is astringent and mucilaginous. It is recommended as a medicine for bowel complaints, as a gargle for sore throat, as a wash for sore eyes, as a cure for baldness, and when made into a decoction, as a lotion for boils, sores, and ulcers.

For internal use, a decoction of 1 ounce of the root boiled in 1 pint of water may be taken in wineglass doses. The effectiveness of such medicine is questionable; there does not seem to be any record of pond lily having been listed in American pharmacopoeias. It seems to be a folk medicine, pure and simple.

The following medicinal instructions appeared in Good's *Family Flora* a century ago:

It [*Nymphaea odorata*] is particularly excellent for removing morbific matter of every kind from every portion of the animal frame, being well calculated to promote the healthy action of the organs, and of course the result of its use will be the recovery of tone to the system. . . . In all cases the poultice is an excellent sedative to ease pain, and where there is a high state of inflammation, to reduce the swelling. The poultice may be prepared in the following manner: To a teaspoonful of the fine powder (from the dried root—Ed.), add a gill of boiling water, a teaspoon full of slippery elm *(Ulmus fulva)*; stir well together, then thicken with Indian meal, or what is better, Boston crackers made fine . . . The proper time to gather the root of this plant is in the fall, after the stalk is withered and the ponds are low.

Oenothera biennis

Evening primrose, cabish, cureall, tree primrose, tall sundrop

The specific name of this plant indicates that it does not bloom until the second year after the seed germinates. It may be found either in the first-year stage as a rosette of leaves, or in the summer of the following year as a tall, erect plant, bearing lance-shaped leaves and sunny yellow, primroselike flowers. An American plant widely scattered and growing in dry open fields, it is (in one form or another) often grown in gardens, especially abroad.

For medicinal purposes, the entire plant is gathered and dried, and an infusion is made of 1 teaspoonful to 1 cup of boiling water. It may then be drunk cold. This infusion is mucilaginous, astringent, and sedative. Thus we find it listed as a treatment in cases of asthmatic coughs and whooping cough. Further, it is said that salves made of it may be of help in eruptive skin diseases.

A survey of the literature about evening primrose indicates that it is used as above in France as well as England, and that there are some other species of *Oenothera* used in Mexico. From all of the evidence, it is hard to see why it is called cureall and king's cureall. But it is a lovely plant, however evanescent the flowers, or however slight its curative properties.

CACTACEAE

Prickly pear, Indian fig

There are only two genera of Cacti
which are found remote from the subtropical parts of our country, but one
genus the Opuntia, grows from Massachusetts south and west. The ground-
hugging species *Opuntia humifusa*, under good conditions, has a yellowish
flower, followed by a pear-shaped fruit
which, when ripe and despined, is flat-
tasting but edible. This is the fruit
which coming from other, larger growing species, is sold as the prickly pear.
In Mexico the plants are known as
Nopal, the fruit *tuna*.

Not too much value is placed on Cacti generally, yet the mucilaginous quality of the fruit does seem to function as an emollient.
Further, the fruit appears to have a diuretic effect. Jacobs mentions
that the fruit is used as a "refrigerant in pleuritic affections, in mental disturbances, nausea, coldness, and joint pains." Grieves adds
that a tincture from the flowers and the wood relieves affections of
the spleen, and diarrhea.

Formerly some use was made of the extracted juices of another
member of the Cactus family, the night-blooming *Cereus*. Youngken
says that a few physicians treated "neurogenic disturbance of cardiac rhythm, in neuresthenia and nicotinism, with Cereus, but he
adds that such use is now obsolete.

One member of the *Cactaceae* which has been referred too in the
popular writings of Aldous Huxley and others, is the peyote or mescal
button *(Lophophora Williamsii)*. Although this hallucinatory drug
is used by the Indians of the Southwest in religious ceremonies, it is
potentially a dangerous alkaloid, proscribed in many states. Huxley
represents the controlled use of this plant as being more desirable
(in not being habit-forming) than nicotine or alcohol, but it is considered too dangerous for release to the general public, and too
scarce for any great supply to be furnished from the wild.

Panax quinquefolius

ARALIACEAE

Ginseng, sang, tartar-root, five-finger, red berry (American Indian name—*Garantoqueen*)

The name of the genus, *Panax*, is very closely related to our word *panacea*; indeed that is the meaning of *Panax*—all healing. So this should be a plant of real value. Certainly it has been known and respected for centuries, for in Ezekiel (xxvii, 17) we find that the Jews, "they traded in the market wheat of Minnith, and *Pannag*, and honey and oil and balm."

Ginseng, meaning "wonder of the world, is so valued by the Chinese as a medicine that the latest statistics available show that 122,000 pounds of the root were exported to China from America in 1947.

Yet with all of this history, philology, and folklore, ginseng does not appear in western pharmacopoeias, and the best authority (Youngken) says that it is only "used by the laity as a stimulant and aromatic bitter. The Chinese employ it as an aphrodisiac and heart tonic but without scientific justification."

The American species of *Panax* grows in rich and cool woods throughout much of the Eastern and Central U.S.A., and is distinguishable by the erect stems, each bearing a whorl of three palmately compound leaves. Inconspicuous flowers are followed by red fruit. The root, the part used, is very slow in growing, taking from five to seven years to attain usable size.

To repeat, these valuable roots have no known values in Western medicine. Then, the reader may ask, why is the plant discussed here? Because it is one of the commonly collected medicinal plants and one which has been grown commercially on quite a large scale for sale to the Oriental trade. And, as one still finds reference in advertisements to the money which may be made by growing it, it is well to add a word of caution. The purveyors of roots for sale to prospective growers of ginseng tell much about the high monetary value of the roots (which may be true), but they do not tell about the years of waiting for the roots to grow, or of the very special conditions necessary, of disease, etc. Think twice before you go into the ginseng business.

UMBELLIFERAE

Parsley

Gray's *Manual of Botany* lists this otherwise common garden plant as being "occasional as an escape." Of Mediterranean origin, it is mentioned by early Greek writers as having ceremonial use, and later by Pliny as an important plant of his time. It seems to have been connected in antiquity with death and oblivion. Some sort of similar superstition persists, for modern writers indicate that transplanting parsley plants brings bad luck, and that the normally slow germination of parsley is due to the fact that the seeds "must visit the nether regions three times to obtain permission to grow in the earth." From the standpoint of the gardener, the truth here is that parsley has a single taproot and does not transplant well, as is true with all taproot plants.

Where parsley is subject to frost damage, the medicinal principle is extracted from the old roots, or in some cases an oil, apiol, is extracted from the fresh seeds. It is not practicable to prepare such an oil at home, nor should it be taken without medical advice.

However, one could prepare a tea from the dried or fresh leaves, or, more easily, chew a quantity of leaves. All authorities agree that parsley is a good diuretic, with aromatic and stimulating properties. There are many references to its use as a kidney stimulant. Mrs. Quelch says that parsley taken with boiled onions is good for gall stones, while another writer substitutes juniper berries for onions. There are a number of suggested minor values, but for the author, the culinary and decorative uses are quite sufficient.

Harris writes that "the bruised leaves have been used as a fomentation and to cure bites and stings of insects and the seeds to kill vermin in the hair. It is said to be poisonous to birds." Also, some people are allergic to parsley, which is a not too distant relative of the deadly Poison Hemlock.

LORANTHACEAE

American mistletoe, false mistletoe, goldenbough

The parasitic mistletoe which grows so widely southward from New Jersey, over into Texas, and up into the Mississippi valley is probably called "false mistletoe" to distinguish it from the European genus, *Viscum album.* The uses of mistletoe medicinally are not too great, but the variation in properties between the American and European genera are noteworthy. They illustrate the fact that the writings of European herbalists are not necessarily valid for America.

Heber Youngken's *Textbook of Pharmacognosy* makes these statements:

Phorodendron flavescens "acts as a powerful stimulant to smooth muscle, producing a rise in blood pressure and increasing the contractions of the intestine and uterus. It has been recommended as an oxytocic in post partum hemorrhage and menorrhagia and as a circulatory and uterine stimulant."

Viscum album he says is "used for the reduction of blood pressure in arteriosclerosis in the form of various galenical preparations."

Note then that our American species causes a *rise* in blood pressure, and the European causes a *reduction* of same; but both are known as mistletoe, belong to the same family, and have substantially the same appearance.

One reference to the American mistletoe mentions the antispasmodic action, and indicates that it has been highly esteemed as a remedy in epilepsy and other nervous diseases, and then continues "the leaves have been chewed to relieve toothache and the berries have produced death." Wide possibilities here, one would say.

For many of us the chief value of mistletoe is in promoting New Year osculations. Such a belief, of course, follows thinned-down ceremonies of ancient origin. If you are interested in the whole enthralling story of mistletoe, try to borrow a book by Geoffrey Grigson, *Gardenage* (Routledge—1952) and read the chapter entitled "The Mistletoe Bough."

PHTYOLACCACEAE

Pokeweed, scoke, garget, pigeonberry, crowberry, jalap, pocan bush, inkberry, cancer root

Not too often do we find in the scientific name of a plant any reference to its value as a dye, but *phytolacca* is a Greek-based name (*phyton*—plant; *lacca*—crimson lake, a dye color. This may help us remember the name, as we associate it with the beautiful color of autumn leaves and the crimson juice of the berries. It is said that in Portugal and France there was once a law requiring the bush (an herbaceous perennial, it grows large and shrublike) to be cut down, so that the berries would not be used to color cheap wine, a practice the natives followed.

Pokeweed is indigenous to most of this continent, growing in fairly rich soils in fence rows and the like, where it can remain undisturbed. The stout shoots which arise in early spring are as good as, or better than, asparagus as a spring green. However, from that time on the plant is valuable only as medicine. The thick roots are highly poisonous, as may also be the purple leaves in autumn.

But, as noted in *U.S.D.A. Bulletin 77*, these roots are collected in the fall for the drug trade and used in treating rheumatism and as an emetic, for which purpose it is valuable because of its slow but unharmful action. Meyer considers that, in home medicinal practice, pokeweed is best as an "alterative," an infusion made with a tablespoon of the root or cut berries to a pint of water to be taken in tablespoon doses.

Many writers on pokeweed feel that its value comes principally for chronic rheumatism. For such use, Dr. Barton, 150 years ago, mentioned that the berries were infused in brandy. He added that he doubted that pokeweed had any value in cancer.

One writer comments that "the leaves are used in ointment for sore eyes and in the form of a poultice for reducing swellings from the bites of poisonous insects." Like so many other plants, it has also been recommended for the treatment of syphilis, but this use also was considered doubtful by Dr. Barton.

Mainly one should remember the narcotic and poisonous quality of the roots, and use them only with great care and respect.

PINACEAE

White pine, Weymouth pine, American or Northern white pine, deal pine, soft pine

There are a great number of species of pine in the United States, each useful or beautiful in its own way, and each identifiable by habit and foliage. The white pine, which is found in cool sections, is known from Georgia to Canada and west to Iowa. With a smoothed-barked trunk when young, grayish and soft-appearing foliage, it can be distinguished by these characteristics and the five needles in each little bundle.

Originally the great forest giant of the Northeast in climax forests, it was decimated by the demands of the British for shipmasts for their ships because it was straight and strong. It was also used for making unpainted Colonial furniture, called "deal," hence the name deal pine.

But it has medicinal values as well. Perhaps the best remembered medicine of the author's childhood is the family bottle of "White Pine, Honey, and Tar Cough Syrup" on the kitchen shelf. All contemporary reputable writers regard it as a valuable stimulating expectorant generally combined with other materials. The dried and powdered outer bark from which the cork and pieces of inner wood have been removed may be infused at the rate of a teaspoonful to a cup of boiling water, and taken as often as necessary. But most books indicate that it is best used in combination with other expectorants, each having slightly different effects. Thus we find wild cherry and sassafras mentioned, as well as spikenard, bloodroot, balm of Gilead, honey, etc. (and in the cases of proprietary medicines, sometimes with codeine). There is an astringent property to this bark which is helpful, as well as the expectorant quality.

Other possible medicinal uses include using a decoction of the buds as a purgative, pine tar for burns and the itch, with additional notations as to the use of the pitch for treatment of gonorrhea and in kidney complaints.

PLANTAGINACEAE

Common plantain, Englishman's foot, way-bread, great or greater plantain, devil's shoestring, bird seed, snake weed, rib or ripple grass, and many another name

Here is a plant of European origin which is widespread and which gardeners with lawns know well as a weed. One name, "white-man's foot," is said to have been applied by the Indians, for it seemed to spring up everywhere the Europeans went. The Latin name *plantago* itself means *sole of the foot* because of the shape of the leaf. There is, in fact, much of interest in the various local names for plantain, all indicating associations with ceremonies, with magic, and with healing. How far back this goes it is hard to say, but in Shakespeare we find:

ROMEO: Your plantain leaf is excellent for "that," Benvolio? For what, I pray?

BENVOLIO: For your broken shin.

Thus one sees illustrated the complete agreement of all writers that the plantain leaf is a vulnerary (a wound plant) and that in everyday use it is excellent for relief from stings and bruises, an alleviant for nettle stings. A most careful investigator of Southwestern Indian medical practice, Edith Murphrey, says that the Shoshone Indians make poultices of the whole plant and apply for "battle bruises." In some cases, she says, the poultices are combined with the foliage of wild clematis, to the same effect. Another authority on Indian usages, Dr. Sidney Riggs, tells the author that the Indians of southern Massachusetts learned to apply plantain leaves both for wounds and to draw out the poison of snakebites. This is the sort of usage one finds noted everywhere.

The whole plant is used, and the leaves are soaked a bit after being washed, and bound to the sore spot. For internal use in diarrhea, an infusion is made of an ounce of the plant to a pint of boiling water, taken in wineglass doses. Writers from both our Southland and from Mexico suggest that an ointment made from the leaves is good for sore eyes.

Berberidaceae

May apple, wild jalap, mandrake, hog-apple, ground lemon, Indian apple, vegetable mercury, umbrella plant, duck's foot, vegetable calomel, yellow berry

The names of this plant quickly suggest the uses to which it has been put. In all of the literature on May apple, it is always listed on a cholagogue, this being a medicine which promotes the discharge of bile. *Podophyllum* has been an official drug since 1840, but disappeared from the *Pharmacopoeia* in 1930, probably in favor of supplanting synthetic products.

The May apple is a delightful plant to discover in the wild, and is found over a great part of North America in moist, wooded spots, massed in colonies. It is a rather curious plant in that it has two leaves; one a flowering stem with a leaf of from 3-7 parts, while the other palmate leaf has from five to nine lobes or parts; and both leaves grow to the same height. The plant grows only about a foot in height and the whole colony spreads out as a flat-topped ground cover. The flowers are followed by a yellowish lemonlike fruit, sweet-ish and edible. The period of ripening is the time to dig the roots, which are dried, then used as infusions or decoctions. Meyer gives a dose as a teaspoonful of the root, cut small, to a pint of boiling water, taken one teaspoonful at a time as required.

As one writer says, *Podophyllum* is a "medicine of most extensive service; its greatest power lies in its action upon the liver and bowels. . . . In congested states of the liver, it is employed with the greatest benefit, and for all hepatic complaints is eminently suitable, and the beneficial results can hardly be exaggerated."

The reference to "jalap" indicates its similarity to that plant in its slow but certain cathartic action. Its most beneficial action appears to be obtained by small doses frequently given, as large doses may cause violent evacuations and debility.

Cautions—the leaves are said to be poisonous, and that large doses of the drug are apt to be dangerous. But of the many plants of this book, few are more reputable and useful than the lovely May apple.

POLEMONIACEAE

Greek valerian, Jacob's ladder, blue-bells, sweatroot, abscess root

Generally growing from our northern borders to Georgia, in woods, damp soils and along shady river banks, this medicinal plant has only minor values. It is a low-growing (1 foot) perennial with a creeping rootstock. The leaves are pinnate with up to seven pairs of leaflets. The terminal flower heads are a delightful shade of blue, making the *Polemonium* one of the few medicinal plants to introduce into a blue perennial border or garden.

In herbal practice, the rootstocks are dried and powdered and an infusion prepared at the rate of about an ounce to a pint of boiling water. Taken warm as a diaphoretic, this infusion will produce sweating (note one of the common names).

Polemonium in addition to being diaphoretic, is an astringent, alterative, and expectorant. As a drug, it has been recommended by various writers for use in febrile and inflammatory diseases, pleurisy, etc., while one writer notes its value in snakebite—a doubtfully reliable recommendation. Taken as a whole, *Polemonium* seems to be not in the least poisonous, and as a diaphoretic has value in home use if other plant drugs are not available.

Polygala Senega

POLYGALACEAE

Senega snakeroot, milkwort, mountain flax, rattlesnake root, senega root

This rather small, slender, unattractive weed grows in dry woods in many parts of the United States, more widely in the southern states than elsewhere. It is a perennial with a hard, branching, and knobby root which, for medicinal purposes, is gathered in the fall just before frost. The several stems grow about a foot high and terminate in tiny pinkish flowers.

In the early part of the eighteenth century, a Scotch doctor in Pennsylvania heard of its use by the Seneca Indians in cases of snake bite and investigated its merits. He discovered that an infusion of the dried roots would actively promote salivation, desirable in chronic catarrh, croup, asthma, and lung disorders. It was accepted by the *U.S. Pharmacopoeia* as early as 1820, and remained on that list until recently.

A recommended infusion is 1 ounce of the dried root to a pint of boiling water, taken as needed, in doses of a tablespoon or more. Its value as an expectorant and sialagogue indicates its use in sore throat and for the conditions mentioned. A laboratory analysis shows that it contains methyl-salicylate, a principal constituent of wintergreen.

Caution: in very large doses it can have poisonous reactions; irritating, causing vomiting and purging, and having other side effects.

The "snakebite cure" aspect of senega seems to have been lost sight of since its adoption as an official drug. Whether or not it has such values does not appear in any of the many references to this valuable plant.

Populus balsamifera
also
P. deltoides
P. tacamahaca
SALICACEAE

Balsam-poplar, hackmatack, taccamahac,
balm of Gilead, Carolina poplar

This tree may be found across the
country to Wisconsin and south to
about North Carolina, growing along
the borders of rivers and swamps and
occasionally as an undesirable tree.
It grows to 90 feet with ovate and thickish leaves up to 5 inches long, round at
the base and whitish beneath. This might be considered a general
description of the genus under discussion, but even the botanists are
not agreed as to names and descriptions of many species. In fact, so
many hybrids have crept into the genus that, for the purposes of this
book, the most distinguishing feature of the balsam-poplar is its
resin-coated large winter buds. Those buds may be collected in
February or March, and used in the preparation of a stimulating and
expectorant medicine.

Buds of all poplar trees like those on left of illustration contain medicinal resin.

These buds are known by pharmacists as "Poplar bud" and are
used by them in compounding such cough preparations as Compound Syrup of White Pine. The balsamic resin which is extracted
is also used in the preparing of soothing ointments and plasters.

For internal use as an expectorant, a teaspoon of the buds to a cup
of boiling water provides a soothing and stimulating potion, but for
use in salves and ointments the resinous property is extracted as a
tincture.

The author cannot leave the discussion of this poplar and its hybrid variations without saying a word about the destructive effects
and general undesirable qualities of these rapid-growing poplars as
landscape trees. Not only are they coarse and dirty, but the power of
the huge shallow-growing roots in uprooting sidewalks, and the brit-
tleness of the limbs add up to making it the worst of all trees for
use in home landscapes.

Populus tremuloides

SALICACEAE

Aspen, quaking aspen, white poplar, trembling asp, cottonwood tree, old wive's tongue

Quite generally distributed, especially in cooler sections, the aspen tree grows up to a hundred feet tall. The branches are concerned with pale greenish yellow bark; the broad, ovate leaves have toothed and hairy edges. The name would appear to come from the tendency of the leaves, with the slightest breath of wind, to dance with that quivering, restless motion characteristic of all poplars, more pronounced in this species than in others. While we moderns attach no significance to such motion, the Celts and other groups in early Christian times believed that the leaves could never rest, trembling for shame that Christ, so 'twas said, was crucified on a cross of poplar wood.

Medicinally, the part used is the bark, which is reputed to be excellent for the treatment of fevers. Leaves have also been recommended. Because of its balsamic and soothing quality, it also is listed as a tonic. The bark is quite bitter, and, because of this, an extract of the bark has been used as a substitute for quinine. Potter in fact says that it has none of the drawbacks of cinchona bark. He goes on: "For all cases of debility, indigestion, faintness, hysteria, etc., it may be freely given. It is used also in urinary complaints."

An infusion of a teaspoonful of the leaves or bark to a cup of boiling water is suggested, several cupfuls a day appearing to be a useful dose. Externally a soothing wash may be prepared by adding a little borax to a strong tea made of the bark.

In literature, many references are found to the appearance and to the trembling quality of the aspen, and in South Europe it has (in other species) been long known for its medicinal values. Of interest as summing up the story of the fluttery but valuable qualities of the aspen are the lines from Sir Walter Scott:

> Oh, women! in our hours of ease
> Uncertain, coy, and hard to please,
> And variable as the shade
> By the light quivering aspen made,
> When pain or sickness rends the brow,
> A ministering angel thou.

ROSACEAE

Silverweed, argentine, goosewort, wild tansy, crampweed, moor grass, silvery cinquefoil

Like so many other medicinal "weeds," this plant is an introduction, its probable origin being Eurasia. It is now growing in this country across the northern tier of states, in sandy banks or moist roadsides. A low-growing, silvery and powdery-leafed plant, its toothed and fern-like leaves make it a delight. The small yellow flowers and seeds are unimportant; the plant spreads largely by runners, much in the manner of its relative, the strawberry.

Like other plants, too, silverweed has an interesting scientific name. *Potentilla* means "little powerful one," while *anserina* brings in the word goose, it being said that geese and other creatures like to browse on the plant. But not only geese use silverweed; there are well-documented stories of the eating of the roots by Northern peoples in times of famine. In fact, the plant has been cultivated for its slightly enlarged edible root, called in Gaelic, "the seventh bread."

Medicinally, the most reputable use of silverweed is in cases of difficult menstruation and in diarrhea, the constituents of the plant being tannin, several glycosides, tormentol, etc., as Youngken reports. This abundant tannin in the plant explains its use in country medicine as a lotion for piles; and as an infusion for all conditions where an astringent is indicated. An infusion of silverweed, to which honey has been added, constitutes an excellent gargle for sore throat.

A strong distillation of the herb is said to be excellent to take away freckles, pimples, and is valuable (as one might expect) in cases of sunburn.

The whole top of the plant is gathered in June, very carefully dried, and then tightly stored, as the least mildew will cause it to lose its values. An infusion may be made of a teaspoonful of the dried herb to a cup of boiling water, taken cold, one or two cupfuls a day.

There is much in the literature about the values of this and other species of *Potentilla*, and it thus should be noted as one of the standard items in Northern herbal cabinets.

Prunella vulgaris

<small>LABIATAE</small>

Self-heal, heal-all, brown wort, sickle wort, carpenter's herb, hook weed, wound wort, blue curls

Nearly every one of the above names is concerned with healing (sickle-, hook-, and carpenter's- all refer to wounds made with tools). One would assume therefore that it is a pre-eminent healing plant, yet *Prunella* is not found listed in the pharmccopoeia, nor is it adjudged to have much more than a psychological value. However the resemblance of parts of the flower to a carpenter's bill-hook was so noticeable that the plant was assigned certain values as a curative agent by the *Doctrine of Signatures*. And early belief in this doctrine was so strong that it has long persisted.

Like most members of the Mint family, *Prunella* has a medicinal-seeming, pungent and bitter quality, and a slight astringency as well. These factors suggest that it may be good as a gargle for throat irritations, and possibly the same astringency *would* heal small cuts, much in the manner of a styptic. One usually reliable writer suggests that a teaspoon of the herb placed in a pint of brandy or whiskey for a few days, then taken several tablespoons at a time, is a good medicine. Taking the relaxing and possible medicinal values of alcohol into account, this suggestion is probably good.

Reviewing all of the literature, self-heal is variously noted as an aromatic, a carminative, diuretic, anthelmintic, and astringent. But the emphasis on recognized value is so slim that it cannot be highly recommended, except as the name heal-all recommends it.

Prunella is a plant of roadsides, fields, and waste places, and on introduction from Europe, spread widely. It grows variously from 1 foot to 2 feet with a downy, bristly stem and purplish two-lipped flowers in terminal spikes, the flowers growing in clusters of three.

Nicholas Culpeper in 1653, talking about self-heal, says: "The juice hereof used with oil of roses to anoint the temples and forehead, is very effectual to remove headache and the same mixed with honey of roses, cleanses and heals all ulcers, in the mouth, and throat, and those also in the secret parts."

ROSACEAE

Rum cherry, wild black cherry, Virginia prune-bark, whicky cherry, coke, or chokecherry

One finds the wild cherry tree mostly along fence-rows, country roadsides or the banks of streams. It grows to a height of forty or more feet, but in the fall its bunches of grape-cherries bend the branches toward the ground. Were it not for the regrettable attraction of the rum and chokecherry trees to tent caterpillars, we might consider it desirable. It has shiny leaves, white flower clusters, and edible fruit with a bitter but vinous flavor which is so good as a meat-course jelly.

One of the most neatly-wrapped statements about the value of wild cherries is made by Saunders: "Every holder to the old traditions is loyal to Wild Cherry bark. . . . An infusion of the dried bark (gathered preferably in autumn) in cold water, in the proportion of one-half ounce of bark to a pint of water, enjoys a reputation both as a mild sedative suited to cases of nervous excitability and as a tonic adapted to debility and impaired digestion."

The outside layer of the tree bark should first be removed, the green layer then stripped off and carefully dried. Young, thin bark is best for medicinal purposes. Dried bark more than a year old is apt to have lost its potency and should be replaced. And further it should be noted that, used in any excessive quantity, cherry bark could be poisonous because of the hydrocyanic acid found as one of its constituents. The Indians, who used both dried rum and chokecherries as an ingredient of pemmican, soaked the acid out of the fruit before drying.

Cherry bark is often a basic ingredient in cough medicines, seemingly because of its sedative action; its function as a bitter has made it useful in treating dyspepsia and as a part of general tonics. A teaspoonful of the dried inner bark to a cup of boiling water is recommended as an infusion to be drunk cold, one or two cupfuls a day.

ROSACEAE

Chokecherry, Virginian cherry, black cherry

In considering this tree, one should read all that has been written about *Prunus serotina*, as these two species are closely related and often confused. They grow generally in the same locales, and are much the same in appearance, except as the leaves of *P. virginiana* have sharper teeth on the margins, the bunches of fruit are a little shorter, and ripen a little later. Fernald says also that the bark of the chokecherry is nonaromatic, and notes other variances important to the botanist but not readily seen by others.

The medicinal properties of the chokecherry are similar to those of the rum-cherry; again it should be pointed out that the hydrocyanic-acid content of cherry bark puts it in the class of poisons to be used discriminatingly.

The American Indians knew all this, yet considered it an important tonic, and the fruit was basic to the making of pemmican. One of the first to investigate chokecherry as a medicine was the reliable Dr. Barton, whose comments (written 1804) are worth quoting at some length, as they represent statements still made about this tree.

"The bark of Prunus Virginiana . . . is considerably bitter and astringent. These qualities are accompanied with some aromatic warmth. . . . This bark also possesses an evident narcotic quality, to which it is highly probable, that some of the useful qualities of the medicine, in certain cases, must be ascribed.

To go a step further in our discussion of both the rum-cherry and the chokecherry (assuming the medicinal value of a draught of brandy), it is interesting to notice that the addition of the ripe fruits to brandy make a tasty and potent drink. Walter Beebe Wilder in his *Bounty of the Wayside* gives this recipe:

"They were stripped from the stems, crushed, and boiled with a cup of water to each quart of fruit for half an hour. Sometimes half a lemon was added. The juice, after being run through a jelly bag (thoroughly squeezed), was mixed with sugar, a quart to a pound, and then with brandy, a pint of juice to a quart of brandy."

RUTACEAE

Wafer-ash, wing seed, shrubby trefoil,
hop tree, swamp dogwood, stinking ash

Ptelea illustrates a fact well-known in
perfume chemistry: the name "stinking
ash" might apply to flowers close up,
yet the perfume wafted from a distance
is delightful. Similarly the generally delightful fragrances of narcissus and
some other flowers seem well-nigh pu-
trid if sniffed close up. Actually, the
wafer-ash comes by its fragrance hon-
estly, as it is a "kissin' cousin" of the
edible orange (as well as of the herb,
rue). The odor of orange blossoms can be overwhelming too.

Ptelea is 8-10 feet high, with trifoliate leaves, greenish-white flowers appearing in June, followed by an aromatic, bitter fruit (wafers)
which has been used as a substitute for hops. It grows in the wild
generally throughout the East and Midwest (abundantly west of the
Alleghanies), and has been widely cultivated as a shrub.

The bark of the root will release its properties to an infusion, or
more easily with alcohol as a solvent. All writers agree that the action
of *Ptelea* as a bitter tonic is mild and nonirritating, that it has, indeed, a soothing influence on the mucous membranes, and promotes
appetite. It has been employed in dyspepsia, general debility, and all
diseases involving fevers.

A simple infusion is a teaspoon of the bark, cut small, to a cup of
boiling water, taken cold in tablespoon doses three or four times a
day.

It is interesting to note in a discussion by Youngken that this bark
has often been an adulterant of the bark of the Wahoo or burning
bush *(Euonymus atropurpureus)*, an American shrub elsewhere
discussed in this book; its root bark provides a "cholagogue cathartic in torpid liver and constipation." Because of an irritant quality, euonymus must be taken carefully, and is not recommended for
the home medicine shelf.

Pyrus Malus

Rosaceae

Apple

Science News Letter for December 9, 1961 has a headline in bold type which says: APPLE A DAY MAXIM CONFIRMED BY RESEARCH. It describes a study made of 1300 students at Michigan State University which proved that the apple-eating group was definitely healthier having less "upper respiratory infection" than in the student body as a whole, and less "tension-caused" illness. The article continues: "the investigators said the ascorbic acid (Vitamin C) in the apples might have accounted for the benefit, and that perhaps some naturally occurring tranquilizer in the apple might have accounted for lessening the tension pressure."

Whether there is any correlation between an apple a day keeping the doctor away and the fact that the doctor today keeps the apple away, is hard to say. The apple is hardly the sort of medicine which the druggist can hand over the counter or which looks like a prescription on the doctor's chit, but the apple has long been regarded as a health preservative, containing as it does a high content of iron, potassium, sodium and vitamins, all known to be beneficial. The malic and tartaric acids are of great benefit to persons of sedentary habits in assisting digestion and stimulating the liver. One reads that "in countries where unsweetened cider is used as a beverage, kidney stone or calculus is unknown."

Valuable also is the substance found in the apple core not usually eaten by the "apple-a-dayers." This substance, pectin, is one which every housewife depends on in making jellies or jams, either using it as derived from fresh apples or as prepared pectin powder or liquid. This particular apple product is an "official" drug. It is used as an emulsifying and jelling agent, and enters into such products as pastes for external application, hair pomades, dentifrices, etc.

An old-time remedy for diarrhea is to simmer apple parings in boiled milk, a half-cupful drunk warm every hour until relieved.

Yes, an apple a day may well keep the doctor away.

F AGACEAE

White oak, stone oak, tanner's oak

The scientific name of the oak genus is said to be derived from the Celtic *quer* (fine) and *cuez* (tree); and surely "fine tree" would sum up the status of the whole oak family. It is not possible in these lines to discuss the sacredness with which oaks have been surrounded, the many myths growing up around them, nor to describe the many historic and majestic specimen oaks found in this and other countries. Their symbolic and historic part in English history is a story in itself, while the economic value of the oak as a timber tree and as a source of tannin is well-known.

Each country has its own oaks which have economic values. In this country the oak with the most medicinal value is the white oak. With age, a spreading sturdy tree, it grows to nearly a hundred feet, and is found generally throughout the Eastern United States.

The bark of all of the oaks contains tannic acid, that from our present species being generally used by tanners. For medicinal purposes, the inner bark of the oak is cut, dried, powdered, and used as an infusion. As might be supposed, the inherent astringency which makes the bark valuable for tanning and diarrhea suggests its value in dysentery. Potter gives a dose as a decoction made from 1 ounce of bark to a quart of water, boiled down to a pint, and taken in wineglass doses. As a gargle for sore throat, as a possible mild hemostat, and as a vaginal douche, the same astringency would be operative.

The bark from a number of species of *Quercus*, such as the red oak, the black oak, and other native and hybrid forms may also be useful. But Meyer suggests that, while such bark may be used as an external astringent, they are "rarely employed internally, as it is liable to derange the bowels."

One notes in studying a book of drug formulas that tannic acid is a usual ingredient of healing ointments, and, from personal experience, the author can vouch for the efficacy of a healing herbal salve containing the extract of oak bark.

The same valuable property of astringency is found in oak galls and in the acorns, which latter, in powdered form, were an ancient remedy for diarrhea.

Rhamnaceae

Buckthorn, alder buckthorn, black dogwood, bird cherry, arrow-wood

This is a shrub, introduced from Europe, which grows to about 10 feet, has smooth, obovate, and olive-green leaves about 2 inches long. A distinguishing characteristic of the plant is the elongated, whitish marks (lenticels) which appear on the branches. In the fall, there appears black fruit, each with three seeds. It is now quite common in wild hedgerows and, according to one writer, "likely to become obnoxious."

Medicinally the part used is the dried and seasoned bark, seasoned (it is suggested) from two to three years, as the new bark is not only cathartic in action but likely to cause violent pains, vomiting, and other affects. Bark properly aged, however, and prepared as a remedy for chronic constipation in a decoction of 1 ounce of bark in 1 quart of water boiled down to 1 pint, is helpful taken in tablespoon doses. Doses may be decreased as the condition is remedied. Use with caution, however, and (much better) under the advise of a competent herbal doctor or other practitioner.

One other reason for caution is the fact that there also may be found growing in the East, at least, plants of the slightly similar *Rhamnus cathartica,* the common buckthorn, one of the principal distinguishing characteristics of which is that each black fruit has four rather than three seeds. But watch out! for *R. cathartica* does not bear the name of *Purging buckthorn* for nothing. Although it has at times been prescribed, it is so violent in its action that it is dangerous.

Both of the shrubs above are plants of the East and Midwest but persons who live on the West Coast will be more apt to know another member of the genus, *Rhamnus purshiana,* the cascara buckthorn, or cascara sagrada. The meaning of *cascara sagrada* is "Sacred bark," and it was doubtless so named by the Spanish missionaries who first learned of its value. Many people have heard of this milder and commonly prescribed laxative, which works principally on the large intestine and seems to be excellent for chronic constipation.

Anarcardiaceae

Scarlet sumac, smooth sumac

The sight of the brilliantly colored leaves and the maroon-red clusters of hairy fruit on this 10-foot-high shrub is a familiar one in dry rocky places over all but the central parts of the United States. And many people know it from finding it in their landscape-architect-designed shrub plantings. The stems of the species *(R. glabra)* are smooth, while those of the equally valuable *R. typhina* staghorn sumac) are very hairy, and its fern-like foliage very beautiful.

These two forms of sumac are desirable in many ways. The tannic acid which they contain has been much used in dyeing, and it is the tannic acid which brings the species into the field of medicinal plants. But a caution should be given here; not all members of the family are so desirable. The cashew family includes the all too familiar poison ivy, poison oak, and the quite similar looking poison sumac. Although poison ivy does have listed medical properties, little need be said about the poison forms of *Rhus* except a word as to distinguishing features. It is notable that, in the poison forms, one usually finds the seed stalks coming from the leaf axils along the stem, but in the useful species they are usually terminal. The fruit of the poison forms is gray-green or white, but red in the forms in which we are interested. Again, the number of leaflets of the poison kinds runs from 3 to 13, while from 9 to 31 leaflets are found on the species under discussion.

The medicinal use of the poison ivies mentioned is, for practical purposes, limited to the injection of the poison from the plants into the system as an antidote. One hears stories of persons who have chewed the leaves for the same purpose. The effects of both poison and cure are, however, so variable that one is best advised to leave the decision on treatment to the medical profession. Literature on this subject has quite a bit to say about the value of various substances as cures. Plantwise, there is some evidence of the real value of the juice of the jewel weed, *Impatiens pallida* (q.v.) which is often found growing in swamps where poison ivy is so happy. If contact has been made with ivy, crush stems of the jewel weed on the parts, or boil down a mess of the juicy plants and apply this decoction as a lotion. No harm will be done and quite possibly *you* will be protected.

The above caution having been given, we can return to the species which do not have bad characteristics. The plant known as the smooth or scarlet sumac, and to many as just plain sumac, has values recognized by official pharmacopoeias, and is recommended in many herbals. For those who can not find plants of *Rhus glabra*, it is noteworthy that the staghorn sumac, *R. typhina*, is equally of value.

The chemical property which gives sumac its value is one of astringency, and a drug made from the dried ripe fruit is a component of gargles. Using its refrigerant qualities, a drink made from sumac is also a cooling draft for those with fevers. Seemingly, the healing quality is found in the bark as well as the fruit. One authority recommends a dose of a teaspoon of the bark decocted in boiling water and taken a mouthful at a time to relieve throat irritations. With this same quality in mind sumac has also been recommended for various skin irritations or, as with so many other plants, for the treatment of gonorrhea. The Iroquois Indians considered it a general alterative. The bark may be boiled in milk and used as a healing wash for bad burns, in the absence of more potent remedies. Decoctions in large doses are said to be cathartic in effect.

It seems certain that the Indians were the ones who recommended this plant to the early settlers, for the native Americans early enjoyed the use of a drink made from the fruit. For this, the fruit heads are first crushed and the juice strained to remove the fine hairs, sugar is added to taste, and one has a palatable and pink-lemonade type of drink. It is said that the Indians dried the berries in the summer to assure a supply of the acid drink in the winter, such a potion having further value for the lessening of throat irritations.

ROSACEAE

Japanese rose

For the benefit of those who do not live along coastal sections where *R. rugosa* is happiest, note should be ma⁻ ⁻ of a few rose species which have values similar to this plant: *R. acicularis, R. cinnamonea* and *R. canina.*

The hips (heps) or the fruit of roses is, in varying degrees, a major source of Vitamin C. To quote Robert Rodale, editor of "Organic Gardening": "Several common hips are as much as 60 times richer in vitamin C than oranges, and oranges are generally recognized as just about the richest common source of vitamin C."

The three species mentioned above are almost as high in vitamin content as the *R. rugosa* of these notes, but the fruit is smaller and not so convenient for use. The often escaped and common garden species, the Japanese rose, is almost an evergreen, is a dwarf, free blooming, and a wholly desirable shrub, as useful as it is beautiful.

In the sense that an ounce of prevention is worth a pound of cure, this page is intended to call attention to the use of these and other rose hips in the maintenance of health, rather than as a curative. Reviewing all of the writings on the use of rose petals as an astringent, and the usefulness of rose oil in medicine, no great claims has been or could be made for the use of either, but the knowledge of the value of rose-hips is quite enough.

The best plea for these fruits (which can easily be made into a preserve or jam) is from an English publication. The English should know, for, during World War II, they and the Scandinavians, in the complete absence of citrus fruits, depended solely on rose hip jam for "C" and other vitamins so well combined in roses. The article states that not only are rose hips richer than oranges but "there are hidden dangers in citrus fruits because of the citric acid content. Citric acid is a strong acting compound that can cause cavities in the teeth, intestinal disturbances, itching rectum, etc. The Vitamin C (in roses) prevents scurvy, protects the health of all the body tissues including skin, teeth, gums, bones, blood vessels, eyes . . ."

Rubus (all species)

Rosaceae

Blackberry

Considering that *Gray's Botany* lists, for the central and northeastern United States alone, over 200 distinguishable species of blackberries, and also suggests the presence of many hybrids, there is small use in getting into any taxonomic argument by mentioning one or another particularized species of blackberries. Anyone who has tramped the summer woods knows how variable blackberries are. Therefore this discussion is relative to the medicinal properties of *any* blackberry or dewberry. Youngken does say that, commercially, most of the root bark used in the drug trade comes from *Rubus villosus, allegheniensis,* or *cuneifolius.* This dried blackberry bark contains "tannin, gallic acid, and villosin," which properties add up to an excellent astringent, particularly useful in decoction for diarrhea. To a less extent the juice of the fruit is also used thus; while the leaves, although containing less of the valuable properties, may also be infused or decocted.

One recipe for preparing an astringent potion from the dried root-bark of blackberries calls for an ounce of the root to be boiled down in water or milk from 1½ pints to a pint, taking half a teacupful every hour or two in cases of diarrhea. Of fresh root, a larger dose would be required. This astringent drink is reputed to be helpful also in cases of whooping cough.

For many people a convenient and safe-keeping form of blackberry as a medicine is in the form of blackberry brandy, or cordial, which is made with the juice of fresh berries, sugar, and a few spices, boiled together, with brandy added.

On the value of any form of blackberry extraction, there seems to be complete agreement. No household should be without one or another form of such a simple remedy for unexpected intestinal upsets.

Within the genus *Rubus* there are other berries, but none as valuable as the blackberry group. *R. idaeus* is the raspberry which, having a mild astringency, is useful for treating children. There are also several unsubstantiated references to its usefulness in pregnancy.

Polygonaceae

Sheep sorrel, sorrel, red weed, cuckoo bread, wood sorrel, sour dock, sour grass, etc.

A perennial weed of general distribution, sorrel came to this country from Europe and has, in sum, little to recommend it, although it has been mentioned medicinally for centuries. The 350-year-old illustration, reproduced from Gerard's Herbal (a photograph would do no better) shows the character of the foliage, but not the usually red or brownish leaves, nor the triangular seed pods. It does, however, suggest the long tap root which, in the poor soils where sorrel grows, goes down to great depths and makes it hard to eradicate.

This long root imparts a red color to boiling water, and it is reportedly used in France for coloring medicines. The plant itself is also esteemed by the French as a principal ingredient of their *Soupe aux herbes*.

Medicinally, the leaves of sheep sorrel are known to be refrigerant, antiscorbutic, and diuretic, but in every case, only mildly effective. It is an acidulous plant, containing, according to one analysis, oxalic, citric, malic, tartaric, gallic, and prussic acids.

Perhaps about the only paean of praise to sheep sorrel (and a good example of how a discussion of a noxious weed can be raised to the status of literature) is the paragraph in the monograph on salads, written in 1699 by John Evelyn:

"Sorrel sharps the appetite, assuages heat, cools the liver, and strengthens the heart; it is an antiscorbutic, resisting putrefaction, and in the making of sallets imparts a grateful quickness to the rest as supplying the want of oranges and lemons. Together with salt, it gives both the name and relish to sallets from sapidity which renders not plants and herbs only, but men themselves, and their conversations, pleasant and agreeable. But of this enough, and perhaps too much! lest while I write of salts and sallets I appear myself *insipid*."

Rumex crispus

Polygonaceae

Curled or yellow dock, narrow-leaved dock, bitter or sour dock, out-sting, rumex

The U.S. Department of Agriculture calls this a "troublesome weed," probably because of its deep root, but to the writer this is the spring green deemed by his parents to be superior to spinach. A native of Europe, it is now widely spread. It is easily identified by the curly leaves and the tall, warm brown seed stalk, a boon to flower arrangers.

It has for some years been listed in the *U.S. Pharmacopoeia*, the part used being the root, which is collected late in the summer or autumn, split, dried, and stored, to be used as a gently tonic astringent, laxative and alterative, and externally in itching, etc.

For the relief of itching and eruptions on the skin a simple ointment may be prepared by boiling the root in vinegar and then mixing the softened pulp with lard (or Vaseline), to which sulphur may be added. Although this is not a native American plant, the Indians of our country were not adverse to using dock, and we find that in the Far West, Mrs. Murphey reports—that the Blackfeet Indians mashed the roots into a pulp and applied it to human sores and swellings and also to their horses for saddle sores. Similar use among the Navajo is mentioned by Wyman and Harris, and it was used by the Iroquois as a food.

Just as with *Rumex acetosella* (q.v.), early writers were enthusiastic about *R. crispus*, Culpeper in 1653 says about dock (which he also calls Blood-wort), "All docks being boiled with meat, makes it boil the sooner: Besides Blood-wort is exceeding strengthening to the liver, and procures good blood, being as wholesome a pot herb as any growing in the garden; yet such is the nicety of our times, forsooth, that women will not put it into a pot, because it makes the pottage black; pride and ignorance (a couple of monsters in the creation) prefering nicety before health."

RUTACEAE

Rue, garden rue, herb-of-grace

A plant mentioned in the Bible, referred to by Greek writers, known and used by the Romans, important in Medieval times, and in the present day familiar to everyone with an herb garden, this is a plant introduced to America and now found escaped and widely cultivated. It is a perennial with thickish, pinnatifid leaves of a pleasing bluish-gray, notable for the presence of tiny oil glands. It grows variably to 3 feet in height and does best in a dry, slightly shaded spot. The leaves have a bitter, not unpleasant taste.

Of few plants is it ever noted that they "cure old age," but directly and indirectly this statement is made by a number of writers about rue. And of few plants also is reference made to curative properties for eye conditions; yet it has been said that rue "bestows second sight, and it certainly preserves ordinary sight, by strengthening the ocular muscles" (Leyel).

Actually, the most likely and reputable use for rue is as a tonic with sedative qualities, in colic, and for ammenorrhea. An infusion (recommended by several) would be about a teaspoonful of the dried herb (the whole plant is dried) to a cup of boiling water, taking such a quantity in the course of a day in doses of a tablespoon.

Externally the leaves of fresh rue are irritating and thus as a counter-irritant have been recommended to be rubbed on the forehead in cases of headache.

There is a great deal of real interest in the extensive literature relating to rue. The name "herb-of-grace" comes from the fact that this was a plant used in exorcisms by the early church, and before that, ceremonially by those outside the church. Because of its strong odor it was also deemed to be a protection against pestilence, and was usually provided on the desk of the judge in courts of law to protect against infections from criminals. And, quite curiously, there is a tradition that many gardeners will appreciate: it is said that plants of rue grow best when they are stolen from another's garden. All "cutting-snitchers"—please note.

Sagittaria latifolia

ALISMACEAE

Arrowhead, Duck Potato

To nature-lovers who tramp the woods it is always a delight to come upon a hidden shallow pond and find on its banks the bold foliage of the Arrowhead, so well named after the shape of the leaves. This boldness of foliage somehow suggests the tropics in northern waters, and probably it should, for most of the thirty species are natives of southern and hot climates in the Western hemisphere, only one species *S. sagittifolia* being found in Europe.

Here in the north we find this species somewhat variable in size of foliage and even in flower, for sometimes the highly fragile lovely white flowers are doubled. Down in the mud under all the plants one will find a number of tubers which (as many water animals well know) are quite edible, the Indians calling it Wapatoo or Katniss. In China and Japan Arrowhead tubers have long been used for food, in fact, great medicinal value is not ascribed to Arrowhead.

Some of the writers of the last century list *Sagittaria* as a diuretic and antiscorbutic, because of the acrid principle found in the plant. In Devonshire, England, says Grigson, the natives make a "strengthening tea" using exactly 9 leaves to each brew. Probably knowing the astringency of the leaves, they attached this magic number to the recipe or, perhaps this is just the number which reflects the mixture of superstition and medicine which pervades so many of the folk practices of all nations.

LABIATAE

Sage, garden sage, meadow sage, true sage

So far there has been no attempt to discuss cultivated herbs, a subject covered in more specialized books, but some observations on the cultivated (and sometimes escaped) garden sage are appropriate here. Dried herbs are likely to be found on every kitchen shelf, ready for use in stuffing turkey, wild duck, or pork roast.

The reason for such culinary use of sage is not often considered, except that one assumes it is pleasant and spicy. Actually, sage is used in stuffing because it is effective as a carminative and as an aid in the digestion of rich dishes. Sufferers from flatulent indigestion may be helped if they eat a sandwich with dried sage, or drink a cup of sage tea.

Other uses include gargling with sage and vinegar to alleviate ulcerated gums, or with sage and cloves to relieve toothache. Youngken says that sage is also used in hair dressings (as a darkener), in sausage stuffings, where its oils have a preservative effect on meat, something that was important before refrigeration.

In medieval times there was a saying:

> He who would live for aye
> Must eat Sage in May.

And Mrs. Quelch says, "beyond doubt sage does much to prolong life by strengthening the body, clearing the blood, and aiding digestion."

The oil which volatilizes when the fresh leaves are crushed and deeply inhaled is powerful, and may indeed cause giddiness. Or, when smoked, it may says one writer, "cause intoxication and giddiness of the brain."

We see that one of the commonest kitchen herbs is also a good medicament, as is attested by a body of commendatory literature. Keep sage in mind the next time someone has dyspepsia. To make a pun, *be sage—use sage.*

Sambucus canadensis

CAPRIFOLIACEAE

Elderberry, American or common elder

The elderberry shrub, with white flower heads followed by black-purple fruits, is a strong-growing member of the honeysuckle family, usually found in moist soils on the edges of meadows or swamps. It is known by discriminating people to be wonderful for pie as well as wine. The various medicinal properties are less well known, however.

The dried inner bark of the stem has been used for centuries as a dependable active purgative, which should be used cautiously because it is emetic in large doses. The bark of the *root* is violently purgative and dangerous.

Although there are alkaloids and poisons in the leaves, which make them safe only for external use, an oinment made from the leaves is recommended for bruises and sprains. In ancient times, the juice of the leaves was used as an eye-wash. A countrywoman writes that for headaches her grandmother "warmed the leaves of elderberry and applied them to the forehead."

The heat-thickened juice of elderberries forms "an invaluable cordial for coughs and colds," while a draught of hot elder wine before bed is soporific and promotes perspiration, helping to ward off the effects of a chill.

It is, however, the *flowers* of elder which receive the most favorable notice, being the part of the plant which is recognized in the *National Formulary*. When carefully dried and cleaned of stems, says Youngken "the fresh flowers are employed as a diaphoretic and stimulant and in the preparation of elder flower ointment and water."

Elder-flower water, for which there are a number of recipes, was once used as a cosmetic to remove freckles, alleviate sunburn, and relieve itching.

One home recipe for elder-flower ointment says to take the flower heads without leaves and rub them into the purest lard until no more blossoms can be pushed in. Place in a clean baking tin, and dry in a moderate oven until the flowers are quite brown. Strain through muslin and store in small jars. Such an ointment will beautify complexions, heal sores, and keep away flies.

PAPAVERACEAE

Bloodroot, red, yellow, or white puc-coon, Indian plant, tetterwort, coonroot, sweet slumber, red root

In deciding which plants to discuss one must consider borderline plants. Poisonous, or otherwise dangerous plants have been rigorously excluded, and some of the plants discussed are on a low level of value. The object of this particular entry is to present bloodroot, so common in the woods in spring, and so beautiful, that it seems wise to talk about it, however marginal its nature. Low-growing and early blooming, from each bud of the root stalk it sends up a stem with a leaf attached, and another stem with the flower. The easiest and surest identification is the orange-red juice which copiously flows from a broken root. This juice contains the active ingredient from which the plant's main medicinal properties are derived. In large doses the juice is strongly emetic and has narcotic effects. In small doses, it is a stimulant, tonic and expectorant.

To make an expectorant, Meyer suggests steaming a level teaspoonful of the root in a pint of boiling water for half an hour. After straining and cooling, the dose is one teaspoon 3 to 6 times daily.

Bloodroot has been used for catarrh, scarlatina, jaundice, dyspepsia, ringworm and affections of the respiratory tract. As an external remedy in cases of ringworm, fungoid tumors, the powdered root or a tincture of the root is said to act energetically. One writer suggests that in polypus of the nose the dried powdered root may be an effective snuff.

Yet, as Dr. Barton wrote some 160 years ago, "the most prominent effect of the medicine is to induce vomiting," even when taken in moderate doses. Perhaps as a warning, nature has provided sanguinaria with a bitter taste.

Saponaria officinalis

Caryophyllaceae

Soapwort, bouncing bet, bruisewort, Boston or chimney-pink, Fuller's herb, Londonpride, latherwort, dog cloves, world's wonder

Another plant not native to the States, soapwort was early introduced in the colonies, probably for its medicinal value. A member of the family of pinks, it is a roadside perennial and is often found in the cultivated parts of a garden. Growing about 15 inches tall, it has pink single (and sometimes double) flowers.

A decoction made from the root or leaves is used medicinally. The principal characteristic of such a decoction is a readily produced foam resembling soap bubbles. In the absence of other soap, when one is in the wild, the use of soapwort may prove to be important in the care of an injured person. This knowledge will be of special interest to Scouts and campers.

A recommended decoction is 2 ounces of root boiled in 1 pint of water to be used as an internal dose, or external application.

Taken internally, soapwort may be valuable in the treatment of venereal diseases, jaundice, gout, and rheumatism. While the thickened juice was given as a treatment of gonorrhea, such use preceded the discovery of modern and effective drugs such as penicillin.

Several writers on *Saponaria* note its effectiveness as a treatment for skin diseases. Mrs. Quelch says that "countless numbers of skin diseases, boils and abscesses and other form of blood troubles, have been cured, when the sufferers have taken an infusion of soapwort regularly over a considerable period. . . . When there is much skin irritation, a strong decoction of the root may be used for outward application with advantage."

Because of its soapy property, this plant was formerly used in making beer, to produce a good "head." Meyer notes that "as a substitute for soap in shampoo compounds, it is excellent."

Soapwort is a delightful, if sometimes weedy, plant for our gardens and one of considerable value medicinally.

LAURACEAE

Sassafras, ague tree, saxifrax, cinna-monwood, saloop

Probably no plant was ever more closely connected with American exploration than sassafras. G. B. Emerson in *Trees and Shrubs of Massachusetts* (1894) says, "this tree has the credit of having aided in the discovery of America, as it is said to have been its strong fragrance, smelt by Columbus, which encouraged him to persevere, and enabled him to convince his mutinous crew that land was near." Historical writers generally agree that the Spanish explorers discovered sassafras in Florida, that its uses were learned from the Indians by French Huguenot refugees living there, and that it was described by the botanist Nicholas Monardes of Seville in 1574. It was used in Germany by 1582 and within a few short years, it became the "universal specific," especially for treating syphilis.

The demand for sassafras was so great, that ships sailed to the New World in search of it. As early as 1603 the Englishman Gosnold, finding it growing on Martha's Vineyard, dug up the roots, and took them back to England, making Sassafras the first export from the States. In the pamphlet *Good News from Virginia*, written in 1612, another explorer, Whitaker, says of sassafras was "called by inhabitants Winauk, a kind of wood of most pleasant sweet smell and of rare virture in phisick for the cure of many diseases."

There are, indeed, many references in the literature of Indian medicinal practices to the use of sassafras. The following quotation from *Iroquois Herbalism* (W. N. Fenton, Smithsonian, 1942) sums up practices which were evidently common from Florida to Canada and as far into the west as the tree grows:

"Living at the northern extremity of its range, Iroquois uses of sassafras were typical of tribes farther south. Seneca warriors carried the powdered leaves, women employed it as a tonic after childbirth, it was used in cases of rheumatism, and as a diuretic: and drinking sassafras tea as a spring tonic has so long ago become a part of life on the American frontier that the Iroquois herbalists have regularly peddled the root bark on the doorsteps of their white neighbors."

By 1800, however, the well-educated Dr. Barton of Philadelphia had begun to question some of the more extravagant claims for sassafras. In his essay of 1804 he says, "the oil of Sassafras, when externally applied to the body in rheumatic . . . affections, is remarkable for its power of shifting the pain from its original seat; but not always to the advantage of the patient . . . I believe, however, that it is a medicine well adapted to many cases of rheumatism in its chronic stage; though even here it may prove injurious."

What about sassafras today, 400 years after its discovery? It was an acceptable drug in the *U.S. Pharmacopoeia* from 1840-1910, and is presently listed in the *National Formulary*. Youngken says that as it is used as an aromatic, as a diaphoretic in the preparation of sassafras tea, as an antiseptic in nasal and throat sprays, and as a repellent for ants. Other writers tell of a sassafras decoction which is soothing when applied to inflamed eyes. It is also used as a mild diuretic, and as a flavoring for less palatable medicines. Its early use as an antidote for venereal diseases is generally discounted.

In the North sassafras is a shrub, but in the South it often attains a height of 100 feet. The leaves vary; some have three lobes, others have only one lobe on the side: these are shaped like mittens. The yellowish green, fragrant flowers are borne in clusters which appear in early spring. Male and female flowers are borne on different trees. The fruit appearing on the female tree is dark blue, and pea-sized. All parts of the tree are aromatic.

The medicinal root bark is in reasonably constant demand from collectors. It is gathered in spring or autumn, the outer layer having been discarded. In the south eastern part of the country there is a small industry concerned with the distillation of sassafras oil—the ingredient used in the drug and flavoring trades.

In home medical practice, sassafras tea or infusion made from the dried root bark, cut or chopped into tiny pieces and used at the rate of a teaspoonful to a cup of water is a reputable stimulating, flavorful and warming tonic.

LABIATAE

Mad-dog skullcap, madweed, blue pimpernel, hood wort, hooded willow-herb, Quaker bonnet

A plant native to all but special climatic sections of the country, this perennial member of the mint family with toothed, lance-shaped leaves, grows from one to two feet high, and with blue or whitish flowers appearing in late summer. Like most mints, it is found in damp places and along roadsides and has a number of close relatives (including some European species), all generally with the same properties .

For medicinal purposes the entire plant is collected in early summer, well dried, powdered and stored tightly. For many years an "official" drug, it is still considered, by one writer, at least, to be "one of the finest nervines ever discovered." The druggist would rate it only as a bitter tonic and antispasmodic. Potter's *Cyclopedia* mentions it in treating hysteria, convulsions, hydrophobia, St. Vitus dance and rickets. From its use as a treatment of hydrophobia, came its name of "mad-dog" skullcap.

A recommended dose is one teaspoon of leaves to a cup of boiling water, drinking a half-cupful frequently.

Literature about this plant suggests that warm infusions have a sedative effect and help to alleviate symptoms of nervous and spasmodic conditions. Although no poisonous principle has been discovered in *Scutellaria*, an overdose could cause excitability, wakefulness and similar conditions as does the caffeine in tea and coffee. Use this plant drug in moderation.

Silphium perfoliatum

Compositae

Cup plant, ragged cup, rosin weed, Indian cup

So many of the plants mentioned are native of the East, with a range extending West, it is nice to have a plant whose main habitat is the Midwest, "extending under naturalization to New England." A member of the great composite or daisy family, *Silphium* is a tall (to 7 feet) perennial having a number of terminal yellow flowers in August. Usually found on rich soil and banks of stream, it may be further identified by the horizontal-growing fleshy root (rhizome) which, in medicine, is the part used.

Looking at its names we find "rosin-weed," derived from the resinous and gummy exudation of the stems and roots. For administration, a decoction of the dried powdered root at the rate of 4 ounces of the root to a quart of water is prepared and taken a little at a time.

Although it does not appear to have ever been an herbal medicine of great repute, *Silphium* has been listed for over a century as a tonic, diaphoretic and alterative. The gum which is collected from *Silphium* is rated to be a styptic and antispasmodic, which, when chewed, will sweeten the breath, it having, one writer says, a perfume like frankincense.

Although it bears the name of "Indian cup," no references have been found to its medicinal use by the Indians. "Cup" refers to the cuplike depression which is made by the attachment of the opposite leaves to the stem.

Silphium, then, is a good example of a plant with no great merit, but is one like hundreds of others, which might have been included in this work, has had some slight reputation as a curative plant.

COMPOSITAE

Sweet-scented goldenrod, blue mountain tea

When Linnaeus, the great stabilizer of botany looked for a name for this genus of the daisy family, he found from its reputation at the time, the word *Solidago*, meaning "I make whole." There was but one known European species of goldenrod, which was recommended as an aromatic and carminative. The type species does not grow in this country but is the only one that doesn't.

Some attempt has been made to suggest the appearance of *S. odora* in the sketch opposite, but it should be remembered that botanists consider *Solidago* one of the "most difficult genera." *Gray's Manual* describes 75 recognized species and suggests many hybrids inbetween.

The true fragrant goldenrod is one which grows with a somewhat inconspicuous head on a solitary stem, 18-36 inches high, with narrow leaves gently scented like anise. Each flower head has only 6-8 flowers and is likely to be overlooked when compared with many of the showier types, even though it grows throughout the States.

The leaves of this plant are harvested in summer, dried and prepared as a tea, using, as with real tea, a teaspoon of leaves to a cup of boiling water. This infusion acts as an aromatic stimulant, a carminative and diuretic and might well be a good addition to other less pleasant herbs to disguise disagreeable tastes.

Saunders in *Useful Wild Plants*, says that in California a species native to that state, *S. californica*, is prepared in lotion form for "sores and cuts on man or beast, finishing off with a sprinkling of the powdered leaves."

Perhaps Gerard's statement about another genus applies to goldenrod too. He said that physicians, "when they have found an approved medicine and perfect remedy near home against any disease, yet not content therewith they will seek a new farther off and by that means many times hurt more than they helpe. Thus much have I spoken to bring those new fangled fellows backe againe to esteeme better this admirable plant. . . ."

***Sphagnum* (all species)**

SPHAGNALES

Sphagnum moss, peat moss

Because some 300 species of this section of the moss family have been identified, and because many common species are equally valuable, it is only necessary to say that we are referring to the rather beautiful light green (to cream-white) mosses that are the cause and constituent of bogs around the world.

Great bogs of peat moss which grew thousands of years ago provide us with the dried peat moss so much in demand by gardeners, while the green-topped moss of last year's growth finds other uses in garden and greenhouse. This moss is popular because its leaves, when dry, can absorb 200 times their own weight in water.

This basic absorptive power of peat moss, then, should immediately suggest its value in medicine. Youngken notes, in the *Textbook of Pharmacognosy*:

"*Sphagnum* has proven a more excellent absorbent than cotton and as such has been employed in surgery in the form of pads. It is now used in the manufacture of some sanitary napkins. Its saturation time is but ⅓ to ½ that of absorbent cotton and it possesses the additional advantage of being antiseptic because of its iodine content, and less expensive."

This authoritative statement describes the use of sphagnum moss as emergency bandaging material. Such use would aid in the clotting of blood, and is possible that the high acid reaction of sphagnum (ca. pH 4.3) helps in the healing process.

It is probable that all the useful properties of *sphagnum* are still unknown. *Science* (Jan. 8, 1960) reports an investigation of the use of mosses as a possible source of antibiotics. The authors report positive results, and note that earlier investigations have shown that "certain products of Sphagnum . . . have inhibitory powers."

Why there has not been a wider inclusion of the uses of moss in the herbals is hard to understand, considering their medicinal value.

Woundwort, all-heal, hedge-nettle, dead-nettle, rough weed, marsh woundwort, clown-heal, panay, wood betony

A plant introduced from Europe which may be found growing in ditches, wet roadsides and waste places, wound-wort and all its subspecie relatives are notably rank smelling. It grows to 3 feet, with lanceolate, hairy leaves, and, like other members of the mint family, square stems. The flowers are reddish purple and grow in whorls.

Woundwort is an herb of ancient and exceptional reputation, but *no* verified value. It does not appear in the *U.S. Pharmacopoeia*, nor in the *National Formulary*, nor do the more modern writers make any claims for it.

This discussion of woundwort is included to show the continuation of ancient beliefs in the face of contrary evidence. There is a record that a physician to one of the Roman emperors wrote a treatise on its medicinal uses and this treatise, plus the disagreeable (and therefore, by implication) medicinal smell of the plant was enough to perpetuate a belief in its worth. Remarkable instances of healing, described by Gerard and others may have been the result of natural processes and the inherent healing capacity of people. But woundwort got the credit for healing, and its reputation was maintained and sustained. This sort of occurrence has also backed up so-called cancer cures, while actually natural retrogression had taken place. The example of this plant should serve to warn the reader that while many herbs have *known* medicinal values, others have only *reputed* ones.

To return to woundwort, the claims made for it are as an "antiseptic and antispasmodic" and as an "expectorant, emmenagogue, emetic and vulnerary." Gather and dry the tops in mid-summer and take an infusion—if you think it will do any good.

Euphorbiaceae

Queen's delight, queen's root, silver leaf, yaw root, nettle potato, cock-up-hat, marcony

This member of the spurge family is found south of Virginia and west of Texas, growing in the sandy soils of open woods. Spurges are plants having a milky juice which is often poisonous. A perennial herb, it has an angled stem, growing to 4 feet. The yellow flowers come on a terminal spike followed by a small encapsuled seed. The root is thick and grows to a length of about four inches. The oils in this root, when taken in large doses cause vomiting and purging.

A pharmacological authority says that it "is used *empirically* as an alterative," meaning that queen's delight is a "hand-me-down" medicine of doubtful value. On the other hand, another herbal authority calls it a "certain and valuable remedy." With this plant, as with so many others, the reader must make his own best judgment.

The root is used medicinally. Even when dried, it should be reasonably fresh. The properties are best extracted in alcohol, but may be taken as a simple infusion, consisting of "a teaspoon of the root to a cup of boiling water, taken a mouthful at a time." It is most often taken combined with other plant medicines, and is generally considered valuable in scrofular conditions.

Grieve's herbal says that chewing pieces of the fresh root daily has permanently and effectively cured bronchitis and laryngitis, and that "one drop on the tongue three or four times daily has been found successful for severe attacks" of croup.

Stillingia also functions as a sialagogue, expectorant, emetic, cathartic, and diaphoretic.

BORAGINACEAE

Comfrey, healing herb, knitback, ass-ear, knit or nip-bone, consolida

This European plant is now naturalized in the States in the Northeast. It is a close relative of heliotrope, mertensia, borage, and the anchusas, and, like these it prefers a moist habitat. Comfrey grows about 2 feet tall, its leaves are large and broad at the base and lancelike at the terminal, where the tail-shaped head of white to purple flowers grows. Its most distinguishing characteristic is the fine hair on the leaves, which cause itching.

The name *Symphytum*, given to the plant by Dioscorides, comes from a Greek word meaning "to unite," and for a long time the plant was reputed to aid in the knitting of bones. Such a reputation does not, however, represent the assessment of modern medicine which, rates comfrey, because of its high mucilaginous content, chiefly as a demulcent, a remedy in pulmonary ailments and a soothing ingredient in herbal preparations.

One reference notes that, as a strong decoction, it is recommended in cases of internal hemorrhage "whether from the lungs, stomach, bowels or free bleeding piles." A dose of one wineglassful taken every two hours until relief is obtained is suggested.

For more healing decoctions, the thick root is preferred, although ordinary infusions may be made of the leaves. Such an infusion is useful in treating chronic catarrh and nasal congestion.

A poultice made by beating the whole plant to a pulp, when applied to sprains, swellings and bruises, promotes the development of boils and abscesses. The most recent investigation credits this healing power to a substance in the plant called *allantoin*, and its use by some doctors confirms its reputation as a vulnerary.

The Swiss writer, Dr. Vogel, places great faith in comfrey and comments on the salve made from it for cosmetic purposes, saying, in fact, that "wrinkles," "crow's feet" or ageing skin damaged by cosmetics will be regenerated by its continuous use.

Symplocarpus foetidus

Skunk cabbage, meadow cabbage, devil's tobacco

If there is a true harbinger of spring, it is surely the bright green skunk cabbage, found in swampy areas. Long before other growth is noted, the pointed rockets unfold into the beautiful spathe (flower) of the skunk cabbage. This arum is found throughout eastern North America, and often is not half appreciated.

Our first knowledge of the value of skunk cabbage came from the Indians who called it "skota" and for whom it was a source of medicine and food. It found its way into our own pharmacopoeia under the name of "dracontium," and was listed as an emetic, narcotic and antispasmodic. An overdose is poisonous, but the fetid odor is apt to repel the unknowing and give warning of its content.

Herbal authorities consulted agreed on the medicinal properties mentioned, and listed its possible use in cases of asthma where the narcotic properties come into play.

Records indicate that the ground-up, powdered roots of skunk cabbage were used by the Indians as a styptic, and it appears they included it in other medicines to cover up unbearable tastes.

The part of the plant usually used is the root, although there is record of the seeds being medicinally potent. The dried root is cut, broken, and powdered just before use. Meyer suggests a dose of one teaspoon of root cut up and simmered in boiling water, "a mouthful of this being taken regularly during the day." It is suggested that mixing it with honey makes it more palatable and more useful.

One caution: Skunk cabbage is most often found growing alongside a similarly bright green plant, the swamp hellebore *Veratrum viride*, which is highly poisonous when taken internally. The distinctive features of this hellebore are the grossly ribbed leaves and the absence of the spathe. Watch yourself!

COMPOSITAE

Tansy, bitter buttons, ginger plant, hind heal, English cost, scented fern

Although there are several native species of *Tanacetum*, this particular plant is an introduction, now grown or escaped to the wild over much of the country. The pungent, fern-like foliage, topped by composite heads of button-like flowers is familiar to many. Although tansy *roots* have been used, medicinally an infusion or tincture made of the plant *tops* is of primary importance. Either such an infusion or the essential oil is used as a stomachic, an emmenagogue, and a stimulating aromatic bitter.

To expel worms in children, a recommended treatment is an infusion of 1 ounce of tansy to a pint of boiling water, one cupful given each night and morning to the subject who is meanwhile fasting. The seeds, likewise, are reputed to be anthelmintic.

Care should be taken against overdoses, which might cause dizziness, headache, nausea and general upset. It is said that many animals avoid tansy because of its bitter volatile oil. This repellent quality explains why tansy, rubbed on the body, is an insect repellent.

Tansy was once considered a culinary herb, some writers suggesting that the leaves, sprinkled on food was a substitute for pepper—this was important when pepper was an expensive rarity. It is still mentioned as a minor ingredient in salad herbs.

Tansy is one of those plants which although never achieving official recognition, has long been known in domestic medicine. As a "strewing herb" it was widely used in churches in Medieval times, and was one of the plants associated with the Virgin Mary. In England during the seventeenth century cakes containing tansy were eaten ceremoniously at Easter, hinting that eating tansy would be good for the stomach after the fasting of Lent. These cakes were also eaten at Passover as a remembrance of the bitter time the Jews had in Egypt. Such mixtures of religion, gastronomy and medicine make plant lore interesting.

COMPOSITAE

Dandelion, blowball, doon-head clock, yellow gowan, priest's crown

No other plant covered in this book has as much written about it as dandelion. Gardeners who regard this lovely flower as a weed should read of its many values, reputed and real. Reliably described by Theophrastus (ca. 300 B.C.), it is said to have been known and used by the Egyptians, but medically it was the Arabian physicians who in the tenth century prescribed its use and named it *Taraxacon*, later adapted by Linnaeus.

In America dandelion was for a hundred years an official drug and still is noted in the *National Formulary*. It may, as Youngken suggests, be chiefly "a simple bitter, and a mild laxative in catarrhal jaundice," but, comparing the recommendations of some twenty texts, one finds that it has been credited as a diuretic, laxative, hepatic, antiscorbutic, sialagogue, tonic, aperient, alterative and stomachic.

If the practices of generations of southern Europeans are to be believed, the eating of young dandelion green in the spring is certainly tonic. Its French name *Pissenlit* (English *piss-in-bed*) indicates a diuretic quality.

Although the milky juice of the plant contains the bitter principle, taraxicin, the plant tops, when young, may be used medicinally. Pharmacists extract a tincture from the dried root which roots should not be more than a year old.

An infusion of one teaspoon of root to a cup of water may be prepared and taken freely. Or a decoction may be made by boiling the solution for fifteen minutes. Several cupfuls of this stronger medicine should be taken each day and may be made more palatable with honey. However, Fernie, in *Herbal Simples*, recommends that dandelion tincture is the most useful dose, as the alcohol dissolves "resinous parts not soluble in water. From 10 to 15 drops of this tincture may be taken in water, three times a day."

The reader should regard this page of notes as only suggestive of the many values and interesting facts about this common but lovely plant.

PINACEAE

*Arborvitae, white cedar, tree of life,
thuja, American arborvitae*

This is an evergreen tree native to the
northeastern United States, west to Wisconsin, and in limestone mountain for-
mations down through the Carolinas. A
distinguishing characteristic is the flat-
ness of the leaf sprays, which, when
young, are gathered and dried for me-
dicinal purposes. Their pungent, balsamic odor, and their bitter taste
betrays the presence of various volatile oils which are the medicinal
agent.

In the drug trade cedar-leaf oil is distilled from the young foliage
of arborvitae. The oil, commercially steam-distilled, is used for the
perfuming of soft soap liniment and also as an insect repellent.

In domestic medicine, an infusion made of the tender leaves (1
ounce to a pint of boiling water), taken a tablespoon at a time, acts
as a uterine stimulant, emmenagogue, and diuretic. One writer notes
that stronger decoctions have been used in cases of intermittent fever,
rheumatism, dropsy, coughs, and scurvy, while, as a uterine stimulant, it "may produce abortion . . . by reflex action on the uterus
from severe gastrointestinal irritation."

For external application, a quantity of leaves boiled in lard makes
a salve which serves as a local application to relieve rheumatism. The
oil, which may be distilled at home, bears a good reputation as a
vermifuge.

It is worth noting that the essential oil is powerful, and a large
dose, while not poisonous, produces unpleasant effects. Just smelling
the crushed leaves for any continued period is unpleasant, if not
sickening. This should not, however, restrain us from using and ap-
preciating this northern evergreen which, in its many horticultural
variations, is such an attractive landscape tree.

Trifolium pratense

LEGUMINOSAE

Red clover, honeysuckle, meadow or purple clover, cleaver grass, sweet clover, bee-bread, trefoil

Go into any health-food store, or see the list of any purveyor of herbs, and you will find the dried tops of red clover prominently displayed. To those of us brought up in the country, this was our first taste of natural sugars, for the florets which make up the flower head produce a delightful mild "clover honey." Red clover is not native to the United States but has long been cultivated here as a forage crop, and may be found in almost every section.

The medical profession gives little attention to the medicinal properties of clover, yet the plant, for a long time, has been employed domestically as an antispasmodic, as an expectorant and as an ointment for local application to ulcers.

One may wonder how much of the reputed value of red clover is based on inherited beliefs in the magic power of certain plants. It is not uncommon to find otherwise practical people wearing dried four-leaved clover for good luck. In parts of England the leaves of red clover are worn as a charm against witches and evil, and in Ireland the leaves of another species of *Trifolium* is the lucky, sanctified, and emblematic shamrock. Surely a "good luck" plant *must*, by inference at least, have medicinal values.

The red clover does, in any case, have a demulcent action which is soothing to coughs. Specifically, for whooping cough, a syrup of red clover may be prepared by adding freshly gathered (or dried) clover flowers to a simple sugar syrup (an ounce of flowers to a pint of syrup). Boil and strain, and take several times a day. Skin eruptions of children may be cured by bathing the affected part in a strong infusion of clover, and, for adults, a poultice of the flower is recommended for ulcers. For such a poultice, bruise a quantity of flowers and steep them in a little water for three hours. The mixture is applied warm to the ulcer.

As an alterative and tonic, a simple infusion is recommended.

LILIACEAE

Bethroot, birthroot, Indian shamrock,
wake-robin, Indian balm, ground lily,
lamb's quarter, rattlesnake root, three-
leaved nightshade

This plant, native to America, is one
of a number of species all with more or
less the same properties. The plant is
distinguishable by the erect (to 15
inches) habit, its three leaves, and its
solitary tripartite flowers, varying from
white to maroon. It is found growing
in damp, shady woodlands, flowering in
May and June.

The part used medicinally is the thick
rhizome or root which is dried and powdered. Internal ingestion of the raw
leaves or roots is a dangerous and possibly poisonous procedure. But there is
considerable evidence of the medicinal
use of *Trillium* by the Indians and early
settlers. The names "beth" and "birth-
root" originated because it was used by the Indians as an aid to
parturition. The Shakers, too, grew and prepared the roots as a
medicine.

The unofficial claims for *Trillium* include its use as an astringent,
alterative, pectoral, and tonic. It is reported to be useful in cases of
internal bleeding, profuse menstruation, and pulmonary complaints,
and as a general astringent to the uterine organs.

Potter's Cyclopoedia recommends that *Trillium* be prepared as an
infusion "by pouring 1 pint of boiling water on a tablespoon of
powder." Then, it "should be drunk freely in most cases when it is
required as an astringent in doses of a wineglassful or more."

For external use as a poultice for skin diseases, the recommendation is to boil a handful of leaves in lard and apply to ulcers and
tumors.

Actually, the acrid constituents of *Trillium* are very powerful, and
Grieves says that "merely smelling of the freshly-exposed surface of
the red bethroots will check bleeding from the nose."

PINACEAE

*Hemlock, hemlock spruce, tanner's bark,
Canada pitch tree*

This fine and often majestic evergreen
is found in the northern tier of states
and along mountain ranges south to
Alabama. The soft foliage and rich dark
green contrasted with the warmth of the
red bark put this tree in quite a different
class from its cousins, the fir and spruce.
One of common names, tanner's bark, hints at the medicinal property of this tree; any extract of the bark is powerfully astringent.
The only detailed instructions for the use of the bark in medicine was
found in *Potter's Cyclopoedia.*

"Used as an astringent injection in female complaints, such as
leucorrhea, falling of the womb, etc., in the shape of an infusion of
2 ounces of crushed bark to 1 pint of water, or the fluid extract may
be diluted with four times its weight in water and so used."

The exudation of bark juice is made by boiling and skimming, to
produce Canada pitch or Canada balsam, used professionally by the
drug trade.

There is an additional reason to consider hemlock in this book.
Many persons have heard that Socrates was "given a cup of hemlock"
to drink and assumed it came from this tree. Actually, the hemlock
referred to comes from one genera of the parsley family (either
Conium or *Cicuta*) both highly poisonous. The hemlock tree is not
dangerous in any way, except that an overdose of any astringent
might be upsetting.

Of etymological interest the generic name *Tsuga* is a pure Japanese
word meaning larch. There are a number of other species of *Tsuga*
native to the Far East, and it is likely that this name was given to
the genus by the German who introduced many Eastern plants,
Philipp von Siebold.

Compositae

Coltsfoot, coughwort, Tussilago, foal's foot, horsehoof

An introduced, persistent perennial with creeping rootstocks, coltsfoot may be found escaped in northern states, growing in gravelly but moist soils. The generic name, *Tussilago*, means "cures a cough," and it has long been used for this purpose. One common name, "son before father," refers to the bright yellow dandelionlike flowers which appear in the spring before the foliage, and later come up with large leaves shaped like the hoofs of domestic animals.

The parts preferred medicinally are these large leaves, gathered in June and July and carefully dried. Analysis shows that they contain a large percentage of mucilage, plus tannin and various acids, all of which are soothing. A decoction made by steeping an ounce of leaves in a quart of water boiled down to 1 pint, when sweetened with honey, provides, as Mrs. Quelch says, "a medicine for the relief of coughs, or, indeed any irritation of the lungs and air passages (which) cannot be praised too highly." Youngken suggests that it is only used by the laity but its long reputation and obviously soothing ingredients recommend such use.

Some writings on coltsfoot note that in the Old Country, sufferers from asthma or bronchitis often found relief by smoking an herbal tobacco, of which coltsfoot was the principal ingredient. According to Mrs. Quelch, it was prepared with coltsfoot leaves and dried leaves of rosemary, thyme, lavender, camomile and betony, rubbed together until fine, made into cigarettes or smoked in a pipe.

Coltsfoot, a native of Europe and Asia, attained an early reputation in medicinal practice; in France, a picture of coltsfoot leaf painted on a door was the sign of the druggist. Listed in the *British Pharmacopoeia*, it is often recommended as an ingredient in cough syrups.

Ulmus rubra (syn. Ulmus fulva)

Ulmaceae

Slippery elm, red elm, moose elm, gray elm

Not found as far west, south, or north as the American elm, the range of the slippery elm nevertheless extends beyond the Mississippi valley, and from a medicinal standpoint, is possibly the most valuable tree mentioned in this book. It may be distinguished by its medium size; its reddish-brown bark; its dark green leaves—larger than those of the American elm, hairy beneath and rough above. Above all it is distinguished by its inner bark which, when separated, reveals a slippery mucilaginous content, a slight pinkish color, a fibrous texture, and a taste resembling the herb lovage.

Much of our knowledge about slippery elm came from the Indians, who appreciated its diuretic, emollient and demulcent qualities. Potter rates it "one of the most valuable articles in the botanic practice, and one which should be in every household." It is chiefly used in cases of diarrhea and other irritated conditions of the stomach and intestines, for coughs due to colds and for skin irritations. It is an important ingredient in suppositories. In its simplest form, slippery elm may be taken as an infusion of one teaspoon of powdered bark to a cup of water.

Actually, the most use can be made of the powdered bark, which although difficult to prepare at home, may easily be secured commercially. In this form slippery elm is a starch, with mucilaginous properties and nutritive values as well. In treatment of inflammation of the stomach, it may combine as medicine and food, given as a gruel flavored with honey and a little nutmeg. One writer says that it contains as much nutritive value as oatmeal, and that it is the basis of many patent foods for invalids and infants.

As an injection for diarrhea, combine equal parts of elm powder and skullcap to three parts of bayberry, infuse, add a little tincture of myrrh, and use lukewarm. As an enema for constipation, elm, warm milk, water, and olive oil is a helpful combination.

URTICACEAE

Nettle, stinging nettle, stingers

In 1672 nettle was mentioned in *New England Rarities*, the first book about the flora and fauna of America. It was already common at that time, having been introduced with imported cattle by the first English settlers. A native of Eurasia, nettle is commonly found in waste places around the United States, often associated with present or former habitations. It is a perennial plant with persistent, spreading roots and is recognized by anyone who has been stung by its needlelike hairs, each of which is a hypodermic needle loaded with virulent venom. The flower stalks grow from the leaf axils and are dioecious, the one-sexed flowers appearing either on the same stem or on a different plant.

The nettle has many valuable characteristics. In Scotland and in parts of Europe the nettle was treated much like flax, the fibers making a cloth similar to linen. In World War I, with cotton imports cut off, the Germans utilized nettles for weaving.

The young shoots and leaves provide a good spring green, Walter Beebe Wilder says in *Bounty of the Wayside:*

"In the spring we often had the young leaves (picked with gloves on) cooked in the manner of spinach in just their own wash water and served with salt, pepper, a little vinegar or lemon juice."

It is noticeable that the poisonous property of the hair disappears with either cooking or drying. In fact, using nettle water provides what Mrs. Quelch calls a wash for "clearing the complexion of all blemishes, and giving added brightness to the eyes."

A number of references to nettles refer to an infusion of the leaves as a treatment for rheumatism. On the method of "counter-irritation," there are records of using bundles of fresh nettles as whips to beat rheumatism sufferers on the affected part, the pain of the nettles (and possibly the acid injections) covering up, if not curing the rheumatism. The seeds also, have been given as an infusion for coughs and shortness of breath, and for many years they were used to treat consumption.

Valeriana officinalis

VALERIANACEAE

Valerian, garden-heliotrope, phu, set-wall, all-heal, amatilla, nard, cat's love

Like many plants which have come to America as medicinal herbs or garden flowers, valerian brought its history with it by way of its names. There are several American native species of valerian, all having somewhat the same constituents, but in the drug trade the rhizomes of *V. officinalis* are preferred. The plant grows, in good soil with plenty of moisture, and may be found growing wild in our Northern states. It is a rather coarse and tall-growing (to 5 feet) perennial with fragrant, pinkish-white flowers on erect stems, and opposite, pinnate leaves. As indicated by its names, valerian is a cultivated flower.

The pharmacist knows it as a calmative for nervousness and hysteria, and as a carminative. He prepares his prescriptions from the dried roots which contain volatile oils and several alkaloids. Because of the effect of valerian on the nervous system, it should be used cautiously. An excessive dose may cause headaches, illusions, giddiness, and spasmodic movements. When properly used, it has an antispasmodic effect which gave it a considerable reputation as a treatment for epilepsy. *Potter's Cyclopedia* says that it "allays pain and promotes sleep. Is strongly nervine without any narcotic effects. . . . The infusion of 1 ounce to 1 pint of boiling water is taken in wineglassful doses," referring to an infusion of the dried root (rhizome).

The name "all-heal" indicates the great store set by valerian in medieval times; the name "phu" was one given by the physician Galen as a reaction to the strong scent of the roots or crushed plant. The scent in some Asian species was strong *and* pleasant; and *spikenard*, which was the biblical name of valerian, was called a perfume "brought from the East." To some people the smell is not objectionable, and the roots in earlier times were used to perfume linen.

Interestingly, valerian acts upon cats much as catnip, but unlike catnip it affects rats in the same way. It is said that the secret of the Pied Piper of Hamelin was the roots of valerian in his pocket.

Scrophulariaceae

*Common mullein, flannel-plant, velvet or
mullein dock, candlewick, Aaron's rod,
lungwort*

At least five species of *Verbascum*
grow wild in the United States, all naturalized from Europe. *V. Thapsus* is
certainly one of the nicest of our wild
flowers. It is beautiful in winter with its
rosette of gray-white woolly leaves,
noble in summer with its spike (to 7
feet) of yellow flowers, and a boon to
flower arrangers in dried bouquets.

But these qualities are outside the
realm of medicine. We find that for
many centuries mullein has served as a
demulcent and emollient, as it contains
mucilage and a few other valuable constituents. Most useful are the
leaves, which are dried and reduced to powder. The flowers, when
fully opened, are also collected and dried, and are equally effective
in the making of soothing infusions.

In the old days, before tuberculosis was better controlled, mullein was often used to relieve coughs and ease expectoration. It is
recommended that a milk infusion be made with an ounce of dried
leaves to a pint of milk, boiled for 10 minutes, strained and given
warm, with honey or sugar added to make it palatable and more
effective. A simple water infusion can be made in a similar manner.

In addition, the dried leaves can be smoked in a pipe or cigarettes
to ease throat congestion. Wyman and Harris say that the Navajos
called mullein "big tobacco." They mixed it with real tobacco, and
smoked it to alleviate mild mental disturbances such as thinking or
talking bad or running away.

Such use is for men, but there are several suggestions for the
ladies. A correspondent writes:

"In Wisconsin in the early part of the century, girls, before going
to dances, would rub their cheeks with mullein leaves to make them
rosy. No rouge in those days for "proper girls." Also, in ancient
Rome and later in Germany, an infusion of the flowers was used to
provide for the hair golden or blond color."

Verbena officinalis

Blue vervain, wild hyssop, herb of grace, herba veneris, simpler's joy

V. officinalis is from Europe and is the more renowned species of *Verbena*. It is found as an introduced plant in the States, while the similar *V. hastata* is indigenous to this country. These species of *Verbena* are rather tall, erect plants with terminal heads of small purplish-blue flowers. The constituent which brings *Verbena* into the medical field is a bitter glucoside and tannin, a simple infusion (2 teaspoons to 1 pint) being employed as a diaphoretic, tonic, and expectorant. There are, in herbal literature, no *strong* claims made for its efficacy. Some of the above species may be found in waste places over the country and should be noted if not used.

An exploration of the story of vervain leads us down some ancient avenues and provides an explanation for belief in the efficacy of the plant in herbal medicine. This plant was first used by the Romans. They gave us the name "verbena," which to them meant any one of a number of plants used in sacrifices, purgation and supplications. Finally the name was attached to one particular plant, and the virtues ascribed to *Verbena* by the Romans were passed along through the centuries, until, in the Middle Ages, it was said to have been a plant which, growing on the Mount of Calvary, staunched the wounds of the Saviour. The transferral of virtues from pagan to Christian (it has happened in our Christmas celebrations) was not unusual, and verbena early became one of the holy herbs associated with St. John.

Pliny said, "if the dining chamber be sprinkled in water in which the herb Verbena has been steeped, the guests will be merrier." Such a story lead to a belief in its efficacy as a cure against the plague, and as a remedy for almost anything. It even had supposed supernatural powers. Several Welsh names have meanings such as "devil's hate" and "enchantment herb." An ancient couplet goes

Vervain and Dill
Hinder witches from their will.

CAPRIFOLIACEAE

*Highbush cranberry, cramp bark, guel-
der rose, snowball tree, squaw bush*

This *Viburnum* is a native of wet
places in the northern United States. Its
European species is often confused with
what *Gray's Manual* classifies as *V. trilobum.* The differences are botanical
ones, not readily noticed. It is a shrub
or small tree growing to 12 feet, with
three-lobed leaves, cream-white flowers
with a disagreeable odor, and clusters of
shiny red berries which appear in August. Birds like these berries, and, although bitter, they are used to make
sauce. Their appearance gave them the name "cranberry," although
they are in no way related to that plant.

For medicinal purposes, the thin bark of the shrub is dried and
later used in a tincture, or in a decoction which is made with ½
ounce bark to a pint of water, a tablespoonful taken as required.
Once an official drug, it was recommended, and is still well regarded,
as an antispasmodic and uterine sedative. As the name implies, it is
effective in cases of cramps, convulsions, and spasms. It has been
employed to treat nervous complaints, debility and, in connection
with other drugs, "palpitation, heart disease, and rheumatism," says
Grieve's Herbal.

In Japan, where the true *V. Opulus* grows wild in cold regions, the
white, fine-grained, flexible wood of the branches is used mostly for
toothbrushes.

Fernald and Kinsey, in their book on edible plants of the United
States, point out that the fruit of the true native form *(V. trilobum)*
is much less bitter than the introduced species, and that jelly made
from fresh, ripe berries has a delicious flavor and beautiful color.
With its more bitter taste than the true cranberry, it is an excellent
accompaniment to meat dishes.

It is suitable for planting in a large shrub border and especially
for attracting birds.

Viburnum prunifolium

CAPRIFOLIACEAE

Black haw, sweet haw, stag bush, sheep-berry, cramp bark, American sloe

The scientific name *Viburnum pruni-folium* indicates that the shape of the small fruits are plum-shaped. The shrub may be found growing from New England south to Florida and west to Texas in moist and open woods. It grows to 15 feet in height, has toothed oval leaves, and white flowers in early spring.

The part used in medicine is the bark of the root or stem. For some years this bark appeared in the *U.S. Pharmacopoeia*, having, according to Youngken, a definite function as a uterine sedative in threatened abortion. He also notes that the bark of several other species of *Viburnum* may be and have been substituted for this bark, as they have similar but less potent properties. He mentions *V. nudum*, *V. cassinoides* and *V. lentago*, and says that the bark of a maple, *Acer spicatum* may also be used.

To prevent possible miscarriage, black haw should be given four or five weeks before the expected event. Several writers give a drinkable infusion as one ounce of powdered dried root bark to a pint of boiling water, taken in doses of a tablespoonful several times daily. Potter says that "it checks pain and bleeding, and is an excellent remedy for dysmenorrhea and after pains of childbirth."

VIOLACEAE

Violet

Attention was originally focused on the violet as a cancer cure because of several reported cases. Most notable of these was the case of General Catharine Booth of the Salvation Army, who, suffering from advanced cancer, is said to have found alleviation of pain with violet foliage. In 1586 Vigo reported that violets had actually cured a victim of cancer. Modern medicine places no credence on those accounts.

Incorrect use should not discredit the value of violets as a medicine. Going back to the Romans, Pliny recommended that a garland of violets be placed on the head to cure headache or hang-over, while somewhat later Dioscorides tells of its value for stomach ailments and other complaints. Exploring the medical lore of France, India, Chile, and Mexico, we find recommendations for violets as an emetic or laxative. Hahnemann, the father of homeopathic medicine, recommends *Viola tricolor*, pansy, as a treatment for skin conditions and as a laxative for children.

Violets are variable in leaf shapes and the tendency for natural hybridizing may make identification difficult.

Of the 20 species of the genus, *Viola*, all are listed as emetic, the activating principle found in the roots. More than half are listed as laxative, and one assumes that this is true of all. The species *V. pedata*, bird's foot violet, is mentioned as a nutrient, expectorant, and demulcent, while *V. blanda, V. canadensis* and *V. obliqua* are mentioned as alteratives.

The characteristics indicated seem to be derived from an acrid principle found in the violet which has been named "violin" or "violine." Fernie, a leading writer, indicates that because of this acrid quality the extracted juice of violets can treat boils, impetigo, ulcers, and other eruptions. Several authors mention the function of violets as a "vulnerary" or as helpful in "psoriasis," "cutaneous eruptions," and "skin troubles." In view of these recommendations, violets might be tried if other cures fail.

Violets have been mentioned as a cure for "consumption"; for this syrup of violets was recommended. Some years ago (in England, at least), this was an important part of the pharmacists' stock, and there grew up quite an industry near Stratford-on-Avon for the growing of violets to be converted into syrup. A recipe advises "one pound of flowers of the freshly picked sweet violet stirred into 2½ pints of boiling water. This is to be left in a glass jar for infusion for 24 hours, the resulting liquid to be poured off and strained through muslin. Then add double the weight of sugar and make into syrup."

This syrup can be used as a coloring agent for candy or as a laxative which, because of its mildness, can be given to children at the rate of ½ to 1 teaspoon of the syrup to equal parts of oil of almonds.

Another writer recommends leaves (and flowers) of *V. papilionacea* as an alterative and expectorant. One teaspoon of dried leaves infused in 1 cup of boiling water, taken a teaspoon at a time 3 times daily.

VITACEAE

V. labrusca—*Foxgrape, the parent of Concord and of Moore's early*

aestivalis—*Summer or pidgeon grape*

riparia—*Frost grape*

vulpina—*Fox grape*

rotundifolia—*Muscadine or scuppernong*

vinifera—*European grape (not a native form but will grow in siutable American climatic zones)*

The medicinal value of grapes comes from their antiscorbutic, refrigerant, and nutritive properties, especially the latter. Current advertising is stressing the quick action of the juice of the grape in producing "sugar-energy," and all authorities attest to this. The leaves seem also to have some value as an astringent. Among people from the Near East, grape leaves are rated valuable as a wrapping for meat balls. The release of chemicals in the foliage helps to tenderize the meat as well as to import desirable flavor.

Of grapes, it was the Foxgrape, found in abundance all along the coast, which caused the Viking explorers to name the country Vinland, and (as well)to cause Gosnold, the Englishman, to name an island (in 1603), Martha's Vineyard. In short, it was grapes which helped to establish this *terra incognita* as a fruitful land.

In Europe, when spas were popular, some health centers along the Rhine specialized in the grape-cure. Persons were placed on a diet of grapes only, with excellent results reported. The juices worked on the kidneys and bowels. Evidence indicates grapes are a healthful food and should be used for the preservation, if not the restoration, of health.

Fernie, a reputable English herbalist, says that "the sap of the vine, named *lachryma*, "a tear," is an excellent application to weak eyes and for specks in the cornea. The juice of the unripe fruit, which is "verjuice," was much esteemed by the ancients and is still in good repute for applying to bruises and sprains."

CHAPTER VI

SEVENTY-SEVEN LESS WELL KNOWN SPECIES

Your sore, I know not what, be not foreslow
To cure with herbs, which, where, I do not know;
Place them, well pounc't, I know not how, and then
You shall be perfect whole, I know not when.

Anon

ESCRIBING all the wild plants of the country which have been used medicinally would be impossible in one book for their number is legion. The original 175 was selected because the plant had "official" recognition or widespread use. The following chapter presents a further but still selective list of plants of the Eastern United States which are less commonly used. Space permits the listing of only the scientific name, a few of the common names, and a brief mention of the reputed values.

Alnus crispa

Green alder, mountain alder
Drinks made from it have been used for eruptive skin diseases, cuts, sores, and ulcers.

Anaphalis margaritacea

Everlasting, pearly everlasting, ladies' tobacco, poverty-weed, silver button

Leaves, plant, and fresh juice are used as astringent, expectorant, diaphoretic, and to relieve ulceration of the mouth. Used as

226

a fomentation for ulcers and swellings, is aphrodisiac, aromatic, antiseptic, and vulnerary.

Antennaria margaritacea

Everlasting cottonweed, cudweed

Flowers are said to be anodyne, pectoral, astringent, and vermifuge.

Anthemis Cotula

Mayweed, dog-fennel, stinking chamomile, poison daisy, dilly

Active tonic, sudorific, stimulant, anodyne, and emetic.

Aralia spinosa

Devil's walking stick, prickly ash, Hercules club

The fresh bark of the root is emetic and cathartic when given in an infusion. The oil of the seed is used in earache, deafness.

Argemone mexicana

Mexican poppy, prickly poppy, thorn apple

The plant is said to be emetic, purgative, narcotic, milky acid juice has been used for cutaneous diseases.

Armoracia lapathifolia

Horse-radish

Grated with sugar and used for hoarseness; also as a warm stimulant.

Arnica acaulis

Leopard's bane

Stimulant, emetic, cathartic.

Artemisia vulgaris

Sailor's tobacco, common mugwort, motherwort

Leaves are used in nervous and spasmodic affections. Decoction is used for stomach ache, headache, diarrhea, rheumatism, fever, bronchitis, sore eyes, poison oak, and to heal wounds.

Asclepias amplexicaulis

Clasping milkweed, rabbit's milk
Kills warts.

Asparagus officinalis

Asparagus
Young shoots are diuretic and gently laxative.

Baptisia tinctoria

Wild indigo, indigo-broom, horsefly weed, dyer's baptisia
The plant is astringent, antiseptic, febrifuge, emetic, diaphoretic, purgative.

Bidens bipinnata

Spanish needles, beggar's ticks, cuckolds
Whole plant is expectorant, pectoral, and an emmenagogue.

Bignonia capreolata

Crossvine, trumpet flower
The root has substituted for sarsaparilla in patent medicines. The decoction has been used as a detergent, alterative, aperient, diuretic.

Cacalia atriplicifolia

Wild caraway, pale Indian plantain
Is used as an emollient, like mallow.

Calendula officinalis

Garden marigold, calendula
The tincture is used for cuts, bruises, sprains, wounds.

Caltha palustris

Marsh marigold, cowslips, mare-blobs, palsywort

A decoction of the herb has been used for dropsy and in urinary affections. Said to be expectorant, pectoral (good for diseases of chest and lungs) and useful in cough syrups. Poisonous, but the poison may be removed by boiling.

Cassia occidentalis

Styptic weed, Florida coffee

A diuretic and vermifuge in a decoction, applied to itch, irritation, and inflammation of the rectum.

Celastrus scandens

False bittersweet, fever twig, climbing staff tree

The bark of the root possesses emetic, diaphoretic, narcotic, stimulant properties; reportedly useful in venereal diseases.

Cephalanthus occidentalis

Button-bush, honey balls, mountain globeflower

Tincture of the fresh bark used for intermittent and remittent fevers. The root is boiled and mixed with honey to make a syrup which is effective in lung diseases.

Chamaecyparis thyoides

Southern white cedar

The leaves are a stimulant, an aromatic, a diaphoretic, and stomachic.

Chelidonium majus

Celandine, tetterwort, wart-weed

An acrid purgative, with diuretic, expectorant and diaphoretic properties. Used as an irritant to treat warts and hepatic eruptions.

Chenopodium Botrys

Ambrose, feather geranium, hidin-heal

Expectorant. Used in catarrh and asthma, for coughs, as an emmenagogue, solvent, and carminative.

Chrysanthemum Leucanthemum

Field daisy, ox-eye daisy

To restore color after jaundice, for wounds, asthma, consumption, tinea, salt rheum, cutaneous eruptions, irritations, and as an insect powder.

Cirsium arvense

Canada thistle, blessed thistle

Plant is boiled with milk and used for dysentery; an emetic, tonic, diaphoretic and astringent.

Collinsonia canadensis

Horse balm, healall, ox balm

The whole plant is tonic, astringent, diaphoretic, and diuretic.

Convolvulus arvensis

Field bindweed

The root is a purgative, hydragogue cathartic, and diuretic.

Cornus Amomum

Silky cornus, kinnikinnik, swamp dogwood, red osier

It is valuable in dyspepsia, diarrhea, and to check vomiting in pregnancy.

Cynoglossum officinale

Hound's tongue, gypsy-flower, Canadian burr, tory weed

Used in hemorrhages, dysentery, as a demulcent and sedative in coughs, externally in burns, ulcers,

Diervilla Lonicera

Bush honeysuckle

The leaves are used as a gargle in catarrhal angina. Diuretic and astringent.

Epigaea repens

Trailing arbutus, mayflower

Remedy in lithic acid gravel and all diseases of the urinary organs. The tincture is used.

Eryngium aquaticum

Button snakeroot, rattlesnake weed, fever weed

The Indians used this drug as an emmenagogue and, in the form of a drink, as an emetic at festivals as a part of their rituals.

Erythronium americanum

Yellow adder's tongue, dog's tooth violet, yellow snake root, adder leaf, deer's tongue

The herb is emetic, emollient, and was used by the Indians for breast complaints.

Eupatorium aromaticum

Wild horehound, white snakeroot

The root is diaphoretic, antispasmodic, expectorant, aromatic, diuretic.

Eupatorium hyssopifolium

Justice weed, hyssop-leaved boneset

The entire plant is antivenomous and may be used as a remedy for bites of reptiles and insects by bruising and applying to the wound.

Euphorbia Ipecacuanhae

American ipecac, ipecac spurge

The Indians used the roots as an emetic and as a hydragogue. May be dangerous.

Fagus grandifolia

Beech, American beech

A decoction of the leaves is used for burns, scalds, and frostbite.

Ficus Carica

Common fig

The fruit is used as a nutrient, demulcent, laxative, and emollient.

Geum virginianum

Virginia avens, chocolate root, cure-all, throatroot

It is said to be a tonic, powerful astringent, styptic, febrifuge, stomachic.

Gillenia trifoliata

Indian physic, Bowman's root, false ipecac

The bark of the root is a mild and efficient emetic.

Helenium autumnale

Sneezeweed, false sunflower

Herb is tonic, diaphoretic, and febrifuge.

Hieracium venosum

Hawk-weed, robin's plantain

Entire herb is tonic, mucilaginous, and astringent.

Hypericum punctatum

Flux weed, spotted St. John's wort

An astringent in diarrhea and dysentery.

Illicium floridanum

Starry anise, anise tree, star anise

A tonic, stimulant, and diaphoretic. The bark and fruit are spicy, aromatic, and a bitter tonic.

Lamium album

White dead nettle, white archangel

A tincture of the leaves and flowers has been used upon the female generative organs to cause inflammatory excitement.

Lemna minor

Duck's meat, duckweed, lesser duckweed

The entire plant is demulcent and is used in poultices.

Liatris odoratissima

Vanilla leaf, deer tongue

Leaves are tonic, stimulant, aromatic, and diaphoretic.

Liatris spicata

Gay feather, button snakeroot, backache root, blazing star

Root is diuretic, stimulant, diaphoretic and an emmenagogue.

Linum usitatissimum

Flaxseed, flax, linseed

In the form of a poultice, it has been used for burns, boils, carbuncles, and old sores. The seed is laxative, emollient, demulcent, and is the source of linseed oil.

Lonicera Caprifolium

Honeysuckle, American woodbine

Used in asthma and lung troubles. Will relieve bee sting.

Lycopus virginicus

Bugle weed, gypsy-weed, water bugle

Sedative and astringent.

Magnolia macrophylla

Great-leaved magnolia, umbrella tree, great magnolia, or cucumber tree

The bark acts as a gentle stimulant, aromatic, tonic, diaphoretic, and stomachic.

Melilotus alba

Sweet white clover, sweet melilot, sweet lucerne

Mild expectorant, diuretic, emollient. Keeps moths out of clothing.

Monotropa uniflora

Indian pipe, convulsion weed, ghost flower, beech drops

The root is tonic, sedative, nervine, and antispasmodic. It is ophthalmic for sore eyes. The tincture of the whole fresh plant has been used.

Nicotiana Tabacum

Tobacco, Virginia tobacco

The leaf is poisonous due to the nicotine content. It is a habit forming narcotic.

Orobanche uniflora

Beech drops, cancer root, clap-wort

Used for bowel upsets, cancerous ulcerations, as a powerful astringent, in canker of the throat, syphilis, gonorrhea, dysentery, and hepatic affections.

Ostrya Virginiana

Iron weed, hop hornbeam

The bark is a bitter tonic, alterative, and antiperiodic.

Oxydendrum arboreum

Sour wood, lily-of-the-valley tree

The leaves have a pleasant acid taste and, in the form of a decoction, are used to allay thirst; is a refrigerant drink in fevers.

Polygonum aviculare

Knot grass, goose grass, bindweed, beggarweed

A decoction of the plant mixed with oak bark used as a substitute for quinine.

Portulaca oleracea

Purslance, purslane

Used widely in medicine as a diuretic, antispasmodic, esculent, vermifuge, refrigerant, antiseptic, and aperient.

Prenanthes alba

Rattlesnake root, gall-of-the-earth, white lettuce

Root of this perennial leafy plant is a bitter tonic; used for dysentery. Reputed antidote for snake and insect bites.

Quercus velutina

Black oak, quercitron

The plant is used as an astringent and corroborant.

Ribes triste

Red currant

The fruit is acidulous, diuretic, refrigerant, and febrifuge.

Rudbeckia laciniata

Cone disk, cone flower, golden glow

The herb is diuretic, tonic, and balsamic.

Scrophularia marilandica

Figwort, healall, scrofula plant, pile wort

The entire herb is considered tonic, diuretic, diaphoretic, discutient, and anthelmintic.

Silene stellata

Starry campion

Has cordial, nervine, and vermifuge properties. Was used by the Indians in sexual disorders.

Silene virginica

Fire pink, catchfly, Indian pink

The root has anthelmintic properties.

Smilax Bona-nox

Bristly smilax, bristly greenbrier

The root is edible and is reputed to have alterative and depurient properties.

Solanum Dulcamara

Bittersweet, nightshade, poison bitter sweet

Bittersweet has alterative, narcotic, diuretic, and diaphoretic properties. The fruit is poisonous.

Sonchus oleraceus

Low thistle, milk thistle, snow thistle, sow thistle

The juice is bitter and diuretic as well as a powerful hydragogue cathartic.

Stellaria media

Common chickweed, stitchwort

The plant is refrigerant, demulcent, mucilaginous, discutient, and alterative.

Swertia caroliniensis

American colombo, Indian lettuce, meadow pride

Powerful, bitter, lacks aroma, an emetic, and a cathartic. The root is a tonic, febrifuge, and antiseptic. The powdered plant is used for ulcers.

Veronicastrum virginicum

Culver's root, physic root, cubeno physic

The rhizomes and roots of this perennial herb are cathartic and a cholagogue.

Viburnum alnifolium

Hobble-bush, tangle legs

The bark is antiperiodic and diuretic.

Viburnum dentatum

Arrowwood, mealy-tree

The bark is diuretic and detergent.

Xanthium spinosum

Clot-bur, bur-weed

Diuretic, sialagogue, diaphoretic, and antiperiodic.

Yucca filamentosa

Adam's needle, bear grass, Spanish bayonets

The tincture of the root said to be good for rheumatism and gonorrhea.

CHAPTER VII

MEDICINES IN HOUSE AND GARDEN

What have you in your house or in its surroundings that can give you swift, sure and reliable help? Your medicine chest is big or small, according to your domestic circumstances. It may stretch from the kitchen to the store-room, from the cellar to the loft. Should you have a garden, you will find many valuable things there, too. If you live out in the country, then field, wood, and common offer you more abundant help.

Dr. H. C. Vogel
in *The Nature Doctor*, Switzerland, 1959

T IS the purpose of this of this book to bring to the attention of the reader the many *wild* medicinal plants which are generally found in America. But not only wild plants have curative values. Without going beyond the author's self-imposed limits, it seems appropriate to take at least a quick look at the medicinal values of many "medicines" which are usually within arms-reach of the American housewife, cures which are ready at hand in the garden or on the pantry shelf. Surely many of these recommendations are known to people who were brought up in the country, or who possess the heritage of one or another of the European cultures.

What, for instance, in the way of simple medicines can one find in the kitchen garden or the home orchard?

Here are a few suggestions.

238

Apples

See *Pyrus Malus*.

Asparagus

Almost everyone who likes to eat asparagus is aware that this vegetable is a powerful diuretic, thus valuable medicinally.

Black currants

Regretfully the law, in all sections where the white pine grows, prohibits the growing of the black currant. But, when it can be obtained, the juice, mixed with honey, is possibly the finest of all medicines for alleviation of throat irritations, from whatever cause. Ben Harris, *Kitchen Medicines* provides an excellent recipe for a throat tablet. Those who can not make their own are directed to the use of the English-made Allenburys Pastilles.

Carrots

Nutritionists are well aware that the carotin principle found in carrots was used during the war to help aviators overcome night blindness. Thus one can consider this vegetable a useful medicine.

Cucumbers

There are a number of suggestions as to the value of cucumbers. Among them is its use in hand lotion made by combining expressed cucumber juice with Irish moss.

Figs

A good food, an excellent laxative.

Grapes

There is a considerable body of literature on the value of grapes medicinally, and one hears every now and then of *grape cures*, in which the patients go on a diet of grapes almost exclusively. When grapes are taken in quantity, they act freely on the kidneys, thus promoting the expulsion of poisons from the system.

Horseradish

This digestant not only peps up a meal, but is useful medicinally. It has been recommended for dropsy.

Lemon

Hot lemonade is noted as a diaphoretic, thus is good to take on going to bed with a cold. Such a drink also has in addition to the fever-inducing quality, a soporific effect. Some years ago, a German doctor claimed that a glass of lemon juice taken regularly would prolong life. And, not too many years ago, similar claims for the tonic properties of fresh cold lemon juice were made in America. How many presently pursue this regimen one does not know.

Onion and Garlic

Although raw garlic was and is often recommended in cardiac and hypertensive conditions, the use of such a plant medicine as Rauwolfia has made the unpopular garlic treatment obsolete.

Many claims are made for onions as well as garlic—the genus *Allium* in the diet is quite likely to be a preventative of disease if not a cure.

Many other statements are made about garlic, including these:

It is an antibiotic, says Mrs. Beatrice Trum Hunter, author of the excellent *Natural Foods Cookbook*.

Dr. Vogel in *The Nature Doctor* says that half a clove of garlic, placed between the gums, will often take away toothache and that a poultice of garlic will relieve the pains of ear or headache.

For those who violently object to the odor of garlic, it is good to know that the properties have now been confined to inoffensive "Garlic perles."

Papaya

Readers who live in Florida are fortunate in that they can secure fresh papaya fruit, to eat as a digestant or to enjoy as a dessert. Natives of the American tropics long ago learned to wrap meat in papaya leaves, for the papaya contains enzymes which tenderize the meat. Papaya juice and extracts in powder form are sold as meat tenderizers quite generally.

Pears

The delight of eating fresh pears from the garden should not blind the one to the fact that they are laxative.

Potato

Exploring the literature of natural medicines, one finds many claims made for the value of potatoes. One of the most plausible is that raw potato juice cures gastritis, and boiled potato (mixed with a little milk) is an emergency poultice.

It is interesting to note that the raw potato juice is rich in protein, and devoid of starch.

Quince

If your garden is provided with a quince tree, you should know that, in addition to the fruit which is so excellent for jelly or sauce, a quantity of quince seed, simmered in water, will make a healing mouth wash or a soothing application to a burn.

For the ladies in need of a "setting lotion" for their hair, a decoction of the same seeds is as efficacious as any commercial preparation. To prepare, put a tablespoon of quince seeds in a pan with a half pint of water and simmer until the mixture is thick. Strain and add a little Eau de Cologne, bottle, and keep for use. A drop or two on the hair brush will do the trick.

Rhubarb

Anyone, like the author, who has eaten and relished the first "mess" of rhubarb from the garden in the spring knows that, even more than prunes, it is a safe and effective laxative.

Sage

Sage, fresh or dried, is a valuable carminative.

Spinach

Most children (and many adults) look on spinach as a medicine rather than a desirable food. Spinach does contain iron and other minerals all medicinally valuable.

To utilize the iron in spinach, it is recommended that it be eaten with some form of calcium—cottage cheese or a similar dairy product.

*   *   *

Now we go to the kitchen shelves to find the following useful articles:

Almonds

Almonds, by themselves, used in a meal, or otherwise processed, are reputed to be an excellent and safe food for diabetics. The extracted oil in almonds is a base in cosmetics.

Arrowroot

Arrowroot flour, found in many kitchens for baking cookies, should be known for its high digestability by those with severe stomach disorders.

Barley

Patients in a hospital know that often barley tablets or barley water is a "first food." It is equally well known in feeding infants; soothes internal inflammations, is valuable in kidney and bladder disorders. Mixed with lemon, barley water is an excellent drink for those suffering from bronchitis, asthma, and sore throat.

Bread

Bread has often been used with hot milk as a poultice for mild burns. Druggists use it for extending drugs in making certain pills, and, as burned toast (charcoal), is a dentifrice.

Cayenne—Chili powder—Capsicum

Whatever it is called, this product of the true hot pepper of American origin is quite different from the peppercorns of the pepper-grinder. In small quantities valuable as a stomachic, the hot peppers are full of vitamins of many kinds. The seeming monotony of the Mexican diet (corn, beans and peppers) is countered by the healthful values of a great variety of peppers, each with its own vitamin-loaded characteristic.

Charcoal

Charcoal from the embers of the fireplace has definite values in sweetening the breath and clearing up an unhappy stomach. The ability of charcoal to absorb gases has caused it to be used in gas-masks and many other commercial products. Its value medicinally is advertised in the promotion of charcoal chewing gum.

Recently charcoal has been suspected as a carcinogenic factor in the alimentary tract and thus its habitual use is unwise.

Cloves

The home medicine chest often includes oil of cloves as an immediate aid to toothache. A culinary clove may be held against the tooth to provide relief. Cloves steeped as an infusion act as an excellent carminative.

Coffee

Coffee contains the stimulant caffeine, which may be administered to persons who have taken an overdose of barbiturates or other sleeping potions. Naturally, it is used when one wishes to remain awake in emergencies.

Corn

As early as 1672 the soothing quality of the starch of "Indian corn" was first brought to the attention of the public. Josselyn, in *New England Rarities*, says that corn is "excellent in cataplasms to ripen any swelling" and that "the decoction of blew corn is good to wash sore mouths with."

Thus today we know that ordinary kitchen-shelf cornstarch will provide an excellent poultice to relieve skin irritations, combining for the purpose cornstarch and castor oil into a paste. The dry starch is a good baby powder and quite likely is one of the principal ingredients of the powders sold commercially.

Ginger

Ginger taken after a heavy meal is not only a delight, but is a protection against flatulence.

Honey

Honey is, or should be, in every kitchen cabinet, for, beyond its general value as food, it has many medicinal values. Dr. Jarvis, in *Folk Medicine*, points out that honey is a wonderful remedy for producing sleep; that a teaspoon of honey to children on going to bed prevents bed-wetting; that it is one of the best cough remedies; a cure for burns; an alleviant for hay-fever sufferers, and that it has many other uses. Never forget *honey*.

Milk

This is not the place to discuss any of the general health values of milk in the diet, but simply to point out the sedative values of milk taken warm before retiring.

Molasses

There are probably people still alive who were brought up on the spring regimen of doses of sulphur and molasses. Such a combination gave to fresh-vegetable-starved country people a supply of vitamin B, iron, potassium, calcium, sulphur, etc. which the body much needed.

Some of us still believe that molasses is not only good, but good for us; quite likely our grandparents were smarter than we knew.

Mustard

Mustard is not only an agreeable spice but a digestant as well. Also mustard poultices for congestion in the chest, or the addition of mustard to a hot bath when one is thoroughly chilled are well-known cures.

Olive Oil

About the only laxative administered to the author in his youth was a teaspoonful of olive oil. It is mild in its action and can be used safely with children where more potent laxatives or cathartics might be harmful.

Olive oil and wintergreen oil make a mild liniment, and a combination of olive or linseed oil and lime water is recommended for burns.

Pomegranate

The root of the pomegranate tree provides, it is said, an excellent anthelmintic. Harris, in *Kitchen Medicines*, suggests that the dried, finely ground rinds of the fruit be substituted for the roots. He prescribes a decoction of two heaping teaspoonfuls of the dried powdered root to a pint of water. After fasting for a day, the patient drinks two ounces of the medicine every hour for six hours, with a laxative following the last dose. Continue the treatment for three days, lapse for three days, and repeat for three; by then a cure should have been effected.

Prunes

Prunes, as well as raw plums in equal quantities, are a simple and effective laxative which may well be as effective as some of the better known remedies.

Rice

There has been considerable discussion in the medical profession as to the value of a much-touted "rice-diet" for patients with cardiac and hypertensive conditions. Schifferes' recent *Family Medical Encyclopeadia* simply mentions that it is ' sometimes prescribed" and that it is a "low sodium, low calorie, but unpalatable diet."

Salt

Medicinally, the use of salt in the diet has been recently discouraged. But one possible value worth noting is that a tablespoon of salt, dissolved in a cup of warm water, is a quick emetic to administer in case of poisoning. Also, hot salt compresses are said to be useful for sprains and bruises.

One authority on nutrition makes the point in a letter to the author that one should make every effort to secure and use *unrefined* salt such as that evaporated from sea-water which, quite obviously, must contain elements of possible value, including Iodine.

Soap

Soap, it goes without saying, is cleansing, which alone makes it valuable for good health. But one might also mention that soap such as Fels-Naptha or Kirkmans, applied promptly and freely after exposure to poison ivy, may well prevent disastrous consequences. Dry soap, powdered and mixed with honey, makes a simple and satisfactory suppository when shaped into a cone.

A caution here is needed to be certain that one is using real *soap* rather than one of the many *detergent*-soaps now on the market. The dangers to water supplies of the inorganic materials in modern detergents are now the subject of widespread investigation.

Sodium Bicarbonate

This makes a gargle, mouth wash, does well as as toothpowder, and, applied as a wash, takes away the sting of bees.

Tea

The tannic acid astringency of strong tea makes an excellent and easily-come-by dressing for burns. Taken internally, it is helpful in diarrhea. For this purpose it should be taken with warm milk and a little cayenne pepper.

Toast

Burned toast is, in essence, a pure form of charcoal, and, as such, can be used to sweeten the breath, remove gas from the stomach, and as toothpowder.

A mixture of burned toast, strong tea, and milk of magnesia is recommended as an emergency antidote when poison has been taken, the tannic acid of the tea acting against alkaline poisons, the magnesia against acids.

Vinegar

Many people know that vinegar is good for bites and stings, and a more valuable general liniment can be made with vinegar, turpentine, plus a little lemon oil, cayenne pepper, eggs, and water. Vinegar is almost a panacea if one is to believe *Folk Medicine* by Dr. D. C. Jarvis.

Water

Water is such an accepted part of daily life that we use it for drinking and sanitation without a thought. Yet plain, pure, cold water may have medicinal values unsuspected by many. The adjuration of the doctor to those with bad colds to *"Drink plenty of water"* indicates that this use of water may be as adequate a cure for colds as any medicine.

Recently it has been revealed that cold (not icy) water on bad burns is as good a treatment as most, and better than many. *Time Magazine* (October 27, 1961) published a method of treating bad burns and scalds which cover less than 20% of the body and are on treatable extremities.

"Cool the burns fast by removing clothing, if it is loose, and immersing them in cold water [or even milk or soda water—Ed.]. Remove clothing only if it will lift off easily. And cut it away. . . . If the burned part cannot be dipped in water, apply loose, wet, cold dressings. . . . If the patient gets chilled, give him hot soup, but no alcohol. . . . Then call the doctor and ask him to visit the patient rather than interrupt the treatment."

Yeast

Space does not permit more than a suggestion of the great value of yeast as a medicine. As almost everyone knows, there are many varieties, some more easily taken and valuable than others. But, from personal experience years ago, the author can testify to a complete cure of long-standing constipation through the taking of one ordinary yeast cake a day for a period of some months. Research by the English has shown that a "man lasts longer on a pound of yeast extract than on a pound of any other concentrated food."

Most nutritionists agree on the value of yeast, but take care to point out that leavening or bread yeast being "live," feeds on the foods in the intestinal tract and that, to secure the values of Vitamin B which are in yeast, bacteria-killed "brewer's yeast" is recommended.

BIBLIOGRAPHY

The books listed below represent, with few exceptions, the library owned and used by the author in preparing this book. To make the list as helpful as possible, comments have been made on a few titles. It is hoped that readers will wish to acquire at least a few of them to supplement the necessarily short discussions of plants in the preceding pages.

Beyond the books used by the author there are hundreds more of interest in this field, most of which will be found listed in one or another of the following herbal bibliographies:

Bureau of American Ethnology. *American Indian Medicines*. Washington: Smithsonian Institution, 1957. 15 pages of titles devoted to this one subject.

de Laszlo, Henry G. *Library of Medicinal Plants*. Cambridge, England: Heffer and Sons, 1958. 50 close-set pages of book listings on the subject.

Hall, Elizabeth. "List of Herb Literature." *Annual Report:* Herb Society. 1948.

Abshire, A. B. *Catalog of Herbs and Spices*. Pasadena: Old-fashioned Herb Co., 1961.

Ackerknecht, E. H. "No 'Hocus Pocus' in the Medicine Man," UNESCO *Courier*. Sept., 1956.

Andrews, E. D. and F. *Shaker Herbs and Herbalists*. Berkshire Garden Center. 1959.

Bailey, L. H. *Hortus Second*. New York: The Macmillan Co., 1942. A secondary botanical authority for this work.

Barton, Benjamin Smith. *Collections for an Essay Towards a Materia Medica of the United States.* Philadelphia: 1798 and 1804. One of the first studies of Indian uses of wild plants to be made by a leading physician.

Belanger, Emil J. *Modern Manufacturing Formulary.* New York: Chemical Publishing Co., Inc., 1958. A book of formulas and methods, somewhat technical.

Bell, J. W. *Nature's Remedies.* Boston: Charles T. Branford Co., 1958. A slight popular treatise not based on United States plants.

Blunt, Wilfrid. *Art of Botanical Illustration.* London: Collins, 1950.

Boericke and Runyon. *Homeopathic Materia Medica.* Philadelphia: 1922.

Brown, O. Phelps. *The Complete Herbalist.* Jersey City: the author, 1856. A good sample of an American herbal a century ago.

Budge, Sir E. A. Wallis. *The Divine Origin of the Craft of the Herbalist.* London: Culpeper House, 1928.

Christensen, B. V. "Some Drug Plants in Florida," *Bulletin 14,* Department of Agriculture, Florida, August, 1935.

Compain, Michel. *Guide de l'Herboriste-Droguiste.* Limoges: Ed. Compain, 1939. Medicinal herbs from the French point of view.

Coon, Nelson. *Using Wayside Plants.* New York: Hearthside Press, 1957. Its original chapter on medicinal plants was the inspiration for the present volume.

Culpeper, Nicholas. *The Complete Herbal and English Physician Enlarged.* London: 1653.

Emmert, E. W. (translator). *Badianus Manuscript.* An Aztec herbal of 1552. Baltimore: The John Hopkins Press. 1940.

Fenton, Wm. N. "Contacts between Iroquois Herbalism and Colonial Medicine," Washington: Smithsonian Institute, *Smithsonian Report.* 1941-1942.

Fernald, M. D. (ed. and rev.). *Gray's Manual of Botany* (8th ed.). Boston: American Book Co., 1950. The basic authority for scientific names and plant descriptions used in this book.

Fernie, W. T. *Herbal Simples* (3rd ed.). Bristol: John Wright, 1914. An English work, exhaustive and interesting.

Fox, Wm. *Family Botanic Guide.* Sheffield: Fox & Sons, 1916.

Freeman, M. D., *Herbs for the Medieval Household.* New York: Metropolitan Museum of Art, 1943.

Grieve, Mrs. M. *A Modern Herbal.* 2 vols., 888 pages. New York: Harcourt Brace and Co. Inc., 1931. Reprinted in 1960. Complete as to the discussion of medicinal herbs growing in every part of the globe. A standard reference work, although some information has not been updated in the reprint edition. Often referred to as Grieve in this work. Expensive, but a basic reference for herbal enthusiasts.

Grigson, Geoffrey. *The Englishman's Flora.* London: Phoenix House, 1955. Folk stories about many plants in this book. A unique and beautiful volume.

Harper-Shove, F. *The Prescriber and Clinical Repertory of Medicinal Herbs.* (2nd ed.). Bognor Regis: Health Press, 1938. Against a list of physical conditions is set the plants useful for their treatment. Dosages given for more than 500 plant drugs.

Harris, Ben Charles. *Kitchen Medicines.* Worcester, Mass.: The Author, 1955.

Hausman, E. H. *Beginner's Guide to Wild Flowers.* New York: G. L. Putnam and Sons, 1948.

Henkel, Alice. *American Medicinal Leaves and Herbs.* Washington: (U.S. Department of Agriculture Bulletin 219), U.S. Government Printing Office, 1911.

Hill, Albert F. *Economic Botany.* New York: McGraw-Hill Book Co. Inc., 1937 and rev. A standard textbook prepared at Harvard University. Discussing useful plants from around the world.

Jacobs, Marion Lee and Burlage, Henry M. *Index of Plants of North Carolina with Reputed Medicinal Uses.* Austin, Texas: Henry M. Burlage, 1958. Exhaustive and compact. Referred to in this work as "Jacobs."

Josselyn, J. *New England Rarities Discovered.* London: 1672. The first discussion of American plants in which medicinal uses are disclosed. Fascinating.

Jarvis, D. C. *Folk Medicine.* New York: Henry Holt and Co. Inc., 1958. Controversial, yet much which makes sense. Available in paperback.

Johnson, C. P. *The Useful Plants of Great Britain.* London: Hardwicke, 1861. Especially fine illustrations by Sowerby.

Kirschner, H. E. *Nature's Healing Grasses.* Yucaipa, Calif., H. C. White, 1960. The doctor-author believes in prevention through nutritious, organically grown vegetables, wayside weeds, and salts from sea-weeds.

Lee, Chas. A. *Medicinal Plants Growing in the State of New York.* New York: Langley, 1848.

Leyel, Mrs. C. F. *Elixirs of Life.* London: Faber & Faber, 1958.

Lindley, John. *Medical and Economical Botany.* London: Bradbury and Evans, 1856.

Lloyd, J. U. *Origin and History of the Pharmacopoeial Vegetable Drugs.* Caxton, 1929.

Lloyd, J. U. and C. G. *Drugs and Medicines of North America.* Lloyd Library Bulletin, No. 31, 1931.

Martinez, Maximino. *Plantas Medicinales de Mexico.* (3rd ed.). Mexico: Ediciones Botas., 1944. The standard and exhaustive work on medicinal plants south of the border.

Mathews, F. Schuyler. *Field Book of American Wild Flowers.* New York: G. P. Putnam and Sons, 1902, Rev. ed. 1955. Long a standard guide. Well illustrated.

Meehan, Thomas. *The Native Wild Flowers and Ferns of the United States.* Boston: Prang, 1878.

Meyer, Joseph E. *The Herbalist.* Hammond, Indiana: Indiana Botanic Gardens, 1939. Revised edition now available. Excellent and compact.

Murphey, Edith Van Allen. *Indian Uses of Native Plants.* Palm Desert, Calif.: Desert Printers, 1959. Excellent investigation of Southwest Indian plant uses.

National Research Council. *A Survey of Wild Medicinal Plants of the United States—Their Distribution and Abundance.* Pub. by Com. on Pharmacognosy etc. n.d. (Circa 1940).

Parker, Arthur C. *Iroquois Uses of Maize and Other Food Plants.* N.Y. State Museum Bulletin, 144, 1910.

Petrides, George A. *Field Guide to Trees and Shrubs.* Boston: Houghton, Mifflin Co., 1958.

Quelch, Mary Thorne. *The Herb Garden.* London: Faber and Faber, 1941. Interesting, modern, England-based herbal.

Rasey, Ruth M. "Great-Grandfather and the Spanish Fly," *Vermont Life.* XXIV (May, 1959). pp. 22-31.

Santander, Carlos U. *Diccionario de Medicacion Herbaria* (5th ed.) Santiago, Chile, Ed. Nascimento. 1953.

Saunders, Charles F. *Useful Wild Plants of the U.S. & Canada.* New York: McBridge, 1934. Contains much Indian Lore.

Sievers, A. F. *American Medicinal Plants of Commercial Importance.* Washington: U.S. Department of Agriculture. Pub. 77, 1930.

Simmonite, W. J. *The Simmonite-Culpeper Herbal Remedies*. London: Foulsham & Co., 1957.

Step, Edward. *Herbs of Healing—A Book of British Simples*. London: Hutchinson, 1926.

Sweet, Muriel. *Common edible and useful plants of the West*. Healdburg, California: Naturegraph Co., 1962. Fifty of the 115 plant genera of that state are discussed in *Using Plants for Healing*.

Tanaka, Yoshio. *Useful Plants of Japan*. Japan: 1888. Lists and pictures of medicinal plants of that country.

Taylor, Kathryn S. *A Travelers Guide to Roadside Wildflowers*. New York: Farrar Strauss and Co. Inc., 1949.

Theophrastus. *Enquiry into Plants*. Sir Arthur Hort (tr.) 250 B.C. (tr. 1916) London: Heinemann, 1916.

Thompson, Samuel. *The Thomsonian Materia Medica*. (reprint ed.) Lloyd Library No. 11, 1909.

Vogel, Dr. h.c. A. *The Nature Doctor*. Switzerland: Bioforce-verlag, 1959. Medical hints from Swiss folk medicine, plus offerings of proprietary drugs.

Wherry, Edgar T. *Wild Flower Guide*. New York: Doubleday and Co., 1954.

William, L. O. *Drug and Condiment Plants*. Washington: U.S. Department of Agriculture Bulletin 172, 1960. Answers some of the questions about growing drug plants as a business.

Wittrock, M. A. & G. L. "Food Plants of the Indians." New York: *Journal of N.Y. Bot. Garden No. 507*, 1942. Page 76 et seq. has article on Indian Plant medicines.

Woodward, M. *Leaves from Gerard's Herbal*. London: Bodley Head, 1943.

Wren, R. C. *Potter's Encyclopaedia of Medicinal Drugs and Preparations*. London: Pitman, 1956. Referred to as Potter in these pages, the most useful and modern work on the subject, although written from the English point of view.

Wyman, L. C. and Harris, Stuart K. *Navajo Indian Medicinal Ethnobotany*. University of New Mexico Bulletin 366, 1941.

Youngken, Heber W. *Textbook of Pharmacognosy*. Philadelphia: Blakiston Co., edition 1921. et. seq. An authoritative textbook for the pharmacist. Often referred to in the preparation of this book. Ref. Youngken.

INDICES

A certain shepherd lad
Of small regard to see, yet well skilled
In every virtuous plant, and healing herb;
He would beg me sing:
Which, when I did, he on the tender grass
Would sit, and hearken even to constancy:
And in requital ope his leathern scrip,
And show me Simples, of a thousand names,
Telling their strange, and vigorous faculties.

John Milton

On the pages which follow, separate indices are offered in a manner intended to make this book more useful. First appears an index of scientific names for those familiar with the so-called Latin nomenclature. Included here are listings of all the plant families together with the names of the individual genera within those families.

The second index will be useful to those familiar with such of the common names of the plants as have been introduced into the text, while the third index points out the pages on which plants reputedly valuable for various conditions are explored. The glossary itself (page 44 *et seq.*) will serve as a further index to most of the physical anomalies mentioned.

A fourth "Collecting Calendar" will act as a guide to the seasonal gathering of a few of the important plants.

INDEX OF SCIENTIFIC NAMES

Includes the names of families represented in this work, together with 216 genera and 280 species. Synonyms are italicized.

INDEX OF COMMON NAMES

Vine maple, 155
Violet family, *see* Violaceae
Violet, dog's tooth, 231
 fragrant, 223
 wild, 223
Vomitwort, 148
Wake robin, 85, 213
Wahoo, 123
Walnut family, *see* Juglandaceae
Walnut, white, 145
Warnera, 139
Wart-weed, 101, 229
Water, 246
Waterbugle, 234
Water-Chestnut family, *see*
 Hydrophyllaceae
Watercress, 163
Waterlily family, *see* Nymphaceae
Waterlily, fragrant, 165
Water-plantain family, *see* Alismaceae
Waxflower, 104
Wax-myrtle family, *see* Myricaceae
Way-bread, 173
White alder family, *see* Pyrolaceae
Willow family, *see* Salicaceae
Willow-herb, hooded, 201

Wing-seed, 183
Winterberry, 141
 bloom, 134
 green, 104, 128
Witch-grass, 67
Witch hazel family, *see*
 Hamamelidaceae
Witch hazel, 134
Wolf's claws, 149
Wood betony, 205
Woodbine, American, 233
World's wonder, 198
Wormwood, 87
Wormseed, 103
Woundwort, 180, 205
 marsh, 205
 soldier's, 62

Yam root, wild, 117
Yarrow, 62
Yaupon, 140
Yawroot, 206
Yeast, 247
Yellow berry, 174
 root, 112, 139
Yerba Santa, 122

INDEX OF PLANT VALUES

Alterative, 66, 79, 81, 90, 104, 105, 108, 124, 125, 127, 139, 144, 155, 158, 171, 175, 188, 192, 202, 206, 210, 212, 213, 228, 235, 236, 237
Amenorrhea, 103, 193
Anodyne, 115, 227
Anthelmintic, 87, 102, 103, 119, 158, 236, 245
Antiperiodic, 113, 237
Antipyretics, 92
Antiscorbutics, 65, 83, 91, 95, 158, 163, 172, 177, 189, 191, 194, 210, 211, 214, 217, 225
Antiseptics, 87, 90, 92, 118, 124, 143, 199, 204, 205, 227, 228, 235, 237
Antispasmodic, 77, 78, 97, 98, 103, 108, 115, 156, 201, 202, 205, 208, 212, 221, 231, 234, 235
Aperients, 67, 83, 105, 107, 144, 196, 210, 224
Aromatics, 62, 75, 77, 87, 88, 92, 128, 140, 143, 152, 168, 169, 180, 182, 199, 203, 209, 227, 229, 231, 233, 234
Asthma, 64, 70, 89, 98, 115, 117, 122, 133, 143, 148, 151, 176, 208, 215, 233
Astringents, 62, 66, 69, 71, 74, 92, 98, 104, 113, 118, 121, 124, 125, 127, 128, 129, 130, 134, 140, 159, 161, 165, 166, 175, 179, 180, 182, 185, 188, 190, 192, 213, 214, 227, 228, 230, 231, 232, 234, 235, 246

Bee and bug stings, to ease, 193, 228, 233, 246

Carminatives, 75, 78, 85, 88, 92, 135, 152, 154, 157, 164, 195, 203, 218, 230, 241

COLLECTOR'S CALENDAR

Here is presented a list of selected wild medicinal plants mentioned in this book, together with approximate dates for collecting them. These dates will, of course, be subject to adjustment for various sections of the United States, having been made up with the northeastern section in mind. Variances as much as one or two months will be needed. A general rule seems to be that the seasons advance from south to north at a rate of something like a hundred miles per week, but this again must be modified by local factors of altitude, longitude and proximity to the ocean. This list should not suggest that plants may be collected only in the months noted nor is it indicative of the fact that leaves or flowers may be collected in one month and roots at quite a different time. See the text for a discussion of each plant.

April
Chicory
Wild ginger
Scotch broom
Sphagnum
Sassafras
Balsam
Watercress
Witchgrass
Violets

May
Chamomile
Horsetail
Strawberry
Cranes-bill
Clover
Buckbean
Slippery elm
Dandelion
Balmony

June
Foxglove
Lemon balm
Aspen
Silverweed
Coltsfoot
Irish moss
Nettle
Tansy
Sheep sorrel

July
Centaury
Water Plantain
Borage
Alder
Milfoil
Sumach
Lily of the Valley
Blessed Thistle
Boneset
Rosinweed
Cudweed
Mock pennyroyal
Common mallow
Red Clover
Soapwort
Skullcap
Self heal
Evening primrose
Mullein

August
Agrimony
Wormwood
Dogbane
Hollyhock
Uva-ursi
Sweet fern
Worm seed
Yerba Santa
Ground Ivy
Spearmint
Jewel-weed
Peppermint
Elderberry
Goldenrod
Parsley
Rue
Sphagnum moss

September
Apple
Garlic
Marshmallow
Pipsissewa
Bayberry
Sunflower
Horehound
Juniper berries
Partridge berries
Yellow dock
Sage
Seneca snakeroot
May-apple
Catnip
Japanese Rose

October	*October, cont.*	*November*
Gold Thread	Persimmon	Fringe tree
Snakeroot	Witch-hazel	Dogwood
Papoose root	Seven-barks	New Jersey tea
Black Snakeroot	Elecampane	Golden seal
Burdock	Blue flag	Ground pine
Spikenard	Blackberry	White pine
Wild Sarsaparilla	Comfrey	Pondlily
Grapes	Greek Valerian	Viburnum
Honey	Chokecherry	Wafer ash
Male-fern	Valerian	Oak bark